BHAGAVAD GĪTĀ

Translation and Commentary

BHAGAVAD GĪTĀ

Translation and Commentary

RICHARD GOTSHALK

MOTILAL BANARSIDASS
Delhi Varanasi Patna Madras

Head Office: Bungalow Road, Delhi 110 007
Branches: Chowk, Varanasi 221 001
Ashok Rajpath, Patna 800 004
6 Appar Swamy Koil Street, Mylapore,
Madras 600 004

First Edition : Delhi, 1985

ISBN: 81–208–0006–0

Printed in India by Shantilal Jain at Shri Jainendra Press, A-45 Naraina, Phase I, New Delhi 110 028 and published by Narendra Prakash Jain for Motilal Banarsidass, Delhi 110 007.

CONTENTS

PREFATORY NOTE

My translation is from the received text which is conveyed with only the slightest of variations in Radhakrishnan, Gandhi and Desai, Besant and Das, Aurobindo, and Zaehner. I have availed myself also of the variants occasionally noted in these, especially in Zaehner.

My commentary has been developed with little reliance upon other commentaries or the notes of other translators. Nonetheless, in my notes, I have made frequent reference to the most useful of the translations and commentaries/notes among those I have encountered, namely, those by Radhakrishnan, Barnett, Edgerton, Gandhi and Desai, Besant and Das, Hill, Aurobindo, Deutsch, and Zaehner.

Of more importance in shaping my understanding of the *Gītā* over the years has been philosophical conversation with Henry Bugbee, who was teaching at Harvard University when we first met and embarked upon twenty years or so of fruitful discussions.

Of greatest importance in the development of my understanding of the *Gītā*, however, were four persons with whom I never discussed the poem at all, but who were crucial supporting figures in my life. They were my parents, Walter and Naomi Gotshalk, and my maternal grandparents, Mark and Cassandra Smith, who together provided me two homes in which to grow up.

To these last four, all now deceased, and to my daughter Diane, who was killed in a motorcycle accident on April 17, 1982, I would like to dedicate, *in memoriam*, this version of the ancient Hindu poem on life and death and this commentary upon that poem.

INTRODUCTION

In our own (European and American) traditions there seems nothing that is quite parallel to the *Bhagavad Gītā* or *Song of the Lord.* For the *Gītā* is a small fragment of didactic poetry in the *Mahābhārata*, one of the two major epic poems in the Hindu tradition. The closest approximation to such epic poetry in our traditions would likely be the *Iliad* and the *Odyssey* of Homer. The background out of which both sets of epic poems may be seen to have originated is similar in many respects, but most importantly, as involving a tradition of court lays or secular poetry which developed the story of warriors and kings, of heroic exploits and martial struggles. But when, with Homer, the tradition of court lays was developed in the new and changing conditions of the Greek world of the eighth and seventh centuries B.C., and was developed in response to the occasion which certain religious festivals provided for a celebration of that heroic tradition which was a common heritage to the diverse peoples gathered together at the festival, epic poetry of the character of the *Iliad* and the *Odyssey* was born. Such poetry was distinguished in several ways from the traditional poetry which formed its background and upon which it drew. For example, it was no longer merely oral but was written down, authored by one man but recited by many. But the most important difference for the point of comparison here, is that such poetry was composed for recitation on a religious occasion, not simply as part of court life. And yet the *Iliad* and the *Odyssey* are poetry first and foremost, poetry inspired by the Muses, indeed, and with important religious meaning as well as an important religious function, but poetry untouched by priestly concerns.

In contrast, the *Mahābhārata* and the *Rāmāyaṇa* are poems formed around an epic core, but in them that core has been taken up into a religious framework and made to function in subordination to a didactic religious purpose. Focussing upon the *Mahābhārata* as the relevant poem here, one can see its central story to be the account of a struggle between two branches of the Kuru family, descendants of King Bharata. This story, although rendered with a poetic rather than a historiographical sense of truth, apparently has some basis in the early history of the Aryan settlement of northern India, much as the story of the *Iliad* has a basis in the history of the Mycenaean times. But the epic core of the *Mahābhārata* has been almost submerged under a mass of materials, some poetic, some not, which have been interspersed in appropriate places around the account of the central story and which have expanded it in bulk at least fourfold.[1] Due to the size and the character of such expansion, not only is any dramatic unity such as Homer achieves made impossible, but any unity of thought is also lost. For the *Mahābhārata* achieved its ultimate form as the accomplishment of many men over a rather long period of time. The authors themselves are unknown, their separate contributions are not determinable with assurance, but the significantly different understandings of the nature of things and of human life, which color different phases or parts of the poem clearly attest its composite character. Such an origin is also attested in the name of the man to whom authorship of the epic is attributed, Vyāsa, which means, the compiler.

Historiographical conjecture places the original epic story in existence around the fifth century B.C.; but it places the whole epic as we know it today in existence only around the fourth century A.D.[2] Now what characterizes the completed poem as a whole is its emphasis upon Śiva and Viṣṇu (especially the latter), and in general, upon a popular theism. This theistic emphasis places it in contrast with the Vedic tradition that had developed down through the fifth century B.C. and puts it into the stream of that great theistic development (Vedic and non-Vedic alike) that did so much during the centuries in question, to transform the Brahmanism that had developed with the Vedas and which in the fifth century, was being challenged in many directions. The priestly transformation of the original epic core of the *Mahābhārata* over the centuries into a poem of primarily Vaiṣṇavite outlook seems to show stages.[3] In the light of this, and of the fact that the *Gītā* has its focus upon Kṛṣṇa treated as an incarnation of Viṣṇu, scholars have been led to conjecture that the Song in its present form was added in the dramatically appropriate place in the main epic story by the end of the second century B.C.[4]

This small fragment of poetry hidden away in the larger epic came to have a central importance within the Hindu tradition at large in the succeeding centuries. As part of the epic, of course, it does not have the authority of revelation, but belongs within human tradition. Nonetheless the popular influence of the *Gītā* is second to no other part of that tradition, or of revelation. Not only that: the *Gītā* has come to be a work with which all thinkers within the orthodox tradition must make their thought square, just as much as with revelation (the *Vedas,* in particular, the *Upaniṣads*) and with the *Brahma Sūtra* (a concise summary of the Upaniṣadic teaching).

It is not simply that the *Gītā's* theistic emphasis fitted in with the upsurge of a theism that has maintained itself to this day, that accounts for the wide appeal and important place of this small poem in the Hindu tradition. It is, more importantly, that this emphasis was developed in a didactic work that succeeded in offering a certain unitary crystallization of many strands of the tradition antecedent to it, both Vedic and non-Vedic. Seeking to express how all these strands of tradition have a certain place and validity, the teaching of the *Gītā* is an inclusive one, so that most Hindus could then—and have continued to be able to—find themselves acknowledged and affirmed by it, however differently their religious life may be otherwise characterized. Thus from the start its appeal was many-sided, and indeed, so many-sided that otherwise contradictory forms of religion and religious aspiration have been able to claim it as their own.[5]

What is a Western reader to do in the face of a work such as the *Gītā*? The Song is itself a didactic poem integrated into an extended epic poem and has a natural dramatic place in that larger context. Yet the thoughtful articulation of the problematic of human existence which it embodies grows out of traditions which are alien to ours. And not only that, but the poem itself seeks to take certain of those traditions into an account that would be comprehensive, but which is itself susceptible of (and has in fact received among Hindus) a large variety of conflicting interpretations as to its essential meaning. What can we do to find our way here? In part, that will differ according as our interest is that of someone curious about the cast of mind of men of an early phase of another tradition, or that of someone seeking the truth as that by which one must live and considering the poem as possible truth, or that of someone animated by other interests. But whatever the interest that may animate us, there is one thing which we all must do to find our way in the face of the poem, and that is: first of all and last of all, simply plunge in.

In order that this might happen, one must have a text of the poem, written in a language and composed in a style that could give one access to whatever disclosure is being made in the *Gītā* itself. But in order for one to enter effectively through that access into some measure of sharing in the disclosure in question, there are two further indispensable conditions.

First: If one does not belong to the Hindu tradition, one is lacking altogether that heritage of assumptions and presuppositions, which would enter into the vital matrix out of which a contemporary Hindu might find his way into the meaning of the *Gītā* and which would enable that finding to be a returning into the meaning of an element out of one's own vital historical past. Such a heritage could be an obstruction to an effective return as well as a help, but something like it must be available if a reader is to discover the intrinsic historical dimension involved in the *Gītā*. Nonetheless, all such knowledge, which is broadly historiographical in character, can help one gain access to the meaning of the poem only if one further condition is met. This information, external and apart from the vital matrix, out of which one can take anything into oneself and respond to it as oneself, must be secured in its historically-relevant meaning upon the strength and background of one's own participation in life, inflected through one's own traditions and the ways in which one has assimilated and transformed them. Only as in that participation, assimilation and transformation, one can succeed in being oneself and being human in one's own way, can one know others.

Second: one must participate in a specific way in the knowledgeable reading of the poem and listening to its words unfold its story and teaching. This way of participating can be indicated by observing that the *Gītā* is a song, and that its vision of things is expressed in a dramatic dialogue. As with dramatic poetry generally, the *Gītā* works to draw a reader (hearer) up into its unfolding drama, into the action and interplay of characters which such a reader (hearer) encounters in the no man's land created in poetry. One enters that region of encounter as oneself, and only as oneself. But the more one can be there in a way that is responsive humanly, that is, the more one can there center oneself in that common humanity which could make possible what understanding is possible of other men, or the more one can find touch with that openness to what it is to be human which one's own life and one's own individual transformation of one's own tradition can put one in touch with, so the more one can find the *Gītā* speaking to one as uttering another's voice, as uttering a human vision and tradition that are other to oneself and one's own but which can be properly encountered in that otherness only in communion (which is *not* to say, in agreement). That utterance, didactic in its peculiar way, regards matters of ultimate concern to each and every human being in his/her participation in human life. And only as one is in touch with such matters through one's own participation in life, and only as one's reading of the *Gītā* is thoughtful and reflexive with regard to that participation, will one be in a position effectively to hear and to respond to the Song in its disclosive and educative power. I suggest that it is the working of the poem poetically and dramatically that calls a reader (hearer) into the place from which such a discovery of its meaning is possible. What I am speaking of here, of course, is not the character and outcome of a single reading, but the character and outcome of the recurrent participation in reading and study and reflection through which one can become gradually educated more deeply into the meaning or disclosure which is the heart of the *Bhagavad Gītā*.

What I have sought to accomplish in this work as a whole is three-fold, in accordance with the preceding points explicating the preconditions for a Western reader's effective encounter with the *Gītā*.

First, I have sought to provide a translation which would make it possible for a reader to reach the thought of the *Gītā* through an English rendering that expressed the acknowledgement that the poetic character of the *Gītā* is integral to its meaning. But what constitutes that character? Entering into the *Gītā* as a poem in Sanskrit, are at least the following factors: (1) at the level of speaking (reading and reciting) there is the very sound of the words in Sanskrit, there is the meter through which the sounded words are connected in certain patterns, and there is the division of the connected units into verses (*ślokas*); and (2) at the level of meaning, there is the narrative character of the presentation, and with this, a certain grandeur and forcefulness of language reflecting who is speaking, the occasion for the dialogue, and the content of the conversation.

In my translation I have been guided by the notion that in a translation sacrifice of anything of the poetic character of the *Gītā* must concern the level of speaking, not that of meaning. Thus not only have I sought accurate expression of the meaning and thought constituting the content of the conversation, but I have also payed special attention to the dramatic elements, seeking to render them right down to the epithets used of each other by the speakers. Even without such a focus there was, of course, no way to reproduce the sound of the Sanskrit words, and more importantly, the connotations and ambivalences that only the Sanskrit original could convey without intolerable circumlocution. But with such a focus there might have been an attempt to render the *Gītā* in an English poem, as Sir Edwin Arnold did. I have eschewed this for the sake of a simple and direct presentation of the dialogue, thinking to let the meaning and quality of the English bear the burden of incarnating in an alien tongue the living spirit of the poem as poetry. Of the poetic elements at the level of speaking, then, I have sought to retain only the third, the division into verses; and even here, while retaining the division by numbering, I have used spacing to group certain verses together that are not so visually grouped in the Sanskrit but which seem to represent natural articulations in the flow of conversation and thought within each Chapter (*adhyāya*, chapter or reading, lesson, study).

In this, of course, and in other ways, the English presentation reflects an interpretation. For while I have tried as much as possible to keep interpretation to a minimum, often using or mentioning the Sanskrit terms and always seeking such expressions as would admit as many as possible of the varied interpretations that could relevantly be put upon the Sanskrit, no translation can avoid being also an interpretation. In order to make more explicit the understanding that has been involved in my translation, I have appended a commentary. This should be of some assistance to the reader's understanding of the poem, and more to the point here, should enable the reader, after his/her reading, to make allowances for the translation. To help in that task of making allowances as well as in the task of understanding, I have further appended a number of notes, bearing on alternative translations or interpretations of particular words or verses. And further, I would recommend the reading of other translations more or less different in character from the following one.[6] For example, I suggest the relatively poetic rendering by Prabhavananda and Isherwood,[7] which interjects an *advaita* (monistic) Vedānta mode of interpretation into the translation; and in contrast, the fairly straightforward, clear and accurate translation by Hill.[8] In addition, if the reader has a desire to follow the Sanskrit, I suggest recourse to the translations by Besant and Das,[9] by Radhakrishnan,[10] by Gandhi and Desai,[11] and by Zaehner.[12]

Second, I have sought to provide sufficient information to make possible a reader's preliminary orientation to the terms and notions referred to in the course of the poem. That information, primarily of a historical nature, has been placed in the notes. For further information of like character, as well as for indication of how the *Gītā* becomes interpreted by important figures in the Hindu tradition, I would suggest consulting the commentaries by Śaṁkara and Rāmānuja,[13] or that by Aurobindo,[14] as well as the translations (with notes) by Hill, Radhakrishnan, Zaehner, and Barnett.[15]

Third, I have sought to urge—and here repeat my urging—that the reader take the drama as primordial and as the encompassing focus of his/her response. The dialogical whole of the *Gītā* is constituted by a dialogue within a dialogue, that is, by an indirectly narrated dialogue. The main dialogue, that of Kṛṣṇa with Arjuna, is presented through Saṁjaya, whom we overhear relating that dialogue to Dhṛtarāṣṭra, the blind king whose sons are the leading force in the army arrayed over against the army led by Arjuna and his brothers. Saṁjaya, a charioteer, can relate the dialogue to his master while the two are at a distance from the scene, due to supernatural powers given him by Vyāsa for the purpose. The whole, both the inner dialogue and the interplay of narrator speaking in his own person with narrator also voicing the speech of Kṛṣṇa and Arjuna, unfolds in a dramatic way, and this drama it is that fundamentally determines the course of the dialogue and the manner of presentation of the teaching.

In line with this last emphasis, and in order to facilitate the reader's entry into the drama and the dramatic situation, I here offer a brief summary of the relevant part of the epic kernel of the *Mahābhārata*. This will enable the reader to place the *Gītā* in its larger setting. That epic kernel concerns the descendants of King Bharata,[16] and the relevant part goes as follows. After the death of King Pāṇḍu[17] his brother Dhṛtarāṣṭra[17] succeeded to the throne. The latter educated the five sons of Pāṇḍu, the Pāṇḍavas, along with his own one hundred sons. As they grew to be men, the Pāṇḍavas distinguished themselves by their piety and heroic virtues. In consequence Duryodhana, Dhṛtarāṣṭra's eldest son, became jealous and planned to murder them. Duryodhana's scheme was to build a palace in a distant town, and invite the Pāṇḍavas to stay there during a religious festival. The palace was made of specially inflammable materials, so that Duryodhana's servants could easily set it on fire. It burned to ashes, but the Pāṇḍavas and Kuntī, their mother,[18] had been warned in time, and escaped. Duryodhana believed them dead.

The Pāṇḍavas lived in the forest, disguised as *brāhmaṇas*,[19] meeting all kinds of dangers and adventures. One day they heard that a neighboring king was to choose a husband for his daughter. The winner must string a bow of enormous strength and hit a tiny target. The Pāṇḍavas thought they would try. They went to the city in their disguise. Suitors had gathered from all over India, Duryodhana among them. One after another, they failed in the test. At last Arjuna, third of the Pāṇḍavas, stood up, bent the bow and hit the target with the greatest ease. Draupadī, the princess, threw him the victor's garland. But the assembled princes could not accept this humiliation at the hands of a seemingly poor and unwarlike brāhmaṇa. There would have been a fight if Kṛṣṇa,[20] who was present, had not intervened and persuaded them that Arjuna had a right to his bride.

Dhṛtarāṣṭra and his son now knew that the Pāṇḍavas were not only alive but allied by marriage to a powerful monarch. Duryodhana was for carrying on the feud, but Dhṛtarāṣṭra wisely listened to the advice of his uncle Bhīṣma,[21] which was to send for the brothers and offer them half of his kingdom. So the kingdom was divided. The Pāṇḍavas got the worst of the land, a wilderness along the Jamuna River. They cleared it, built a fine city, and crowned Yudhiṣṭhira, the eldest brother, as their king. The five brothers lived in triumph and splendor, and

Duryodhana hated them more than ever. His jealousy hatched a new plot for their ruin. The pious and noble Yudhiṣṭhira had a dangerous weakness—a love of gambling. So Duryodhana challenged him to play dice with a clever gamester named Śakuni, knowing that the king would feel bound in honor to accept. They played, Śakuni cheated, Yudhiṣṭhira lost game after game, staking his wealth, his kingdom, and finally his brothers, Draupadī and himself. All were now the slaves of Duryodhana's vengeance, subject to insult and cruelty, until Dhṛtarāṣṭra intervened and insisted that they be set at liberty and their kingdom given back.

Duryodhana worked upon his father until he obtained permission for another dice-match. The loser was to forfeit his kingdom and to retire to the forest for twelve years, then he must live for a year in the city without being recognized; if he was discovered, the term of exile would begin again. This game Yudhiṣṭhira also lost. So the Pāṇḍavas went back to the forest. They made a virtue of their misfortune, practising spiritual austerities and doing many heroic deeds. When the period of exile was over at last, Yudhiṣṭhira asked for the return of his kingdom; but Duryodhana refused. Yudhiṣṭhira said he would be content with just one village for himself and for each of his brothers. But Duryodhana, in the insanity of his greed, would not agree even to this. The older members of the family tried to arbitrate, and failed. So war became inevitable. Neighboring kings were drawn into the quarrel, until the whole of India was involved. Both sides wanted Kṛṣṇa's aid. To both, Kṛṣṇa offered the same choice: "either you have the help of my kinsmen, the Vṛṣṇis, in the battle, or you can have me alone; but I shall take no part in the fighting." Duryodhana chose the Vṛṣṇis; Arjuna preferred to take Kṛṣṇa himself, as his personal charioteer.

The battle was fought on the plain of Kurukṣetra, or Field of the Kurus, a sacred place of pilgrimage. It was here, just before the armies engaged, that Kṛṣṇa and Arjuna had the conversation which is recorded in the *Gītā*. The battle lasted eighteen days, and ended with the death of Duryodhana and the complete victory of the Pāṇḍavas. Thereafter Yudhiṣṭhira became undisputed ruler of India, and reigned for 36 years. The story ends with the pilgrimage of Draupadī and the Pāṇḍavas up the heights of the Himālayas to the abode of the Lord, and into the true being of God, into true immortality.

BHAGAVAD GĪTĀ
TRANSLATION

CHAPTER I

Dhṛtarāṣṭra said:

*1. My sons and those of Pāṇḍu, what did they do, Saṁjaya, when, eager to fight, they had gathered together on the Field of the Kurus, the field of *dharma*?[1]

Saṁjaya said :

2. Having glanced over the Pāṇḍava troops arrayed in battle-order, Prince Duryodhana approached his teacher and spoke these words :

3. "Behold, my teacher,[2] this great army of the sons of Pāṇḍu,[3]
which has been arrayed by an intelligent pupil of yours,
4. the son of Drupada.[4] In it are to be found great archers
who are equal in battle to Bhīma and Arjuna—heroes like
Yuyudhāna[5] and Virāṭa,[6] and Drupada, a mighty warrior, /
5. together with Dhṛṣṭaketu,[7] Cekitāna,[8] and the courageous
King of Kāśī;[9] then too, Purujit,[10] Kuntibhoja,[10] and the
6. King of the Śibis, foremost of men. And there is also
Yudhāmanyu[11] the strong, and Uttamaujas[11] the brave,
and the son of Subhadrā[12] and the sons of Draupadī,[13] all
of them mighty warriors.

*7. "Even so, O Highest-of-the-Twice-Born,[14] know that we also have distinguished men, leaders in my army. Let me

---

Editorial note: Notes to the Introduction, Translation and Commentary are marked by number, but Notes Concerning Text are marked only by an "*" placed before the verse number. The verse number stands on the line in which the verse in question starts. If the place of that start is not obvious (the beginning of a sentence, say), a "/" will be used to mark the beginning.

name them for you, that we may both know who they are.
8. There is you yourself, and Bhīṣma[15] and Karṇa[16], and
Kṛpa[17] victorious in battle, Aśvatthāman[18] and Vikarṇa,[19]
9. and the son of Somadatta[20] as well. Many other heroes
are also relinquishing their lives for my sake, and armed
with diverse weapons and missiles, all of them are skilled
in fighting.

*10. "Nevertheless, our force, commanded by Bhīṣma, is not
adequate, while theirs, commanded by Bhīma, is quite
*11. adequate. So throughout all the comings and goings of
battle, let all you lords, standing fast in your proper
posts, above all protect Bhīṣma."

*12. To cheer him up, Duryodhana's aged but majestic grand-
father[21] blew his conch, sending forth on high a lion's roar.
13. In sudden response, conches and kettledrums, cymbals and
tabors and horns, all were sounded, and the noise was
*14. tumultuous. Then on the other side, the descendant-of-
Madhu[22] and the son-of-Pāṇḍu[23], stationed together in a
great chariot harnessed with white horses, blew their celes-
15. tial conches. The Lord-of-the-Senses[24] blew Pāñcajanya[25],
Wealth-Winner[26] blew Devadatta[27]. And Bhīma—vora-
cious, of terrible deeds—blew his great conch, Pauṇḍra.
16. Soon Prince Yudhiṣṭhira, son of Kuntī, was blowing
Anantavijaya[28], Nakula and Sahadeva were blowing
17. Sughoṣa[29] and Maṇipuṣpaka[29]; / and they were joined
by the supreme archer of Kāśī, and the great warrior
Śikhaṇḍin, and Dhṛṣṭadyumna, as well as Virāṭa, the in-
18. vincible Sātyaki, / Drupada and the sons of Draupadī, and
the strong-armed son of Subhadrā: O Lord-of-the-Earth,
19. all these blew their own conches. And the tumultuous
noise, filling heaven and earth, rent open the hearts of
*20. the sons of Dhṛtarāṣṭra. Then, Lord-of-the-Earth, with

the fighting about to begin[30], the monkey-bannered son-
of-Pāṇḍu[31], having glanced over[32] your sons stationed
*21. in battle-order, took up his bow, / and spoke these words
to the Lord-of-the-Senses: "Place my chariot between the
*22. two armies, Unshakeable One, / far enough forward for
me to take a good look at[33] those men standing there eager
to fight, with whom I am to engage in this coming
*23. battle. I want carefully to observe[34] those who, about to
fight, are assembled here desirous of accomplishing in bat-
tle what is dear to the evil-minded son of Dhṛtarāṣṭra[35]."

Saṁjaya said:
24. Addressed by Thick-Hair[36] in this way, O Descendant-of-
Bharata[37], the Lord-of-the-Senses placed that excellent
*25. chariot between the two armies, / and when they were placed
facing Bhīṣma, Droṇa, and all the princes, he said: "O
Son-of-Pṛthā[38], behold the assembled[39] Kurus[40] !"

26. The son-of-Pṛthā saw standing there fathers and grand-
fathers, teachers, uncles, brothers, sons, grandsons, com-
*27. panions, / fathers-in-law and friends, belonging to both
armies. And having looked closely[41] at all those relations
*28. standing there, the son-of-Kuntī / was filled with the utmost
compassion[42]. Weighed down by his sorrow[43], he said:

"Kṛṣṇa, seeing my own kin on hand and eager to fight, /
*29. my limbs become weak, my mouth dry, my body trembles,
30. and my hair stands on end. Gāṇḍīva[44] is slipping from my
hand, my skin is burning all over; I can scarcely remain
31. standing, my mind is reeling. I see bad omens, Fair-
Hair[45], and foresee no good that could come from having
32. slain my own kin in war. "I do not crave victory for my-
self, Kṛṣṇa, nor kingdom and pleasures. What is the good
of kingdom to us, Chief-Guardian[46], or enjoyments, or

33. even life? Those for whose sake kingdom and enjoyments
and pleasures are longed for, are entering the fight relin-
34. quishing their lives and riches. Teachers, fathers, sons,
grandfathers, uncles, fathers-in-law, grand-sons, brothers-
35. in-law, and other relations: / though I am slain, I do
not desire to slay them, Slayer-of-Madhu[47], even for the
kingship of the three worlds[48]. Why, then, for the sake of
the earth?

*36. "What pleasure would there be for us, having killed Dhṛta-
rāṣṭra's sons, Exciter-of-Men[49]? Only sin would attach to
37. us if we slayed these men who are ready to kill us. Hence
we ought not slay Dhṛtarāṣṭra's sons, our own relations; for
having slain our own kin, how will we be happy, Descen-
38. dant-of-Madhu? Even if their minds are afflicted with greed
and they do not see the evil of causing the destruction of
39. a family and the crime of harming friends, / why is it
not wise[50] for us, Exciter-of-Men, who see clearly[51] this
evil of causing the destruction of a family, to hold back
40. from this sin? In the destruction of a family, the primeval
family *dharma* disappears, and with the destruction of
41. *dharma*, *adharma*[52] overcomes the whole family. When
adharma conquers, Kṛṣṇa, the women in a family become
corrupt and among fallen women, Descendant-of-Vṛṣṇi[53],
*42. caste-mixture[54] arises. This mixing brings both the family
and its destroyers to hell, for the spirits of their ancestors
fall when deprived of their offerings of rice and water.[55]
43. By these evils of those who destroy a family and create
caste mixtures, the immemorial *dharmas*[56] of caste and
44. family are upset. We have been repeatedly told, Exciter-
of-Men, that a place in hell is allotted[57] for men of a
45. family whose *dharmas* are upset. Alas, we have resolved[58]
to commit a great sin by undertaking to slay our own
*46. kin out of greed for kingdom and happiness. If in battle

Dhṛtarāṣṭra's sons, weapons in hand, would slay me, unarmed and unresisting, it would be better[59] for me."

Saṁjaya said:

47. Having spoken on the field of battle in this way, Arjuna threw down his bow and arrow and sank down upon his chariot seat, his mind agitated[60] with grief.

CHAPTER II

Saṁjaya said:

*1. To him who was thus burdened[1] with compassion[2], his eyes filled with tears and confused, who was sinking into depression[3], the Slayer-of-Madhu spoke these words:

The Blessed Lord said:

2. "Whence came to you this weakness in the moment of crisis ? It is ignoble, Arjuna, and neither leads to heaven
3. nor brings glory. / Have no share in such unmanliness, Son-of-Pṛthā, it does not befit you ! Having relinquished this petty faint-heartedness, stand up, Foe-Destroyer[4] !"

Arjuna said:

4. "Slayer-of-Madhu, Slayer-of-Foes, how am I to fight with arrows against Bhīṣma and Droṇa, both of them worthy
*5. of reverence ? Surely it would be better to be even a beggar in this world than to have slain those venerable teachers. For having slain them, gain-desiring though they are, I would enjoy only blood-smeared pleasures here on earth.
6. We know not which would be better for us, to conquer or be conquered. For having slain those sons of Dhṛtarāṣṭra standing there before me, we would not desire to live.
*7. With my ownmost nature (*sva-bhāva*)[5] stricken by this

fault of pity, with my mind confused about *dharma*, I ask you, which would be better? Tell me decisively, I am your pupil[6]; teach[6] me who have approached you for help.
8. For I do not myself see[7] what would take from me this grief which dries up my senses, even if I would gain sole rule over a thriving kingdom on earth, or even lordship over the gods."

Saṁjaya said:
9. Having so spoken to the Lord-of-the-Senses, and having said to the Chief-Guardian "I will not fight," the Thick-
*10. Haired Foe-Destroyer became silent. Then, O Descendant-of-Bharata, the Lord-of-the-Senses, as it were smiling, said these words to him who was sinking into depression[8] between the two armies:

The Blessed Lord said:
*11. "You grieve for those who are not to be grieved for, yet you speak words about wisdom.[9] The learned[10] do not grieve for the living or for the dead.

12. "Never was I not, nor you nor these rulers of men; and
13. never hereafter will any of us not be. For just as the embodied one comes to childhood, youth, and old age in this body, so he comes to another body: in this matter, the intelligent[11] person is not deluded.

*14. "It is contacts with sense-objects, Son-of-Kuntī, that yield pleasure and pain, hot and cold; but these conditions are not lasting, they come and go. Endure them,
*15. Descendant-of-Bharata! For he whom these do not disturb, the intelligent[11] man who is the same amidst pleasure and pain, he is fit for immortality, O Bull-of-Man.

16. "The unreal is never known to become real, nor the real
to cease being real.[12] The dividing-line[13] between the two
is seen by those who see truth.[14]

17. "Know that that by which all this is pervaded, is indes-
tructible; nothing can work the destruction of this which
18. is subject to no change. What has an end is these bodies,[15]
belonging to that embodied one who is himself eternal, in-
destructible, and immeasurable. Therefore, fight, O Des-
cendant-of-Bharata!

19. "Both he who considers him to be slayer and he who
considers him to be slain, fail to understand[16]: he neither
*20. slays nor is slain. He is never born and never dies, he has
had no coming-to-be in the past, and will have no coming-
to-be in the future. Unborn, eternal, everlasting, ancient, he
21. is not slain when the body is slain.[17] He who knows him who
is indestructible, eternal, unborn, changeless, how and whom
does this man slay or cause to be slain, Son-of-Pṛthā?

22. "Just as a man, leaving old garments behind, takes on new
and different ones, so the embodied one, leaving old bodies
behind, gains new and different ones.

23. "Weapons do not cleave him in two, fire does not burn him,
24. water does not wet him, winds do not dry him. He is not
able to be cleaved in two, burned, wetted, dried; he is
25. eternal, all-pervasive, stationary, immovable, primeval. He
is called the unmanifest, the unthinkable, the invariable;
therefore, knowing him as such, you must not grieve.

26. "And likewise, if you think he is perpetually born and per-
petually dying, even so, Strong-Armed, you must not grieve
27. for him. For to one born, death is certain, and to one dying,
birth is certain. Therefore you must not grieve over what

28. is unavoidable. Beings are unmanifest in their beginnings
and ends, manifest in their middles: what in this is to be lamented, O Descendant-of-Bharata?

*29. ["Marvellous is the one who sees this, likewise the one who also speaks of this; marvellous are those who hear of this, even though no one who has merely heard of this knows it as yet.][18]

30. "This embodied one in the body of each, is perpetually invulnerable: therefore, Descendant-of-Bharata, you must not grieve for any being!

*31. "Moreover, having regard for[19] your own particular *dharma*,
you must not falter. There is no higher good for a *kṣatriya*
*32. than a fight accordant with *dharma*. Happy is the *kṣatriya*,
Son-of-Pṛthā, who meets with such a fight which, coming
33. unsought, throws open the door of heaven. But if you will
not engage in this *dharma*-accordant encounter, then having
forsaken your own particular *dharma* as well as glory, you
34. will incur sin. And further, beings will recount your
unalterable disgrace; and for one who has been held in
35. honor, disgrace is worse than death. Great warriors will
think you withdrew from battle out of fear, and you, having
36. been highly thought of by them, will be made light of. And
your enemies will speak many unseemly words, scoffing at
37. your ability. What could be more painful than that? Either,
slain, you will gain heaven; or victorious, you will enjoy
the earth. Therefore, stand up, Son-of-Kuntī, the decision
made for battle!

38. "Treating pleasure and pain, gain and loss, victory and defeat, as all alike, become readied for[20] battle! In that way you will not incur sin.

39. "This (preceding) understanding[21] is addressed to you in the Sāṁkhya[22] vein; but listen to this (following) understanding[23], addressed to you in the Yoga[24] vein. Imbued[25] with this understanding[26], Son-of-Pṛthā, you will leave behind the bondage of activity (*karman*)[27].
40. In this, no effort is lost, no regress is known; even a little of this practice[28] rescues one from the great fear.[29]

*41. "In this, Joy-of-the Kurus, the *buddhi* which is resolute[30] is unitary; many-branched[31], indeed, and endless is the *buddhi* of he who is not resolute.

42. "Son-of-Pṛthā, the undiscerning[32], who delight in the letter of the Vedas and say, 'there is nothing beyond this', /
*43. who are characterized by desire and have heaven as their chief aim, proclaim that flowery word which gives birth as fruit of activity (*karman*) and offers an abundance of different rites to be performed for attaining lordship and
*44. enjoyments.[33] The *buddhi* of those who are engrossed in lordship and enjoyments and whose mind is captivated by that flowery word, is not established in ingatheredness (*samādhi*)[34] when it forms its resolves[35].

*45. "The Vedas have as their subject-matter, activity within the three *guṇas*[36]; but you, Arjuna, become free of the three *guṇas*, become able constantly to stand in the truly-essential (*sattva*)[37], free of dualities, free of acquisition-and-
*46. possession, self-possessed[38] ! For a *brāhmaṇa* who knows, there is as much use in all the Vedas as there is in a well when water is overflowing on all sides.

*47. "Your rightful claim[39] is to activity (*karman*) alone, never to its fruits; let not the fruit of activity (*karman*) be what impels you, but do not let yourself be attached to inactivity
*48. (*akarman*) either. Standing in disciplined-union (*yoga*)[40],

be active, Wealth-winner, having relinquished attachment
and having gained equilibrium amidst success and
failure. Equilibrium is called disciplined-union (*yoga*).
49. Activity (*karman*) is inferior by far indeed to the dis-
ciplined-union (*yoga*) of *buddhi*, Wealth-winner; seek
refuge in *buddhi* ! Pitiful are those who are impelled by
*50. the fruit of activity (*karman*). One whose *buddhi* is yoked-
in-disciplined-union[41] leaves behind good and evil doing
even while here on earth. Therefore become readied for[42]
disciplined-union (*yoga*) ! Effort-disciplined-within-union
(*yoga*) is skillfulness in activities (*karman*).

51. "Having relinquished the fruit born of activity (*karman*)
and with *buddhi* yoked-in-disciplined-union, having be-
come free from the bondage of birth, the wise[43] arrive at a
*52. state without ills. When your *buddhi* shall cross over beyond
the confusion of delusion, then you will reach a condition of
indifference to what you have heard or what you will hear
*53. (from the Vedas).[44] When your *buddhi*, turned this way and
that due to what you have heard (from the Vedas), shall
come to stand in ingathered-union (*samādhi*), unmoving,
immovable, then you will reach disciplined-union (*yoga*)".

Arjuna said:
*54. "What is the mark of the one who has stable *prajñā*[45], Fair-
hair, of the one who stands in ingathered-union (*samādhi*)?
How would the one of stable understanding[46] speak? How
would he walk, how sit?"

The Blessed Lord said:
*55. "When a man forsakes all the desires[47] that have entered
into his mind, and through himself becomes content in his
self alone, then, Son-of-Pṛthā, he is said to be one of stable
56. *prajñā*.[48] He whose mind is undistressed in the midst of

sorrows, and is free of yearning in the midst of pleasures[49], from whom passion, fear and anger have departed, he is said to be a spiritual man[50] of stable understanding.

57. "He who has no attachment in any direction, and who
neither rejoices nor hates when he meets with something
*58. good or bad, his *prajñā* is firmly established. When this
man, like a tortoise drawing in his limbs on all sides,
withdraws his senses from sense objects, his *prajñā* is
firmly established.[51]

59. "Matters of sense recede from the embodied one who
abstains from feeding on them, but a relish for such things
persists (with mere abstention). Even that relish recedes,
*60. however, when the supreme has been seen. Of course, Son-
of-Kuntī, even the senses of a man who, knowing such a
vision, is still endeavoring to make his way toward fulfill-
ment, may forcibly carry off his mind, in their capacity to
61. create turbulence. Having controlled all these, he should
sit engaged-in-the-disciplined-effort-of-meditation, given
over to me. For he whose senses are submissive, his
prajñā is firmly established.

62. "In a man intent upon matters of sense, attachment to
such matters is born. From attachment, grasping desire
63. is born, and from such desire anger arises. From anger,
a deluding confusion comes to be, and due to such
confusion, remembrance is dispersed. With this dispersal
goes destruction of the capacity-for-intelligent-decision[52].
And because of this destruction, a man is lost.

*64. "But that man finds calm[53], who moves about amidst
things of sense with his senses free from[54] passionate desire
and hatred and submissive to a self which is itself subdued.
*65. And in that calm, the cessation of all his sorrows is engen-

dered. For the *buddhi* of a calm mind quickly becomes
stable-and-firm.

*66. "For the one who is not yoked-in-disciplined-union, there
is no real-*buddhi*[55], nor is there contemplative-steeping-
of-himself[56]. And for one not fostered through such steep-
ing, there is no inward-peace. But how is there happiness
without inward-peace?

67. "Verily, such of the roving senses as the mind yields to,
carries away the person's *prajñā*, like a wind carrying away
68. a ship on water. Therefore, Strong-armed, he whose senses
are on all sides restrained from sense-objects, his *prajñā* is
firmly established.

69. "That which is night for all beings, in that the controlled
one is awake; that in which beings are awake, is night for
70. the spiritual man who sees. He whom all desires[57] enter
in such way that, like waters entering the sea, he is being
filled but stands fast immovable[58], he wins peace, not he
71. who cherishes desires[59]. The man who, having left behind
all desires, moves without yearning, without possessiveness,
*72. without ego, he finds peace. O Son-of-Pṛthā, this is the holy
state[60]; having reached it, one is no longer bewildered.
Having taken one's stand in this state right up to the end
of his time, he attains extinction-in-the-holy-power[61]."

CHAPTER III

Arjuna said:

1. "If to your mind *buddhi* is superior to action (*karman*), O
Exciter-of-Men, then why, Fair-Hair, do you enjoin me
2. to this dreadful deed (*karman*)?[1] You are bewildering my

understanding[2] with an apparently confused utterance. Having made a decision, tell me the one way by which I may gain what is good!"

The Blessed Lord said:

*3. "Long ago, Blameless One, I proclaimed a two-fold way-of-devotedly-applying-oneself[3] in this world, relating to the men of Sāṁkhya (the discipline [*yoga*] of knowledge) and to the men of Yoga (the discipline [*yoga*] of action [*karman*]).

*4. "No man attains freedom from the bondage of activity
(*naiṣkarmya*) simply by not undertaking actions (*karman*);
5. not by mere renunciation does one attain perfection[4]. For
no one even for a moment is absolutely inactive: independent
of their will, everyone is made to engage in activity (*karman*)
6. by way of the *guṇas* born of nature[5]. He who has held in
check his powers of overt-action (*karman*) but, himself
deluded, sits remembering sense objects with his mind, is
7. to be called a man of false conduct. But he who has
controlled his senses by his mind and, without attachment,
undertakes the disciplined-effort (*yoga*) of action (*karman*)
with his powers of overt-action (*karman*), he excels,
Arjuna.[6]

8. "Do your allotted[7] action (*karman*), for action (*karman*) is superior to inaction (*akarman*)! Besides, if you engage in no action at all, you cannot even win the subsistence of your body.

9. "Except for activity (*karman*) engaged in as sacrifice, this
world is subject to the bondage of activity (*karman*). Perform
action (*karman*) in that fashion, Son-of-Kuntī, released from
10. attachment. Long ago, the Lord of Creatures, having
created creatures together with sacrifice, said[8]: 'By this

shall you prosper, let this be the milch-cow for your desires.
11. By this foster the gods, and let the gods foster you: foster-
ing each other, you will attain to the supreme (worldly)
*12. good. For the gods, fostered by sacrifice, will give you the
pleasures you desire. He who enjoys their gifts without
13. having given to them, is nothing but a thief.' Good men,
feeding on the remains of sacrifice, are liberated from
all sins[9]. But those wicked men who prepare food for their
14. own sake alone, eat sin. Beings arise from food, food has
its origin in rain, rain arises from sacrifice, and sacrifice
*15. has its origin in action (*karman*). Know action (*karman*) to
have its origin in holy utterance[10] (the Vedas), and this
to have its origin in the imperishable. Therefore the holy
utterance[10], which reaches to all, is always established in
16. sacrifice. He who on earth does not contribute to the
continued movement of the wheel thus set in motion[11],
lives in vain, Son-of-Pṛthā, his life a sinful delighting in
17. sense. The man, however, who can be delighted, satisfied,
content, in his self alone, he knows no work-to-be-done.[12]
18. There is no advantage on earth for him to gain by what
is done or by what is not done, and there is no being at all
on whom he depends for any advantage.

19. "Therefore, perform the action (*karman*) to-be-done[13],
continually free from attachment, for by performing action
(*karman*) without attachment, a man reaches the supreme.
*20. Indeed, by action (*karman*) alone, it was, that Janaka[14]
and others ascended to ultimate perfection.

"And you also must act, attending to no less than the
21. holding together of the world. For whatever the superior
man does, that other people also do. He sets the standard
22. which the world follows. For me, Son-of-Pṛthā, there is
no work whatever to-be-done in the three worlds, nothing

unobtained which is to be obtained; yet without fail,
23. I am engaged in activity (*karman*). For if I were not
ever tirelessly engaged in activity (*karman*), Son of Pṛthā,
24. men on all sides would follow my path. These worlds
would fall to ruin were I not engaged in activity (*karman*).
I would be author of confusion, I would do harm to
these creatures.

25. "Those who are confined in ignorance (*avidyā*) act, attached
to action (*karman*); the wise[15] should also act, Descendant-
of-Bharata, but without attachment, desiring to act so as
26. to hold the world together. Let him not beget a divided
understanding in the ignorant[16] who are attached to action
(*karman*); let the wise[15] bring the ignorant to relish
all actions (*karman*), themselves performing each action
(*karman*) yoked-in-disciplined-union.

27. "Activities (*karman*) are accomplished[17] wholly by way of
the *guṇas* of nature; yet deluded by the sense of ego[18], a self
*28. thinks 'I am the doer'[19]. But Strong-Armed, he who knows
the truth about the differentiation-and-relation[20] of *guṇas*
and activity (*karman*), thinks: '*Guṇas* are concerned with
guṇas', and does not get attached.

29. "Those who are completely deluded by the *guṇas* of nature,
become attached to the workings (*karman*) of the *guṇas*. Let
not he who knows the whole, unsettle the sluggish, who
do not know the whole.

*30. "Mindful of what is above your self, having renounced
all actions (*karman*) to me and having become free of
possessiveness and craving, fight, your fever vanished !

31. "Men who constantly follow out this teaching of mine,
unmurmuring and full of faith, are released from their

*32. actions (*karman*). But those who murmur against it, who do not follow it out, know those mindless ones, deluded in regards to all *jñāna*[21], to be lost.

33. "Even the one who has *jñāna*, functions in conformity with his own nature; beings follow nature, what will suppression
34. accomplish? One should not allow the passionate-desire[22] and hatred that become established in the senses in regard to the objects of sense, to gain control; for these passions
*35. and hates are his two waylayers. One's own *dharma*, even when not done perfectly, is better than an alien *dharma*, even though well performed;[23] indeed, death in one's own *dharma* is better than that, for it is perilous to seek to perform an alien *dharma*."

Arjuna said:

36. "Then by what is that man bidden, O Descendant-of-Vṛṣṇi, who performs evil even against his will, impelled so-to-speak by force?"

The Blessed Lord said:

37. "Desire[24] it is, anger it is, produced from the *rajas guṇa*, greatly consuming and greatly sin-bringing: know this to be
38. the enemy in this case. For just as fire is concealed by smoke, a mirror by dust, and an embryo by its membrane,
39. so this is concealed by that. Son-of-Kuntī, *jñāna* is concealed by that constant enemy of the wise, that insatiable and pro-
40. tean[25] fire. The senses, the mind, the *buddhi*, are said to be its seat; through these, it deludes the embodied one, having concealed *jñāna*.

*41. "Therefore, having controlled the senses to begin with, O Bull-of-the-Bharatas, slay this evil which brings loss of
42. *jñāna* and of discrimination.[26] The senses are superior[27], so they say, and the mind is above the senses. But there is *buddhi* above mind, and there is also he who is beyond

43. *buddhi*. So having become awakened[28] to the one beyond *buddhi*, having made yourself firm through yourself, slay this protean enemy, Strong-Armed, which is so hard to get at."[29]

CHAPTER IV

The Blessed Lord said:

1. "I proclaimed this changeless discipline (*yoga*) to Vivasvat,
*2. he told it to Manu, and he, to Ikṣvāku.[1] Handed down in this way from one to another, this discipline (*yoga*) was known by the royal sages[2], but, Foe-Destroyer, it became corrupted[3]
3. on earth with the lapse of much time. That very discipline (*yoga*) of old is being proclaimed by me to you today. You are devoted[4] to me, and call me 'friend'. That discipline (*yoga*) is, indeed, the ultimate secret."

Arjuna said :

4. "You were born after Vivasvat: how am I to understand this, that you proclaimed this discipline (*yoga*) in the beginning ?"

The Blessed Lord said:

5. "You and I have gone through many births, Arjuna; I know
*6. them all, you do not, Foe-Destroyer. Though I am unborn and of changeless self, though I am Lord of[5] beings, having taken my stand over[6] my own nature, I am born
7. by my own self's power (*māyā*).[7] For whenever decrease in *dharma* comes about, Descendant-of-Bharata, and a rise in
8. *adharma*, then I create myself. For the protection of the righteous and the destruction of evil-doers, for the purpose of the establishment of *dharma*, I am born from age to age.

9. "He who knows in truth this, my divine birth and action
(*karman*), having relinquished his body, he goes not to re-
10. birth but to me, Arjuna. With passion, fear, and anger gone,
having cleaved to me, being filled with me, many—purified
*11. by the fire of *jñāna*—come to my being (*bhāva*). I appor-
tion to men what accords with their approach to me. Men
12. follow my path in every case, Son-of-Pṛthā. Those desiring
success of their actions (*karman*) on earth, sacrifice to the
gods. Quickly, indeed, comes success in the human world,
13. born of action (*karman*). I created the four castes in terms
of the differentiation-and-relation[8] of *guṇas* and activity
(*karman*).

"Although I made[9] them, know me to be changeless, no
14. maker[9]. Actions (*karman*) do not pollute me, I do not
yearn for their fruit. He who perceives-and-acknowledges[10]
15. me thus, is not bound by actions (*karman*). Having such
jñāna[11], the ancients who desired release were active.[12]
You be active, therefore, just as the ancients were in
earlier days.

16. " 'What is activity (*karman*)? What is inactivity (*akarman*)?'
Even seers are deluded on this point. I will declare to you
that active-effort (*karman*) which, if you know[13] it, you will
17. be released from sin. You must understand[14] not only acti-
vity (*karman*), however, but improper activity (*vikarman*)[15]
and inactivity (*akarman*); the way of activity (*karman*) is
*18. difficult to fathom. He who can see activity (*karman*) in
inactivity (*akarman*), and inactivity (*akarman*) in activity
(*karman*), is a man of *buddhi*, he is yoked-in-disciplined-union,
19. doing action (*karman*) whole. He whose every undertaking
is devoid of the willful purpose of grasping desire, whose
active efforts (*karman*) have been burned by the fire of
jñāna, the awakened ones[16] call him a man-of-learning.[17]

20. Having relinquished attachment to the fruit of action
(*karman*), being constantly satisfied and without dependence,
he does[18] nothing whatever, even though he is engaged
21. in action (*karman*). Without craving, with mind and self
controlled and all grasping relinquished, being active
with body alone, he does not incur sin. Content with
22. what he happens to find, himself beyond the dualities,
free from envy, and the same in success and failure, he
is not bound even though acting.

23. "The activity (*karman*) of the released one, whose
attachment is gone, whose mind has its abode in *jñāna*,
and whose active effort (*karman*) is that of one performing
*24. sacrifice, is wholly dissolved. The act of offering, the
oblation offered, the one who offers, the sacrificial fire, and
what is to be partaken of by him who is ingathered[19] in
the midst of his active effort (*karman*): all these, and the
action (*karman*) itself, are the holy power itself.

*25. "Some men of disciplined-effort (*yoga*) there are, whose
worship is a sacrifice to the gods; others make sacrifice by
sacrificing only into the fire which is the holy power.
26. (Between these extremes)[20] there are some who offer their
senses into the fires of control[21], some who offer sense objects
*27. into the fires of sense[22], / some who offer the workings
(*karman*) of all the senses and of the vital-breath into
that fire of the disciplined union (*yoga*) of self-control
28. which is kindled by *jñāna*. Still others offer as sacrifice
their possessions, their austerity[23], or their meditational
exercises (*yoga*); and the restrained, firmly adhering to
their vows, offer their scriptural study and knowledge as
29. sacrifice. Others, likewise, having controlled the course
of their inbreathing and outbreathing, wholly devoted to
30. breath control, offer the one breath into the other. And

others abstemious in food, offer one vital power into
another.

"All these are knowers of sacrifice, by sacrifice their sins
31. are destroyed. Those who eat the food-of-immortality[24] left
after the sacrifice, go toward[25] the primeval holy power.
This world is not for one who does not sacrifice, how then
*32. any other world, Highest-of-the-Kurus? Thus manifold
sacrifices are spread out in the mouth of the holy power.[26]
Know them all to be born of activity (*karman*): knowing
*33. this, you will be released. The *jñāna* sacrifice is better,
Foe-Destroyer, than the sacrifice made with possessions.
All complete[27] action (*karman*) is brought to completeness
in *jñāna*, Son-of-Pṛthā.[28]

34. "Know such *jñāna* by humble submission, inquiry, and
service. Men of *jñāna*, having themselves seen the true
*35. reality, will explain that *jñāna* to you.[29] You will never
be deluded again, Son-of-Pāṇḍu, when you have gained
it; by it you will see all beings in your self, then in me.
36. Even if you are the most sinful of sinners, you will cross
37. beyond all wickedness by the boat of *jñāna* alone.[30] Just
as a fire reduces its fuel to ashes, Arjuna, so the fire of
38. *jñāna* reduces all activities (*karman*) to ashes.[31] For no
equal to *jñāna* as a purifier is known on earth; through
himself, the one who has perfected himself in disciplined
39. union (*yoga*) finds it in himself with time. He who has
faith[32], whose senses are controlled, who is intent upon
jñāna, gains *jñāna*, and having done this, he quickly
40. attains supreme peace.[33] But he who is without *jñāna*
and does not have faith, his very self being doubt[34], he
is lost: for such a one, there is neither this world nor
41. the following, nor is there happiness. Actions (*karman*) do
not bind, Wealth-winner, when one has renounced all

activity (*karman*) in disciplined effort (*yoga*), has cut out doubt by *jñāna*, and is self-possessed.

42. "Therefore, having cut out with your self's own sword of *jñāna* this doubt which stands in your heart and is born of lack of *jñāna*, engage in disciplined effort (*yoga*) and stand up, Descendant-of-Bharata!"

CHAPTER V

Arjuna said:

1. "Kṛṣṇa, you praise the renunciation of actions (*karman*), and then again, their disciplined undertaking (*yoga*). Which one of these is better: tell me quite decisively!"

The Blessed Lord said:

2. "The renunciation and the disciplined undertaking (*yoga*)
of action (*karman*) both bring the ultimate good, but of the
two, the disciplined undertaking (*yoga*) of action (*karman*) is
3. superior. He who neither hates nor desires, is to be known
as one who constantly renounces. For free from dualities,
4. Strong-armed, he is easily released from bondage. It is the
childish[1], not the men of learning[2], who declare Sāṁkhya
and Yoga to be diverse. He who is engaged properly in one,
5. obtains the fruit of both. That place-and-standing[3] which
is attained by the men of Sāṁkhya, is reached by those
of Yoga also. Sāṁkhya and Yoga are one: he who sees
this, sees truly.

6. "But Strong-armed, (outward) renunciation is difficult to
be equal to without strenuous application (*yoga*)[4]; the
spiritual man who is engaged in the disciplined-under-
taking-of-action (*yoga*) attains to the holy power quickly.
7. Engaged in such undertaking (*yoga*), himself completely

pure and subdued, his senses subdued, his self having become the self of all beings[5], he is not polluted even though he acts.

8. " 'I am doing nothing at all' : so should think the yoked
one[6] who knows truth. Seeing, hearing, touching, smelling,
9. eating, walking, sleeping, breathing, / talking, grasping and
letting go, opening and closing his eyes: he should hold that
10. in these, 'senses are concerned with sense-objects'. Having
placed his actions (*karman*) on the holy power[7], having
relinquished attachment, one who acts is not polluted by
11. sin, just as the lotus leaf is unsullied by water.[8] For self-
purification, men of disciplined effort (*yoga*) are active by
way of the body, mind, *buddhi*, and bare[9] senses, having
relinquished attachment.

12. "Yoked-in-disciplined-effort, having relinquished the fruit of action (*karman*), he attains perfect peace. Unyoked, attached to the fruit by the working[10] of desire, he is bound.

13. "Having renounced with his mind all actions (*karman*), the
embodied one sits at ease, master in the city of nine gates[11],
14. neither acting nor causing action to be done. The one who
presides over the world[12] neither creates actions (*karman*)
nor the condition of being active, nor the connection of
fruit and activity (*karman*); rather, his own nature[13] is
15. concerned with this. This pervasive one does not take on
anyone's sin nor his good deeds either. *Jñāna* is concealed
*16. by lack of *jñāna*: with this, creatures are deluded. But
the sun-like *jñāna* of those whose lack of *jñāna* into their
selves has been dispelled by *jñāna*, reveals the supreme.[14]
*17. With *buddhi* and self open to the supreme, with devoted
application[15] to it as the final end, they attain a condition
of no return, their sins removed by *jñāna*.

18. "Men-of-learning[16] view with equal eye a *brāhmaṇa* of
knowledge and good breeding, a cow, an elephant, and
19. even a dog and an outcaste. Creation[17] is overcome even
here on earth, by those whose mind stands firm in equani-
mity. For the holy power is the same, without defect;
20. therefore they stand firm in the holy power. One should
not exult on gaining something agreeable, nor should one
be dismayed on meeting with what is disagreeable. His
buddhi steady, undeluded, the knower of the holy power
is firm-and-abiding in that power.

21. "The self which is unattached to external contacts, and finds
happiness in himself, he—the self yoked-in-disciplined-
union (*yoga*) to the holy power—obtains an undecaying
22. happiness. For those pleasures which are born of contact
are merely sources of sorrow, possessing a beginning and
an end. The man who is awake[18] takes no delight in
*23. them, O Son-of-Kuntī. The man who here on earth,
before giving up his body, is able to overcome the impetus
24. born of desire and anger, he is yoked, he is happy. That
man of disciplined effort (*yoga*) whose happiness and de-
light are inner, whose light is also inner, having become
the holy power, goes to extinction in the holy power.
25. Those sages who attain this extinction in the holy power
are those whose sins have perished, for whom duality is
destroyed, whose self is controlled, and who take delight
26. in the welfare of every being. Extinction in the holy
power is near for the striving ones who are delivered[19]
from desire and anger, whose mind is controlled, whose self
is known.

27. "Having shut out external contacts and fixed the eye in the
middle between the two brows, having equalized the two
28. breaths moving within the nostrils,/the spiritual man whose

buddhi, mind and senses are controlled, who is intent on release as final end, whose desire, fear, and anger have gone, he is ever released.

29. "Having known[20] me as the Great Lord of All the Worlds, the Enjoyer of sacrifice and austerity and the Friend of all beings, one attains peace."

CHAPTER VI

The Blessed Lord said:

1. "He who does the action (*karman*) to-be-done, but without
dependence on the fruit of action (*karman*), is a man of dis-
ciplined engagement in action (*yoga*) and a man of renun-
ciation, not he who is without sacrificial fire and with-
2. out ceremonial works.[1] What is called 'renunciation', know
it to be the disciplined engagement in action (*yoga*), O Son-
of-Pāṇḍu. For no one becomes a man of disciplined-union
(*yoga*)[2] who has not renounced willful purpose.

3. "Activity (*karman*) is said to be the element[3] of the spiritual
man[4] who desires to ascend to disciplined-union (*yoga*); tran-
quillity is said to be the element[3] of him who has already
4. ascended to such union (*yoga*). For when, having renoun-
ced all willful purpose, one does not become attached either
to actions (*karman*) or to sense-objects, one is then said to
have ascended to disciplined-union (*yoga*).

5. "Let one raise oneself up by oneself, let one not make one-
self sink down; one's self alone is one's own self's friend
*6. or foe. One's self is friend of one's self in one whose self is
subdued by self; but the self of one not so self-possessed will
be hostile like an enemy.

*7. "The higher self of[5] one who is self-subdued and tranquil, is composed[6] amidst cold and heat, pleasure and pain, honor and dishonor.

*8. "The man of disciplined-effort (*yoga*) whose self is satisfied
in *jñāna* and discrimination,[7] who stands on high with senses
subdued, is said to be 'united'[8]: to him, gold, a stone, a
9. clod of earth, are the same. He excels whose *buddhi* is the
same amidst the righteous and the sinful, amidst the well-
disposed, the friendly, the neutral, the indifferent, and the
hostile, amidst enemies and allies.

10. "Let the man making his disciplined effort by way of medi-
tational exercises, engage himself in those exercises conti-
nually[9], remaining alone in a solitary place, his mind and
11. self controlled, without craving and grasping. Let him fix
for himself on a clear place a firm seat, which is neither
too high nor too low, and which is covered with sacred
12. grass, a deerskin, and a cloth. And there, settled down on
that seat, let him engage in his exercises for the purification
of himself, having made his mind one-pointed and having
13. restrained the working of his mind and senses. Let him hold
his body, neck, and head erect, keeping himself steady and
unmoving, not looking around but looking at the base of
14. his nose; / and having restrained his mind and become
mindful of me, let this tranquil fearless man who stands
firm in his vow to a life of holiness, sit, engaged in his
*15. exercises and given over to me. Ever engaging himself in
his exercises in this way, this man of disciplined effort
(*yoga*)—his mind restrained—attains the peace which exists
in me and which ends in extinction.[10]

16. "But such disciplined effort (*yoga*) is not for one who eats
17. or sleeps too much or too little, Arjuna. For one whose en-

joyment of food is disciplined, whose engagement in actions
(*karman*) is disciplined, whose sleeping and waking are dis-
ciplined, the disciplined-effort-of-meditation (*yoga*) be-
18. comes a remover of sorrow. When one's restrained mind
abides in one's self alone, freed from yearning after any
desire, then one is said to be 'united'[11].

19. "Unflickering, like a lamp in a sheltered place: this is the
traditional image for the man of disciplined effort (*yoga*)
exercising himself in meditational exercises (*yoga*), his
20. mind restrained. That in which thinking ceases, stopped by
the practice of disciplined-meditation (*yoga*), and in which—
seeing himself through himself—one is content in himself
21. .../ that in which he knows that which is boundless happi-
ness, beyond the senses but perceivable by *buddhi*[12], and in
which—firm-standing in it—he truly swerves not from it
22. ... / that which, having obtained it, one thinks there is
no further gain beyond this, and that within which, firm-
standing in it, one is not shaken even by heavy sorrow.../
23. let this disengagement[13] of the connection[14] with sorrow be
called disciplined-union (*yoga*). This disciplined-union
(*yoga*) is to be practised with determination, with a heart
*24. free from depression. Having relinquished entirely all de-
sires originating in willful purpose, having exercised control
25. on every side over all the senses by mind alone, / let him
be stilled little by little, through a *buddhi* which has gained
firmness[15]. Having made his mind self-possessed, let him
26. not think on anything further. Having restrained the
mind—restless, unsteady—from whatever it goes out to,
27. let him bring it under the will of his self alone. Indeed, to
this tranquil-minded and sinless man of disciplined-union
(*yoga*), in whom *rajas* is at rest and who has become the
28. holy power, there comes a supreme happiness. Ever exercis-
ing himself in disciplined-meditation (*yoga*) in this way,

the man of disciplined-meditation—his sin vanished—
easily attains to the boundless happiness of contact[16]
with the holy power.

*29. "The one whose self is yoked in disciplined-union (*yoga*),
sees self standing in all beings, and sees all beings in self[17];
30. everywhere, the view is the same. He who sees me every-
where, and sees all in me, I am not lost to him, and he
*31. is not lost to me. That man of disciplined-effort (*yoga*)
who, taking his stand upon oneness, is devoted to me stand-
ing in every creature, exists in me, whatever directions the
*32. turns of his existing take him in[18]. That man of disciplined-
effort (*yoga*) who, because of the likeness in selves, sees the
same everywhere, whether in pleasure or in sorrow, is to
be considered supreme, Arjuna."

Arjuna said:
33. "You have proclaimed a discipline (*yoga*) of sameness, O
Slayer-of-Madhu; but I do not see how the state of sameness
34. can be lasting, due to restlessness. Restless, indeed, is the
mind, Kṛṣṇa, turbulent and powerful and stubborn. Its
restraint, I think, would be very difficult to accomplish,
like restraining the wind."

The Blessed Lord said:
35. "Doubtless, Strong-armed, the restless-and-fluctuating[19]
mind is difficult to restrain, but by practice and dispassion,
*36. it can be held, Son-of-Kuntī. Disciplined-union (*yoga*) is
impossible to attain with an uncontrolled self: so I think.
But it can be obtained with an obedient self which strives
in a skillful way."

Arjuna said:
37. "What way does he go, Kṛṣṇa, who is possessed of faith but

is not restrained, so that his mind is swerved from dis-
ciplined-effort (*yoga*) before he has obtained the ultimate
38. perfection of such effort (*yoga*) ? Fallen from both[20], not
having become firmly established and being bewildered over
the path to the holy power[21], does he perish, Strong-armed,
39. like a severed rain-cloud ? You must cut off completely this
doubt of mine, Kṛṣṇa, for there is none other than you who
can do this."

The Blessed Lord said:
40. "Son-of-Pṛthā, neither in this nor the other world does such
a one know destruction. For, my dear one, no one who does
41. what is fair goes an evil way. Having attained the world of
the meritorious, having dwelled there many years, the one
who has fallen from disciplined-effort (*yoga*) is born into
42. a pure and prosperous house. Or else he is born in a family
of intelligent[22] men of discipline (*yoga*) : though such a birth
43. in the world is more difficult to obtain. In either case, he
gains there the *buddhi*-integration[23] of his previous embodi-
ment, and once more he strives for perfection from there,
44. Joy-of-the-Kurus. By his previous practice[24] alone, he is
carried onward, even without willing this. Even he who
desires the *jñāna* of disciplined-union (*yoga*), is beyond
45. the Vedic rule.[25] But the diligently striving man of discip-
line (*yoga*) who is completely purified of sin, attains perfec-
tion after many births, and then goes to the supreme desti-
nation.

46. "The man of disciplined-effort (*yoga*) is above the ascetic,
and is even considered above the men of knowledge, he is
above the doers of ritual-and-social works too: therefore,
*47. become a man of disciplined effort (*yoga*), Arjuna. Of all
the men of discipline (*yoga*) also, he who is possessed of
faith and devotes himself to me with his inner self given
over to me, I consider him to be the most disciplined."[26]

CHAPTER VII

The Blessed Lord said:

*1. "Hear this, Son-of-Pṛthā, how engaged in disciplined-effort
(*yoga*) with your mind fastened on me, depending on me,
*2. you will gain insight into[1] me fully, without doubt. I will
tell you the whole of this *jñāna* accompanied by discrimination.[2] Having gained this *jñāna*, there remains nothing more on earth to be seen into.[3]

*3. "Scarcely one man in thousands strives for perfection, and of the thousands of those who strive[4], scarcely one knows me in truth.

4. "Earth, water, fire, air, ether, *manas*,[5] *buddhi*, and ego: this
*5. is that nature[6] of mine which is divided eight-fold[7], / my
lower nature[6]. But know now, Strong-armed, my other
nature,[6] higher and endowed with life, by which this world
*6. is supported. Know that all beings have this[8] for their
source. I am the cause of the existence of the entire world,
7. and cause of its destruction as well.[9] There is nothing whatever above me, Wealth-winner. All this is strung on me like multitudes of pearls on a string.[10]

*8. "I am the taste in the waters, Son-of-Kuntī, and the radi-
ance in the sun and moon, the sacred syllable *aum* in all the
9. Vedas, sound in ether, manliness in men. I am the pleasant
fragrance in earth, the glowing brightness in fire, the life
10. in all beings, the austerity in ascetics. Know me to be
the primeval seed of all beings, Son-of-Pṛthā. I am the
understanding[11] of the wise[12], the splendor of the splendid,/
11. that strength of the strong which is devoid of grasping
desire and passion, and Bull-of-the-Bharatas, I am that desire in beings which is not at variance with *dharma*.

12. "And know also that whatever conditions[13] are sattvic,
rajasic, or tamasic, are from me alone. But I am not in them,
13. they are in me. Deluded by these conditions[14] composed
of the three *guṇas*, this whole world does not perceive-and-
14. acknowledge me, changeless above them. For this divine
deluding-power (*māyā*) of mine composed of the *guṇas*, is
difficult to transcend. Those who go forth to me alone, cross
15. this deluding-power (*māyā*). Foolish evil-doers, lowest of
men, whose *jñāna* is carried away by my deluding power
(*māyā*) and who have fallen subject to what is demonic in
its nature, do not go forth to me.

*16. "Men of good deeds who devote themselves to me, Arjuna,
are of four kinds: the oppressed and afflicted, the seeker of
knowledge[15], the seeker of purpose, and also, Bull-of-the-
17. Bharatas, the man of *jñāna*. Of these the man of *jñāna*, cons-
tantly yoked-in-disciplined-union and one in his devotion,
excels. Indeed, I am exceedingly dear to the man of *jñāna*,
18. and he is dear to me. Noble are all these without exception,
but to my mind the man of *jñāna* is my very self. For, his
self yoked-in-disciplined-union, he takes his stand upon me
alone, the unsurpassed way.

19. "At the end of many births, the one who possesses *jñāna* goes
forth to me, aware that 'Vāsudeva is all'. Such a man of
20. great self is very hard to find. Those whose *jñāna* is carried
away by one desire or another, go forth to other gods,
having carried out one or another observance governed by
21. their own nature. I make unwavering the faith of any
devotee who wishes to worship with faith any particular-
22. manifestation-of-divinity[16]. Filled with that faith, he seeks
the propitiation of such a manifestation, and from it he
gains his desires. Indeed, it is I who fulfill those desires.
23. But transient is that fruit of those of little intelligence. Those

who sacrifice to the gods, go to the gods; but those who are devoted to me, go to me.

*24. "Those without understanding think me, the unmanifest,
to be exhausted by a manifestation, not being cognizant of
25. my higher nature, changeless and unsurpassed. Covered by
my magical power (*yoga-māyā*), I do not shine forth for all.[17]
This deluded world does not perceive-and-acknowledge me,
26. unborn, changeless. I know the beings that were, are, and
27. will be, Arjuna, but no one knows me.[18] Foe-destroyer,
Descendant-of-Bharata, all beings at birth enter into delu-
sion through the illusion of duality that springs up in desire
28. and hatred. But those men of meritorious deeds in whom sin
has come to an end, who are thus released from the illusion
of duality and who are firm in their vows, devote themselves
to me.

29. "Having cleaved to me, those who strive for release from
old age and death know that holy power entire, knowing it
in its very self and knowing the whole of its action (*karman*).
30. Those who with yoked mind know me in my relation to
beings and to the manifest world at large and in my relation
to sacrifice, know me even at the time of their departure."[19]

CHAPTER VIII

Arjuna said:

1. "What is that holy power? What is it in its very self? What is its action (*karman*), Supreme Spirit? What is it declared to be in relation to beings and to the manifest world at large?
2. How and what is it in this body in relation to sacrifice, Slayer-of-Madhu? And how are you to be cognized by those with restrained selves at the time of their departure?"

The Blessed Lord said:

3. "The holy power is the imperishable and supreme, and it is
its ownmost (creational) nature-and-being (*sva-bhāva*) that
is its very self[1]; that creating which initiates the existence-
*4. and-nature of beings, is its action (*karman*). In relation
to beings, it is perishable existence, and in relation to
the manifest world at large, it is spirit. And in relation to
sacrifice, it is none other than I, O Best-of-Embodied-
5. Beings, here in the body. And he who departs at the end
of his time, remembering-and-thinking-on me alone, hav-
ing let go his body, goes to my nature-and-being (*bhāva*):
of this there is no doubt.

6. "Otherwise, Son-of-Kuntī, at the end he abandons his body,
and goes to that natural condition[2] alone which he is re-
membering-and-thinking on, ever being made to assume
7. that condition.[3] Therefore remember-and-think-on me at
all times and fight; with your *buddhi* and *manas* joined to
me, freed of doubt you will come to me alone.

8. "Meditating with a mind which is engaged without wander-
ing in the practice of the disciplined-effort-of-meditation
(*yoga*), one goes to the supreme divine spirit, Son-of-Pṛthā.
9. He who remembers-and-thinks-on the ancient seer[4], the
governor[5], who is subtler than the subtle[6], the supporter
of all[7], incomprehensible in form[8], sun-colored and beyond
10. darkness[9]: / he, devotedly engaged in meditation with an
immovable mind and having succeeded by virtue of this
disciplined effort (*yoga*) in making his life-breath go to the
mid-point between his eye-brows, comes to that supreme
divine spirit at the time of his departure.

11. "That which the Veda-knowers designate 'the imperish-
able', which the restrained ones free of passion enter, and

desiring which they undertake the religious life: that abode, I
12. will declare to you briefly. Having closed all the gates[10]
and having confined the mind to the heart, having set one's
self's life-breath in the head and having entered upon the
concentration of the disciplined-effort-of-meditation (*yoga*),/
13. he who utters *aum* (the one-syllable holy utterance) and
remembers-and-puts-his-mind-on me, goes to the supreme
destination when he relinquishes his body and departs.[11]
14. He whose mind is never on anything but me, who constantly
remembers me: for that man of disciplined effort (*yoga*)
constantly engaged in discipline (*yoga*), I am easily reached,
15. Son-of-Pṛthā. Having gone to me, those men of great self
do not come to rebirth in this impermanent abode of sorrow,
but go to the supreme perfection.

16. "The worlds from the realm of Brahmā[12] down, are subject
to rebirth, Arjuna; but having gone to me, Son-of-Kuntī,
17. rebirth is not known. The men who know the day of Brahmā,
long as a thousand ages, and the night of Brahmā, equally
18. as long, are knowers of day and night[13]. All manifest things
arise from the unmanifest at the coming of day, and at the
coming of night they are dissolved there, in what is called
19. the 'unmanifest'. This very same multitude of beings,
having come to be over and over again, goes to dissolution
at the coming of night, Son-of-Pṛthā, and arises at the
20. coming of day, quite apart from their willing this. But
beyond this unmanifest, is another unmanifest nature-and-
being (*bhāva*), primeval, which does not perish even with
21. the perishing of all beings. Called 'the imperishable
unmanifest', they call it the supreme destination, having
reached which they do not return. This is my supreme
22. dwelling-place. / Son-of-Pṛthā, he is the supreme spirit, by
whom all this is pervaded, in whom all things stand. He
is to be gained, however, by unswerving devotion.

23. "But Bull-of-the-Bharatas, I will declare at what time men
of discipline (*yoga*), departing, go and do not return, and at
24. what time they go but do return. Fire, light, day, the bright
half of the lunar cycle, the six months of the sun's northerly
course: departing then, men who are knowers of the holy
25. power go to the holy power. Smoke, night, the dark half of
the lunar period, the six months of the sun's southerly course:
departing then, the man of discipline (*yoga*) reaches the
26. light of the moon and returns. These bright and dark paths
of the world are thought to be everlasting: by the one,
one goes and does not return, by the other, one returns
27. again. The man of discipline (*yoga*) who knows these paths,
Son-of-Pṛthā, is not deluded. Therefore at all times be
engaged in disciplined effort, Arjuna.[14]

28. "The man of discipline (*yoga*) who knows all this, transcends the fruit of merit assigned for Vedic study, sacrifices, austerities and alms-giving, and arrives at the supreme and primal place-and-standing."

CHAPTER IX

The Blessed Lord said:
1. "To you, however, who are not murmuring against what
I am saying, I will declare this most secret[1] *jñāna* joined
with discrimination[2]; having gained this *jñāna*, you will be
2. released from sin. Sovereign knowledge, sovereign secret,
changeless, this utmost purifier is approached directly and
immediately in understanding[3], is accordant with *dharma*,
3. and is quite easy to follow. Men who put no faith in this
practice[4], Foe-destroyer, return to the path of wandering
and death, not having reached me.

4. "This whole world is pervaded by me in my unmanifest
form. All beings stand in me, and I am not lodged in
5. them. / Yet beings do not stand in me. Behold my lordly
magic (*yoga*): sustaining beings, yet not lodged in them, my
6. very self is creator of beings. Know that just as the
mighty wind, going everywhere, stands constantly in space,
so all beings stand in me.

7. "All beings go into my nature[5] at the time of universal
destruction, Son-of-Kuntī, and I send them forth again at
*8. the time of universal beginning. Resting on[6] my own na-
ture[5], I send forth this whole multitude of beings again
and again, at the behest of my nature[5] and not according
9. to their will. And these actions (*karman*), Wealth-winner,
do not bind me, who remain as if indifferent, unattached
10. to these actions (*karman*). Under my supervision[7], my
nature[5] brings forth the moving and the unmoving; it is
due to this cause, Son-of-Kuntī, that the world revolves.

11. "Deluded men, not aware of my higher nature as Great
Lord of Beings, have no respect for me dwelling in human
12. form. Fallen subject to the delusive nature[5] which is fiendish
and demonic, they are mindless, their knowledge, deeds and
13. hopes are vain. But those of great self, who cleave to
my divine nature[5] and who have a mind for no other, are
devoted to me, Son-of-Pṛthā, having become aware of[8]
14. the changeless beginning of beings. Ever celebrating me
and striving, those of firm vows, paying reverence to me
with devotion, attend upon me constantly engaged-in-
*15. disciplined-effort.[9] And others also, sacrificing with the
sacrifice of *jñāna*, attend in manifold ways upon me who
face in all directions, attending with *jñāna* into my oneness
and into my distinctness.[10]

16. "I am the ritual, the sacrifice, the ancestral oblation, the
medicinal herb, the Vedic text, the clarified butter, the fire,
*17. the offering.[11] I am the father of this world, the mother, the
supporter, the grandfather; I am the to-be-known, the
purifier, the sacred syllable *aum*, the three Vedas (*Ṛk*, *Sāma*,
18. *Yajus*). I am the witness[12], the presiding one[13], the sustai-
ner[14], and the final destination[15]; I am the friend[16], the
refuge[17], and the abode[18]; I am the origin and dissolution
19. and continuance[19]: I am the place of rest[20] and the
changeless seed[21]. I give heat, I give and withhold rain;
I am immortality as well as death, being (*sat*) as well as
non-being (*asat*).[22]

20. "Knowers of the three Vedas, having sacrificed to me and
drunk the soma and become purified of sin, pray for the
way of heaven. Having reached the fair world of Indra, they
21. enjoy the pleasures of the gods in heaven. Having enjoyed
that spacious world of heaven, their merit exhausted, they
enter the world of mortals. Thus conforming to the practice
enjoined in the three Vedas, cherishing desires, they gain
22. what is transient. Of the men who attend upon me, think-
ing on me alone, I bring acquisition-and-possession to those
who are constantly engaged in disciplined-effort (*yoga*).
23. Even those who, devoted to other gods, sacrifice filled
with faith, sacrifice to me alone, Son-of-Kuntī, though not
24. according to rule. For I am the enjoyer of all sacrifices,
and the one who presides[23] as well, but they do not perceive-
25. and-acknowledge me in truth, therefore they fall[24]. Those
who are vowed to the gods, go to the gods; those who are
vowed to the fathers, go to the fathers; those who sacrifice
to inferior spirits, go to the inferior spirits. But those
who sacrifice to me, go to me.

26. "He who offers to me with devotion a leaf, a flower, a fruit,

27. water, I accept that devotional offering of a pious self. Make
what you do, eat, offer in sacrifice, give in charity, and
28. undergo as austerity, an offering to me, Son-of-Kuntī. In
that way you will be released from good and evil fruits,
released from the bondage of activity (*karman*); and with
your self engaged in the disciplined-effort (*yoga*) of
29. renunciation, released, you will come to me. I am like-
minded toward all beings, none is hateful or dear to me.
But those who are devoted to me with devotion, are in
30. me, and I am in them also. If a man of very evil conduct
devotes himself to me in undistracted devotion, he too is
to be thought righteous. For he is rightly resolved.[25] /
31. Swiftly he becomes one whose self is *dharma*, and enters
everlasting peace. Recognize, Son-of-Kuntī, that no one
who is devoted to me perishes. For cleaving to me, Son-
32. of-Pṛthā, even those who are born of sin[26], women,
vaiśyas, likewise *śūdras*, go to the supreme destination.
33. How much more, then, meritorious *brāhmaṇas*, and devoted
royal-sages. Having entered this unhappy and inconstant
34. world, devote yourself to me ! Your mind on me, be devot-
ed to me; sacrificing to me, pay reverence to me; having
thus engaged your self in disciplined-effort (*yoga*), given
over to me as final end, you will come to me alone."

CHAPTER X

The Blessed Lord said:

*1. "Listen still further to my supreme word, Strong-armed, which out of desire for your welfare I will declare to you who are taking delight in it.

2. "Neither the multitude of gods nor the great sages know my origin, for I am the beginning in every way of gods and great

3. sages. He who knows me to be the Great Lord of the World,
without birth or beginning, he—undeluded among mortals—is released from all sins.

4. "Understanding[1], insight[2], freedom from delusion, forbearance, truthfulness, self-control, tranquillity; pleasure and
pain, existence and non-existence, fear and lack of fear,/
5. non-violence, equanimity, contentment, austerity, charity,
fame and ill-fame: these varied conditions[3] of beings are
6. from me alone. The seven great sages[4], the four ancients[5],
and the Manus[6] too, had their being from me, being born of
my mind; from them, are these creatures in the world.

*7. "He who knows in truth this pervading-power[7] and magic (*yoga*) of mine, is united to me in unfaltering union (*yoga*); of this, there is no doubt.

8. "I am the origin of all, from me all proceeds; having this,
in mind, the awakened ones[8], full of love, devote themselves
*9. to me. Mindful of me, their lives given over to me, bringing
each other to understand me and constantly conversing
10. about me, they are content and delighted.[9] To those con-
stantly yoked ones who are devoted to me with love, I give
that disciplined-union (*yoga*) of their *buddhi* by which they
*11. attain to me. Out of compassion for them, I stand over
my own nature (*bhāva*)[10] and make their ignorance-born[11]
darkness perish by the shining lamp of *jñāna*."

Arjuna said:
12. "Blessed One, you are the supreme holy power, the supreme
abode[12], the supreme purifier. Everlasting divine spirit,
13. primal god, unborn, pervasive[13]: / all the sages speak of
you as such, likewise the divine sage Nārada[14]. And Asita,
Devala, Vyāsa[15] say this also, and now, you say it to me

14. yourself. I believe all this to be true which you tell me,
Fair-hair. Indeed, O Lord, the gods and demons do not
15. know your manifestation. You alone know your own self,
knowing your self with your own self, O Supreme Spirit;
Source and Lord of Beings, God of Gods, Lord of the World,/
16. you should tell me without omission the pervading-powers
of your self, the divine ones indeed, by means of which you
17. stand pervading all these worlds. How may I, ever medi-
tating, come to know you, Magic One ? and in what condi-
*18. tions are you to be thought on by me, O Lord ? Tell me
further, in full detail, your self's magic (*yoga*) and
pervading-power, Exciter-of-Men; for I am not satiated
listening to that nectar."

The Blessed Lord said:

19. "Come, I will tell you the divine pervading-powers of my
self: the chief ones, O Best-of-the-Kurus, for there is no end
to my extent.

20. "Thick-hair, I am the self standing at the heart of every
being; I am the beginning and middle of beings, and the
21. end as well. Of the Ādityas[16], I am Viṣṇu; of lights, the
radiant sun; of the Maruts[17], I am Marīci; of the lights of
*22. night, the moon. Of Vedas, I am the Sāma Veda; of gods,
Vāsava (Indra); of the sense-powers, I am *manas* (the
23. sixth); of elemental factors, consciousness[18]. Of the Rudras,
I am Śaṁkara (Śiva)[19]. of the Yakṣas and Rākṣasas,
Lord of Wealth (Kubera)[20]; of the Vasus, I am Pāvaka
24. (Agni),[21] of mountain peaks, Meru[22]. Know me, Son-of-
Pṛthā, to be the chief of household priests, Bṛhaspati[23];
*25. of generals, I am Skanda[24]; of waters, the ocean. Of great
sages, I am Bhṛgu; of utterances, *aum*; of sacrifices, I am
the sacrifice of repetition (of the divine's name); of things
26. immoveable, the Himālaya. Of all the trees, I am the Aśvat-

tha[25]; of divine sages, Nārada; of Gandharvas, Citraratha[26];
27. of perfected men, the spiritual man Kapila[27]. Of horses,
know me to be Uccaiḥśravas[28], sprung from nectar;
of royal elephants, I am Airāvata[29], and of men, the
28. monarch. Of weapons, I am Vajra (Indra's thunder-
bolt); of cows, Kāmadhenu[30]; of progenitors, I am
*29. Kandarpa (god of love); of serpents, Vāsuki[31]. Of the Nāgas,
I am Ananta[32]; of sea beings, Varuṇa[33]; of the fathers,
*30. Aryaman[34]; of subduers, Yama[35]. Of demons, I am
Prahlāda[36]; of reckoners, time; of beasts, the king of beasts
31. (lion[37]); of birds, the son of Vinatā (Garuḍa)[38]. Of puri-
fiers, I am the wind; of weapon-bearers, Rāma[39]; of fish,
*32. I am the sea-monster; of streams, the Ganges. Of creations,
I am the beginning and the end, and the middle also,
Arjuna; of forms of knowledge, I am self-knowledge; of
*33. speakers, the speech. Of letters, I am "a"; of compound
words, the dual; I am also undecaying time, and the
34. supporter[40] facing all sides. I am all-devouring death, and
the origin of what will be; of things feminine, I am glory
and prosperity and speech, memory and intelligence and
35. firmness and forbearance.[41] Likewise, of hymns, I am
Bṛhatsāman; of meters, *gāyatri*; of months, I am *Mārgaśirṣa*[42];
*36. of seasons, spring. Of the deceitful, I am the play of dice;
of the splendid the splendor; I am victory, I am resolute-
37. ness[43], of the courageous, their courage (*sattva*)[44]. Of the
Vṛṣṇis, I am Vāsudeva[45]; of the Pāṇḍavas, Wealth-winner;
of the spiritual men, I am Vyāsa; of seers, the seer Uśanas[46].
*38. Of the tamers, I am the rod; of those seeking victory, wise
conduct; of secrets, I am the silence; of those with *jñāna*,
39. their *jñāna*. And further, Arjuna, I am that which is the seed
of all beings; there is no being, moving or unmoving, which
could be without me.

40. "There is no limit to my divine pervading-powers, Foe-

Destroyer; but I have declared for illustration these parti-
41. cular expressions of my pervading-power. Whatever
reality (*sattva*) is possessed of glory-and-power[47], is of high
rank[48], or is merely vigorous[49], understand that to be
sprung from a portion of my flaming splendor.

*42. "But of what use is this detailed knowledge to you[50], Arjuna?
I keep continually pervading this entire world with one
portion (of myself)."[51]

CHAPTER XI

Arjuna said:

*1. "This delusion of mine has vanished, due to the word you
have uttered as favor to me, making known the supreme
*2. secret as it relates to your self.[1] For I have heard in detail
from you, Lotus-eyed, of the arising and vanishing of
3. beings, and also of your changeless majesty. As you say
yourself to be, O Supreme Lord, so it is. I desire to see
4. your lordly form, O Supreme Spirit. If you deem it capable
of being seen by me, O Presiding One, then Lord of
Magic (*yoga*), show to me your changeless self."

The Blessed Lord said:

5. "Behold, Son-of-Pṛthā, my forms, hundreds and thousands,
6. divine, varied in kind and in color and shape. Behold the
Ādityas, Vasus, Rudras, the two Aśvins[2], also the Maruts;
behold many marvels not seen previously, Descendant-of-
7. Bharata. Behold today the entire world of the moving and
unmoving, standing in unity here in my body, Thick-hair,
8. and behold whatever else you want[3] to see. But you cannot
see me with this eye of yours; I give you a divine eye:
behold my lordly magic (*yoga*)!"

Saṁjaya said:

9. Having spoken thus, O King, the Great Lord of Magic
(*yoga*), Hari[4], made visible to the Son-of-Pṛthā his supreme
10. lordly form. With many mouths and eyes, with many
wonderful aspects, with many divine ornaments and uplifted
11. weapons, / wearing divine crowns and raiments, anointed
with divine perfume, a god composed of every marvel,
12. boundless, faced in every direction: / if in the heavens
there would come to be the light of a thousand suns rising
together, that light would be like to the light, of that
13. great self. There, in the body of the God of Gods, the
Son-of-Pāṇḍu then beheld the entire world, divided in
14. manifold ways, standing in unity. Then, Wealth-winner,
filled with wonder, his hair standing on end, having bowed
his head to the god and placed his hands together in suppli-
cation, spoke:

Arjuna said:

15. "I behold in your body, O God, all the gods, and likewise,
crowds of different beings: lordly Brahmā seated on his
16. lotus-seat, and sages all, and celestial serpents. I behold
you, O Lord-and-Form-of-All, who have many arms and
bellies and mouths and eyes, and whose form is boundless
on every side, you who have no end or middle or beginning.
17. I behold you with crown, mace, and discus, glowing on all
sides, a mass of flaming splendor, difficult to look upon,
radiant as a sun and fire glowing all over, immeasurable.
*18. You are to be known as the supreme imperishable, the
supreme place of rest for all this; you are the changeless
guardian of ever-lasting *dharma*, the primeval spirit: so you
are, to my mind.

19. "I behold you who are without beginning, middle and end,
of boundless potency, with limitless arms, with the moon
and sun as your eyes, with your mouth a glowing fire,

20. heating all this with your own flaming splendor. This
interval between heaven and earth, and all the quarters as well, are pervaded by you alone; O One-of-
Great-Self, having seen this wondrous andt errible form of
21. yours, the three worlds tremble. Yonder hosts of divine
beings enter you; certain of them—afraid—praise you,
with hands extended together in supplication; having said
'Hail!' the hosts of great sages and perfected ones
22. praise you with songs of abundant praise. The Rudras,
Ādityas, Vasus and Sādhyas[5] with the Viśvedevas[6],
Aśvins, Maruts and Ūṣmapas[7], the hosts of Gandharvas,
Yakṣas, Asuras[8] and Siddhas[9] : all look on you, and all
23. are amazed. Having seen your great form, with many
mouths and eyes, Strong-armed, with many arms and
thighs and feet, with many bellies and dreadful teeth,
24. the worlds tremble, and so do I. Having seen you touching the sky, glowing and many-colored, with mouth
open and huge eyes glowing, my inner self trembles, I
*25. find no firmness nor tranquillity, O Viṣṇu. Having seen
your mouths dreadful with teeth and like to the flames of
time, I lose my bearings and find no refuge to take. Be
gracious, O Lord-of-Gods, Abode-of-the-World.

26. "All yonder sons of Dhṛtarāṣṭra, together with the hosts
of kings, and likewise Bhīṣma, Droṇa, Karṇa, together with
27. our chief warriors also : / they are all rushing to enter into
your fearful mouths with their dreadful teeth; some of them
are visible caught between your teeth, their heads crushed[10].
28. As the many currents of rivers run towards the ocean, so
those heroes in the world of men enter your flaming
29. mouths. Just as moths with great speed enter into the
flaming fire to meet destruction, so also the worlds with
great speed enter your mouths, to meet destruction.
30. You lick up and devour with flaming mouths entire worlds

on every side; your terrible rays of light fill the entire world
31. with flaming splendors and burn it, Viṣṇu. Tell me who
you are with form so terrible; homage to you, Best of
Gods, be gracious. I desire to understand you, the Primal
One, for your manifestation[11] is not intelligible[12] to me."

The Blessed Lord said:

32. "Time am I, world-destroying, mature in power[13], here
manifest[14] as engaged in fetching back worlds. Even without
you, all the warriors standing over against you will cease
33. to be. Therefore stand up, gain glory; having conquered
enemies, enjoy a prosperous kingdom. By me alone they are
already slain; be you merely occasion, O Ambidexterous
34. One. Droṇa, Bhīṣma, Jayadratha[15], Karṇa, and other
warrior-heroes likewise: slain by me, slay them, do not
tremble ! Fight, you will conquer your adversaries in
battle !"

Saṁjaya said:

35. Having heard this word of Fair-Hair, the trembling Diadem-wearer[16] placed his hands together in supplication and, paying homage and making obeisance before him, spoke to Kṛṣṇa again, in faltering voice, exceedingly afraid.

Arjuna said:

36. "Lord-of-the-Senses, it is fitting for the world to rejoice
and grow passionate in celebrating you. Rākṣasas run in
fear in all directions, while all the hosts of perfected ones
*37. pay you homage. And why should they not do homage to
you, O One-of-Great-Self, who are primal creator, greater
even than Brahmā ? Boundless Lord-of-Gods, Abode-of-
the-World, you are the imperishable, being (*sat*) and not-
38. being (*asat*), that which is supreme. You are first of gods,
ancient spirit; you are the supreme resting-place of all
this. You are the knower and the to-be-known, and the

supreme dwelling-place. By you, O Boundless-Form, all is
*39. pervaded./You are Vāyu[17], Yama, Agni, Varuṇa, Śaśāṅka[18],
you are Lord of Creatures and The Great Grandfather.
Homage, homage to you, a thousand times; homage,
40. homage to you, again and yet again. Homage to you in
front, homage behind, homage to you on all sides, O All.
Boundless in potency, immeasurable in might, you fill-
and-fulfill all, therefore you are all.

41. "I ask your pardon for whatever—in negligence or in
affection—I have rashly called you ('O Kṛṣṇa', 'O Yā-
dava'[19], 'O Comrade'), having thought of you as comrade
42. and being ignorant of this greatness of yours. And I ask
pardon as well for any ill-treatment done in jest while alone
or with others, at meals or when reclining or being seated
or when at play, Unshakeable One, Immeasurable One.
43. You are father of the world of the moving and unmoving,
you are its honorable and reverend teacher; there is no
equal to you, O One-of-Incomparable-Power, how then
could there be another in the three worlds who is
44. greater?[20] Therefore having made obeisance before you and
prostrated my body, I seek your grace, Adorable Lord:
you should bear with me, O God, as father with son,
45. comrade with comrade, dear one with dear one. I am
delighted, having seen what was not previously seen,
but my mind trembles with fear. Show me that (human)
form, O God; be gracious, Lord-of-Gods, Abode-of-the-
46. World. I desire to see you as before, with crown and
mace and with discus in hand. O Thousand-Armed-One,
Form-of-All, become that four-armed form."

The Blessed Lord said:
47. "By my grace, by means of my own self's magic (*yoga*), this
supreme form was shown to you, Arjuna, my form composed

of flaming splendor, universal, boundless, primal, which
48. has been seen before by none besides you. Not by the
Vedas or sacrifices or study, not by gifts or rites or terrible
austerities, can I come to be seen in the world of men with
this form by someone besides you, Hero-of-the-Kurus.
49. Do not tremble or be bewildered, having seen this awful
form of mine. Free from fear and glad at heart, behold
once again this (human) form of mine."

Saṁjaya said:

50. Having spoken thus to Arjuna, Vāsudeva has shown his own form again, and having become again mild in appearance, the One-of-Great-Self has comforted the frightened one.

Arjuna said:

51. "Having seen this mild human form of yours, Exciter-of-Men, I am now returned to my mind, restored to my natural condition[21]."

The Blessed Lord said:

52. "This form of mine, very hard to see, you have seen; even the gods are constantly desirous of the sight of that form.
53. Not through the Vedas nor austerity nor charity nor sacri-
fice can I be seen in this form in which you have just seen
54. me. But by unswerving devotion, Arjuna, I can, in that
form, be truly seen and known[22], and be entered into,
55. Foe-Destroyer.[23] Doing action (*karman*) for me, comple-
tely given over to me, devoted to me, without attachment
and without enmity to any being, one goes to me, O Son-
of-Pāṇḍu."

CHAPTER XII

Arjuna said:

*1. "Those devotees who reverently attend upon you ever
yoked in this way, and those devotees who reverently attend
upon the imperishable unmanifest: which of these know
disciplined-effort-and-union (*yoga*) best?"

The Blessed Lord said:

2. "Those who have brought their minds to enter me and who,
constantly engaged-in-disciplined-effort[1], reverently at-
tend upon me with supreme faith, are considered by me to
3. be supreme in disciplined-effort-and-union (*yoga*). But
those who reverently attend upon the imperishable and in-
definable unmanifest, omnipresent and unthinkable, set on
4. high, immoveable, fixed, / who control the senses, are even-
minded[2] everywhere, and take delight in the welfare of
5. every being, they reach me also. The difficulty of those
whose heart is set on the unmanifest is greater, for the un-
manifest is a destination not easily reached by embodied
6. beings. But those who, intent on me, having renounced
all actions (*karman*) to me, reverently attend upon me,
thinking upon me with unswerving discipline (*yoga*): /
7. their minds having been made to enter into me, Son-of-
Pṛthā, I am soon their deliverer from the ocean of death
and wandering.[3]

8. "Set your mind on me alone, settle your *buddhi* down at
home in me; you will dwell in me alone thereafter, of that
9. there is no doubt. But if you are not able steadily to con-
centrate[4] your mind on me, then seek to reach me by the
discipline (*yoga*) of repeated-practice[5], Wealth-winner.
10. If you are not capable of such repeated practice, be given
over to action (*karman*) for me; engaging in activity (*kar-*
11. *man*) for my sake, you will assuredly reach perfection. But if

you are not capable of doing even this, then resorting to my
discipline (*yoga*), do every action (*karman*) as one whose
*12. self is controlled, the fruit relinquished.[6] [Knowledge is
better than study, concentration is superior to knowledge;
but relinquishment of the fruit of action (*karman*) is better
than concentration, for from such relinquishment comes
peace soon afterward.][7]

13. "Without hate for any being, friendly and compassionate,
without possessiveness or ego, forbearing, even-minded in
14. pleasure and pain, / the man of discipline (*yoga*) who is ever
content, his self controlled, his determination firm, his
buddhi and mind fastened on me: he, devoted to me, is dear
15. to me. He from whom the world does not shrink in fear
and who does not shrink in fear from the world, who is
released from exaltation, intolerance, fear and agitation,
16. he also is dear to me. He who, devoted to me, is without
expectation, pure, able, unaffected, untroubled, and who
17. has relinquished all undertakings[8], he is dear to me. He
who, possessing devotion, neither exults nor hates, grieves
nor desires, who has relinquished good and evil, he is dear
18. to me. The devoted man who is the same toward friend and
foe, toward honor and dishonor, toward hot and cold,
19. pleasure and pain, who is free from attachment, / who
holds in equal account blame and praise, who holds his
tongue, is content with whatever comes, is homeless and
*20. steady in mind: he is dear to me. But those devotees are
exceedingly dear to me who, possessed of faith and given
over to me, partake of this nectar-teaching-about-practice[9]
which I have set forth."

CHAPTER XIII

The Blessed Lord said[1]:

1. "This body, Son-of-Kuntī, is called 'the field'[2], and him who knows it, those who know it call 'the knower of the field'[3].

2. "Know me, Descendant-of-Bharata, to be the field-knower in all fields; *jñāna* of the field and the field-knower: this is what I would deem to be the-insight-of-wisdom (*jñāna*).

3. "Hear from me briefly what this field is, of what character,
what its modifications are, and whence is what, as well
*4. as who he is and what his powers. This has been sung many
times[4] by sages, in various hymns separately, and also in
the well-reasoned and considered[5] verses of the Sūtras[6] on
the holy power.

5. "The (five) gross elements[7], ego, *buddhi*, the unmanifest,
the ten powers (five of sense, five of action) and *manas*, and
*6. the five sensory realms[8]; / desire and hatred, pleasure and
pain, the bodily aggregate, consciousness[9], firmness: this,
in brief, is the field with its modifications.

7. "Absence of pride and of deceit, non-violence, patience,
uprightness, service to one's teacher, cleanness, steadfast-
8. ness, self-restraint, / dispassion toward sense objects, lack
of ego, perception of the evils of birth and death and old
9. age and sickness and pain, / non-attachment, lack of
clinging to son, wife, home and the like, constant even-
mindedness in desirable and undesirable occurrences, /
10. unfailing devotion to me by unswerving discipline (*yoga*),
resort to secluded places, lack of delight in crowds of
11. people, / constancy in *jñāna* concerning one's self, vision
of the purpose of *jñāna* into truth : this is declared to be 'the-

wisdom-of-insight' (*jñāna*), and whatever is other than this,
'lack-of-such-wisdom' (*ajñāna*)[10].

12. "I will declare that into which one is to have insight (*jñāna*);
having gained *jñāna* into this, one attains immortality. This
is the supreme holy power, beginningless, who is said to be
13. neither existent (*sat*) nor non-existent (*asat*). / With hands
and feet, faces and heads, eyes and ears, on every side, it
14. stands in the world, encompassing all.[11] / Appearing to have
qualities of all the sense-powers, yet void of all the sense-
powers[12], sustaining all yet unattached, enjoyer of the *guṇas*
15. yet free from the *guṇas*, / both outside and inside beings,
both moving and unmoving, too subtle to be discerned, far
16. away yet near is this.[13] Undivided, yet standing as if divided
among beings, it is to be gained insight (*jñāna*) into as
sustainer of beings, used to devouring and to producing
*17. beings. / Light of Lights, it is said to be beyond darkness[14];
jñāna, what is to be gained insight (*jñāna*) into, and what is
to be reached by means of *jñāna*, it is seated in the heart of
all.

18. "Thus is the field, the wisdom-of-insight (*jñāna*), and what
is to be gained insight (*jñāna*) into, stated in brief. Devoted
to me, having understood this, one comes to my nature-
and-being (*bhāva*).

19. "Know that nature[15] and spirit are both beginningless;
know also that the modifications and *guṇas* are born of
*20. nature. Nature is said to be cause in respect of the condi-
tion of being active center, the action, and the outcome
of action; spirit is said to be cause in respect of the matter
21. of being enjoyer of pleasure and pain. For spirit, standing
in nature, enjoys the *guṇas* born of nature. Its attachment
to the *guṇas* is the cause of births in good and evil wombs.
22. The supreme spirit in this body is also called: 'Onlooker'[16]

and 'Permitter'[17], 'Sustainer'[18], 'Enjoyer'[19], 'Great Lord'[20], 'Supreme Self'.

23. "He who knows in this way spirit and nature with its *guṇas*
is not born again, whatever turns his existence takes.
24. By meditative concentration[21] some see their selves with
their selves in their selves; others do this by the disciplined-
effort (*yoga*) of knowledge[22], still others by the disciplined
*25. effort (*yoga*) of action (*karman*). However, others, without
knowing (spirit and nature) in this way, worship, having
heard (of these things) from others; and in addition,
taking refuge in what they have heard, they cross beyond
death also.[23]

26. "Whatever actuality (*sattva*), moveable or immoveable, is born, know it to be born from the union of field and the knower of the field, Bull-of-the-Bharatas.

27. "He who sees the Supreme Lord standing the same in all
beings, the indestructible in the destructible, he sees indeed.
*28. For seeing the Lord standing firm everywhere equally, he
does not injure his self through his self; thus he goes to the
supreme destination.

29. "He who sees actions (*karman*) to be done altogether by way of nature, and who likewise sees his self not to be doer, he sees indeed.

30. "When he perceives beings severally existent standing as one and spreading out[24] from just there, then he enters into the holy power.

31. "This supreme self, changeless, without beginning or quality[25], neither acts nor is tainted, even though embodied,

32. Son-of-Kuntī. As the omni-present ether is not defiled by
reason of its subtleness, so the self, abiding everywhere,
33. is not defiled in the body. As the one sun illumines this
entire world, so does the field-owner illumine the entire
field, Descendant-of-Bharata.[26]

34. "They go to the supreme who, with the eye of *jñāna*, know
in this way the difference of the field and the knower of the
field, and the release of beings from nature."

CHAPTER XIV

The Blessed Lord said:

*1. "I will declare still further the supreme *jñāna*, chief among
insights (*jñāna*); having gained this *jñāna*, all spiritual men
2. have gone from that to supreme perfection. Having held
to this *jñāna* and entered into likeness[1] with me, they are
not born at creation nor are they disturbed at dissolution.

3. "The great holy power is my womb; in it, I place the seed[2].
From this, Descendant-of-Bharata, comes to be the birth of
4. all beings. The great holy power is the womb of whatever
forms come to be in any womb, Son-of-Kuntī, and I am the
father who bestows the seed.

5. "*Sattva*, *rajas*, *tamas*: these *guṇas* born of nature fetter the
changeless embodied one in the body, Strong-armed.
6. Among these, *sattva*, due to its spotlessness, is clear and
healthy; it binds, O Blameless One, through attachment to
*7. happiness and to knowledge. Know *rajas*, of passionate
essence, to be the source of attachment in the form of crav-
ing; it binds the embodied one, Son-of-Kuntī, by attach-

8. ment to action (*karman*). But the *tamas* which gives birth to
the lack of *jñāna*[3], know it to be deluding for all embodied
ones. It binds, Descendant-of-Bharata, by heedlessness,
9. indolence and sleep. *Sattva* makes one attached to happi-
ness, *rajas* to action (*karman*); but having covered *jñāna*,
Descendant-of-Bharata, *tamas* makes one attached to heed-
lessness.

10. "*Sattva* waxes strong[4], having overpowered *rajas* and *tamas*, Descendant-of-Bharata; *tamas* also, having overpowered *rajas* and *sattva*, and *rajas*, *tamas* and *sattva*.

11. "When wisdom (*jñāna*) is born, shining out through all the
gates in this body, then it may be known, '*sattva* is strongly
12. developed'. Greed, busyness, enterprise in actions (*karman*),
unrest, yearning: these are born with strongly developed
13. *rajas*, Bull-of-the-Bharatas. Unclarity and inertia, heed-
lessness and delusion: these are born with strongly deve-
14. loped *tamas*, Joy-of-the-Kurus. When the embodied one
goes to destruction with *sattva* strongly developed, he attains
then to the spotless worlds of those knowing the highest.
15. Having gone to destruction in *rajas*, he is born among those
attached to action (*karman*); likewise, gone to destruction
*16. in *tamas*, he is born in the wombs of the foolish. The fruit
of good action (*karman*) is spotless and sattvic; that of
17. *rajas* is pain, that of *tamas* is unwisdom (*ajñāna*). *Jñāna*
arises from *sattva*, greed from *rajas*, heedlessness and
18. delusion from *tamas*, as also *ajñāna*. Those who stand in
sattva, go upwards; those in *rajas*, stay in the middle,
those standing under the working of *tamas*, the lowest
guṇa, go downward.

19. "When the beholder perceives no other factor at work than
the *guṇas* and knows what is beyond the *guṇas*, he attains

*20. to my being (*bhāva*). Having gone beyond these three
guṇas springing from the body[5], the embodied one, released
from birth and death, old age and unhappiness[6], attains
immortality."

Arjuna said:

21. "O Presiding One, by what marks is he who has gone be-
yond these three *guṇas*, distinguished? What is his conduct?
How does he pass beyond these three *guṇas*?"

The Blessed Lord said:

22. "He does not hate clarity and busyness and delusion when
they arise, Son-of-Pāṇḍu, nor desire them when they do
*23. not. He who, seated as if unconcerned[7], is not agitated by
the *guṇas*, who thinks 'only *guṇas* are concerned' and stands
24. fast and does not go out, / who takes his stand in himself,
the same in pleasure and pain, the same toward a clod or
a stone or gold, holding in equal account the dear and the
25. not dear, praise and blame, / good and bad repute, friend
and enemy, who is steady and has relinquished all under-
26. takings[8]: he is said to have gone beyond the *guṇas*. And
he who serves me with unfailing effort (*yoga*) of devotion,
having gone beyond these *guṇas*, is fit for becoming the
*27. holy power. For I am the dwelling-place[9] of that power, of
the immortal and changeless, of everlasting truth[10] and
undivided happiness."

CHAPTER XV

The Blessed Lord said:

*1. "They speak of a changeless fig-tree[1], its roots above, its
limbs below, and its leaves the Vedic hymns. He who knows
2. it, is a Veda-knower. Its branches are stretched out above

and below, grown forth in accordance with the *guṇas*, its
twigs being the sense-domains. And down in the world of
men, it spreads out roots, which have actions (*karman*)
3. as their results[2]. Its form is not perceived here, nor its begin-
ning, end, and foundation; having cut off this strong-
rooted fig-tree with the firm sword of non-attachment, /
*4. then they should seek after that abode from which, when
they come to it, they do not return again. May one go
forth[3] solely to that primal spirit from which this ancient
*5. manifestation[4] came forth. Without pride and delusion,
with the fault of attachment overcome, freed from desires
and from the dualities known as pleasure and pain, the
undeluded, constant in regard to their self, attain to that
6. changeless abode. The sun does not shine on that, nor
the moon nor fire[5]; having come to this—my supreme
dwelling-place—they do not return.

*7. "A primeval fraction of my very self, endowed with life in
the world of life, draws into its power the senses and mind
*8. which stand in nature. The Lord who takes on a body and
also departs, having taken senses and mind to himself, goes
*9. like the wind carrying fragrant odors from a place. Having
inhabited the five senses and the mind as well, this (Lord)
frequents the sensory realms and cultivates the things of
10. sense[6]. The deluded do not perceive him, whether he is
departing or is staying or is taking his enjoyment, joined to
the *guṇas*[7]. They see him, who see with the eye of *jñāna*.
11. The men of disciplined-effort (*yoga*), by making an effort,
see him also, abiding in their self; those whose selves are
unprepared, who are mindless, do not see him, even though
they make an effort.

12. "That glowing brightness in the sun which illumines the
entire world, the glowing brightness in the moon and in fire:

13. know that glowing brightness to be mine. Having reached to
earth also, I support beings by my vital force. And having
become sap-natured soma, I also cause all plants to thrive.
14. Having become the vital-heat inhabiting the body of living
beings and being united with their life-breaths, I digest
15. the four kinds of food[8]. And I am seated in the hearts of
all; from me are memory and knowledge, and their loss[9] as
well. I am also the one alone to be known by way of the
Vedas; the author of the end of the Vedas (= Upaniṣads)[10],
I am also the knower of the Vedas.

16. "There are these two spirits in the world, the perishable
and the imperishable; the perishable is all beings, the
17. imperishable is called 'the immoveable'[11]. But other than
these is the uttermost spirit, called 'the supreme self', who,
as changeless Lord, having entered the three worlds, sus-
18. tains them[12]. Because I surpass the perishable and even
the imperishable[13] I am celebrated in the world and in the
19. Vedas as the Supreme Spirit. He who, undeluded, has in-
sight (*jñāna*) into me thus, as the Supreme Spirit, he—know-
ing all—is devoted to me with his whole being[14], Descen-
dant-of-Bharata.

20. "Thus has this most secret teaching[15] been disclosed by me, Blameless One; having become awakened[16] to this, Descendant-of-Bharata, one will be a man possessed of *buddhi* and will have done what is to be done."

CHAPTER XVI

The Blessed Lord said:

*1. "Fearlessness, essential purity[1], perseverance in knowledge[2]
and action[3], charity and self-control and sacrifice, study

2. of scripture, austerity, uprightness, / non-violence, truth,
freedom from anger, relinquishment, peace, lack of malice,
sympathy for beings, freedom from covetousness, gentleness,
*3. modesty, absence of fickleness, / spiritedness, forbearance,
firmness, cleanness, loyalty, absence of overweening pride:
these belong to one fit by birth for a divine issue[4], Descen-
4. dant-of-Bharata. Hypocrisy, arrogance, overweening pride,
anger and harshness and unwisdom[5]: these belong to one
5. fit by birth for a demonic issue[6], Son-of-Pṛthā. The divine
issue is considered to be release[7], the demonic, bondage;
do not grieve, Son-of-Pāṇḍu, you are fit by birth for a
divine issue.

*6. "In this world there are two creations of beings, the divine
and demonic[8]. The divine has been spoken of at length;
hear me now, Son-of-Pṛthā, concerning the demonic.

*7. "Demonic men know neither the way of action nor the way
of inaction; cleanness, good conduct, truth, are not known
*8. among them. They say that the world is without a truth, a
foundation, a Lord; nor is it produced in orderly fashion.
What else is the case but that it is produced by desire?[9]
9. Resting on this view, such men—lost in self, small in mind,
terrible in deed—come forth as enemies for the destruction
10. of the world. Having fallen subject to insatiable desire, full
of intoxication and pride and hypocrisy, having accepted
untrue notions due to delusion, these men of impure mode
11. of life venture forth in action. Clinging to an unlimited
anxious-concern[10] whose only end is in death, completely
devoted to desire and enjoyment, they are sure 'this is
12. all'[11]. Bound by hundreds of fetters of hope, given over to
desire and anger, they aim at gaining wealth unjustly, for
13. the sake of gratification of desire. 'This was gained by
me today, that desire I will obtain; this is mine, this

14. wealth will also become mine besides; / that foe was slain
by me, and I will slay others besides. I am lord and enjoyer,
15. I am successful and strong and happy. I am wealthy and
well-born, who else is like to me? I will sacrifice, I will
give alms, I will rejoice.' Thus think those deluded, in
16. their lack of *jñāna*. Bewildered by manifold notions, en-
meshed in the net of delusion, given over to the gratifi-
17. cation of desires, they fall into a foul hell. Self-conceited,
obstinate, full of pride and intoxication due to their wealth,
they offer sacrifice in name only, hypocritically and not
18. according to rule. Ego, might, arrogance, desire, anger:
clinging to these, these malicious men show hatred against
me in their own bodies and in those of others.

19. "These men—hostile, cruel, vile, the lowest of men—I am
forever hurling into demonic wombs in their wandering
20. through birth and death. Having entered demonic wombs
and in birth after birth having failed to reach me, these
deluded ones finally reach the lowest destination, Son-of-
Kuntī.

21. "This threefold gateway to hell, the ruin of a self, is gras-
ping desire, anger, and greed. Therefore relinquish this
22. triad! The man who is released from these three gates of
darkness (*tamas*), Son-of-Kuntī, practises what is good for
*23. his self, then goes to the supreme destination. He who,
dismissing the rule of the teaching[12], acts according to his
inclination, does not reach perfection, happiness, or the
24. supreme destination. Therefore, having become cognizant
of the teaching[12] as your standard in settling what is to be
done and what is not, here on earth you should do the
deed called for by the rule of the teaching[12]."

CHAPTER XVII

Arjuna said:

*1. "But what is the state[1] of those who, having dismissed the
rule of the teaching, sacrifice full of faith, Kṛṣṇa?[2] Is it
sattva, rajas, tamas?"

The Blessed Lord said:

2. "Born of their ownmost natures (*sva-bhāva*), the faith of
embodied ones becomes threefold, sattvic, rajasic, and
*3. tamasic. Hear now of this matter. / The faith of each comes
to be conformably to his essence; man here is constituted
by his faith, Descendant-of-Bharata, himself being such as
the faith he has.[3]

4. "The sattvic sacrifice to the gods, the rajasic to the Yakṣas
and Rākṣasas, and the rest, the tamasic, sacrifice to the
host of spirits and ghosts of the deceased.[4]

5. "Men full of the strength of passion and desire, full of ego
and hypocrisy, who engage in dreadful austerity which is
6. not ordained by teaching[5], / mindless men who are
weakening the collection of elemental factors found in their
bodies, and also weakening me standing within their bodies:
know them to be demonic in their intent.

7. "But also the food dear to each is three-fold, and likewise
the sacrifice, austerity, and charity: hear this distinction of
these.

8. "Foods promoting life, energy, strength, health, happiness
and joy, tasty, mild, lasting[6], agreeable: these are dear to
9. the sattvic. Foods which are pungent, sour, salty, over-
cooked, spicy, astringent, scorching hot, which cause pain

and grief and sickness: these are cherished by the rajasic.
10. Food which is stale, tasteless, foul-smelling, spoiled, which
is left over or is not fit for sacrificial use: this is the food
dear to the tamasic.

11. "That sacrifice which is offered in observance of the rule,
by men who do not desire fruits but think simply 'this sacri-
12. fice is to be made': this sacrifice is sattvic. Know that sacri-
fice to be rajasic, Best-of-Bharatas, which is made aiming
at the fruit, and also, is made with hypocritical display
13. besides. That sacrifice is called tamasic which is lacking
in faith, is not observant of the rule, is lacking in
hymns[7], is lacking in distribution of the food, is lacking in
a present for the priest.

14. "Honor for the gods, the twice-born, teachers and wise
men; cleanness, upright behavior, continence, and non-
15. violence: this is bodily austerity. Utterance which is in-
offensive and truthful, agreeable and beneficial, and the
practice of scriptural recitation: this is austerity in respect
16. of speech. Mental clarity[8], gentleness, reticence, self-
restraint, purity of feeling and thought[9]: this is mental
austerity.

17. "This three-fold austerity, practised with supreme faith by
men who are engaged in disciplined-effort (*yoga*) and are
18. not desirous of fruit: this is called sattvic austerity. That
austerity which is practised here for the sake of favor, es-
teem, or honor, and also is done with hypocritical display,
19. is called rajasic: it is fluctuating[10] and fleeting. And that
austerity which is done for self-torment under confused not-
ions, or is done to destroy others, is called tamasic.

20. "That charity which is engaged in under the notion 'this is
to be done', and without expectation of return, and which is

engaged in at the proper time and place and in relation to
a worthy person: that charity is declared to be sattvic.
21. But that which is engaged in for the sake of something in
return, or aiming at fruit, and which is engaged in grud-
22. gingly, is declared to be rajasic. That charity which is
engaged in at the wrong time and place and in relation to
an unworthy person, and is engaged in disrespectfully and
with contempt: that charity is called tamasic.

*23. " '*Aum, tat, sat*' : this is declared to be the three-fold designa-
tion of the holy power, by which the *brāhmaṇas*, the Vedas,
24. and the sacrifices of old were ordained. For this reason,
uttering '*aum*' the expounders of holy utterance ever under-
take the acts of sacrifice, giving, and austerity, which
25. were proclaimed by sacred precept. Uttering '*tat*', the
diverse acts of sacrifice and austerity and charity are done
by those seeking release, without their aiming at the fruit.
26. '*Sat*' is the word used for true being (*sat-bhāva*) and a truly
good nature (*sādhu-bhāva*), O Son-of-Pṛthā, likewise for
27. a praiseworthy action (*karman*). Steadfastness in sacrifice,
austerity, and charity, is also called '*sat*'; and action
(*karman*) for the sake of such steadfastness[11] is also con-
28. sidered '*sat*'. That sacrificial offering, that gift of charity,
that austerity, which is made or performed without faith,
is called '*asat*', Son-of-Pṛthā; it is of no avail here on earth
or hereafter."

CHAPTER XVIII

Arjuna said:

1. "O Strong-armed Slayer-of-Keśin[1], Lord-of-the-Senses, I
desire to know the true nature and distinction of renuncia-
tion[2] and relinquishment[3]."

The Blessed Lord said:
2. "Seers know renunciation to be the giving up[4] of activities
(*karman*) engaged in because of grasping desire; relinquish-
ment, the far-seeing declare, is the relinquishment of the
*3. fruit of all activity (*karman*). Some thoughtful men declare,
however, that action (*karman*) is to be relinquished as an
evil[5]; others say one should not relinquish the acts (*karman*)
4. of sacrifice, charity, and austerity. Hear from me the solu-
tion of this question about relinquishment, Highest-of-the-
Bharatas.

5. "Relinquishment, Tiger-of-a-Man, is to be explained as
three-fold[6]. The acts (*karman*) of sacrifice, charity, and
austerity, are not to be relinquished but to be done; for
sacrifice, charity and austerity are purifiers of the intelli-
*6. gent[7]. But even these acts (*karman*) are to be done, Son-
of-Pṛthā, with attachment and the fruits relinquished; this
7. is my assured and final view. But renunciation of one's
allotted action (*karman*) is not fitting; the relinquishment
8. of it due to delusion is declared to be tamasic. He who
would relinquish an action (*karman*) due to fear of bodily
pain, thinking 'it is painful', having made a relinquishment
which is rajasic, would win no fruit at all for his relinquish-
9. ment. But he who does his allotted action (*karman*),
Arjuna, thinking merely 'it is to be done', having relinqui-
shed attachment and the fruit, he is deemed to have made
10. a sattvic relinquishment. The intelligent man[8], whose
doubt is cut off, who relinquishes full of purity (*sattva*), does
not hate unskillful action (*karman*) and is not attached to
11. skillful action (*karman*). It is not possible, indeed, for the
body-bearer to relinquish activity (*karman*) altogether;
but he who relinquishes the fruit of activity (*karman*) is
12. called a man of relinquishment. The wanted, the unwan-
ted, and the mixed are the three-fold fruit of activity

(*karman*) for the non-relinquisher after death; but there is
no fruit whatever for those who renounce.

*13. "Understand from me, Strong-armed, these five causal
factors in the accomplishment of all activity (*karman*), as
proclaimed in the Sāṁkhya at the end of the *kṛta* age[9].
*14. The seat[10], likewise the active center, instrumental powers
of various sorts[11], various kinds of function[12], and (as
fifth) also the environing-world-at-large-supported-by-the-
15. divine[13]. Whatever activity (*karman*) a man undertakes with
his body, his power of speech, and his mind, whether right
16. or wrong, these five are its causes. This being so, the weak-
minded one who, because of his imperfect *buddhi*, sees self
17. in isolation[14] as in reality the doer, does not see. He whose
nature (*bhāva*) is not egoistic, whose *buddhi* is not tainted,
even though having slain these worlds, he does not slay and
is not bound.

*18. "Congnizance[15], what is to be cognized, and the cognizer,
are a three-fold factor impelling toward activity (*karman*).
The active center, action (*karman*), and the instrumental
power(s), are a three-fold totality in relation to activity
19. (*karman*). Cognizance, activity (*karman*), and the active
center, are said, in the enumeration of the *guṇas*, to be
three-fold also, according to the diversity of the *guṇas*. Listen,
accordingly, to these also.

20. "Know that cognizance to be sattvic by which one sees the
one changeless nature (*bhāva*) in all beings, the undivided
*21. in the divided. Know that cognizance to be rajasic which
knows separately the manifold conditions-and-factors
*22. (*bhāva*) of various kinds[16] in all beings. But that cognizance
is called tamasic which, missing the cause[17], clings to

one causal factor as if it were the whole, and thus is narrow and not conformable to the truth.

23. "That activity (*karman*) is sattvic which is an allotted acti-
vity (*karman*), engaged in without desire of gaining the
fruit, with attachment abandoned, without passionate
24. desire and hatred. That activity (*karman*) is called rajasic
which is engaged in with great strain[18] by one seeking to
25. gratify his grasping desire or by one with an ego. That
activity (*karman*) is called tamasic which is undertaken out
of delusion without regard to consequences, to destruction
and injury, or to what is humanly possible.

26. "That active center is called sattvic which is freed from
attachment and I-speaking, is without agitation in regard to
success and failure, and is filled with strength (of will)[19]
27. and firmness. That active center is called rajasic which is
passionate, desirous of obtaining the fruit of activity
(*karman*), lustful and impure and violent, filled with
28. exaltation and grief. That active center is called tamasic
which is unbalanced[20], unrefined[21], obstinate, deceitful,
dishonest, indolent, despairing and procrastinating.

29. "Wealth-winner, hear the three-fold differentiation (according to the *guṇas*) of *buddhi* and firmness, also, declared fully and one by one.

30. "That *buddhi* is sattvic, Son-of-Pṛthā, which knows the ways
of action and inaction[22], what is to be done and what is
not, the fearful and what is not, bondage and release.
31. That *buddhi* is rajasic, Son-of-Pṛthā, by which one knows
(but not in proper fashion) *dharma* and *adharma*, and also
32. what is to be done and what is not. That *buddhi* is tamasic,
Son-of-Pṛthā, which, covered by darkness, deems as *dharma*
what is *adharma*, and thinks all things in such reversed fa-
shion.

33. "That firmness is sattvic, Son-of-Pṛthā, by which, through
undeviating disciplined-effort (*yoga*), one makes steady the
34. workings of mind, breath, and sense[23]. But that firmness is
rajasic, Son-of-Pṛthā, by which one, desiring fruit, holds fast
to worldly goals (*dharma*, wealth, pleasure) in the manner
35. of attachment. That firmness is tamasic, Son-of-Pṛthā,
by which the unintelligent do not give up dreaming, fear,
grieving, being despondent, and being intoxicated.

36. "But hear now from me, Bull-of-the-Bharatas, the three-
fold happiness; due to repeated practice, one takes delight
*37. therein and enters into the end of sorrow. That happiness
is sattvic which, born of clarity in one's awareness (*buddhi*)
of self, is at first like poison but in the end is the finest
38. nectar[24]. That happiness is declared rajasic which, being
due to the union of sense and sense-objects, is in the begin-
39. ning like the finest nectar but in the end like poison. That
happiness is declared tamasic which, delusive of the self in
the beginning and in the end, arises from sleep, indolence,
and heedlessness.

40. "There is no actuality (*sattva*) either on earth or in heaven
among the gods, which would be destitute of these three
41. *guṇas* born of nature. The works (*karman*) of *brāhmaṇas*,
kṣatriyas, *vaiśyas* and *śūdras*, Foe-destroyer, are distinguished
by the *guṇas* prominent in their own particular natures
42. (*svabhāva*). Tranquillity, self-control, austerity, cleanness,
patience, and uprightness, as well as piety, wisdom[25] and
knowledge[26]: this is the work (*karman*) of a *brāhmaṇa*, born
43. of his own particular nature. Heroism, spiritedness, firm-
ness, resourcefulness, and not fleeing in battle, generosity
and leadership: this is the work (*karman*) of a *kṣatriya*, born
44. of his own particular nature. Agriculture, cattle-tending,
trade: this is the work (*karman*) of a *vaiśya*, born of his own

particular nature; service is the work (*karman*) of a *śūdra*,
born of his own particular nature.

45. "A man, attentive to[27] his own work (*karman*), attains per-
fection[28]; hear in what way he finds perfection, occupied
46. with his own work (*karman*). A man finds perfection by
worshipping—through his own work (*karman*)—him from
whom beings came forth and by whom all this is pervaded.
47. One's own *dharma*, even when not done perfectly, is better
than an alien *dharma*, even though well performed; one
does not incur sin doing the work (*karman*) allotted for
48. one's own particular nature[29]. Son-of-Kuntī, one should
not relinquish the work (*karman*) native to one, even
though it is defectively done; for all undertakings are
clouded by defect like fire by smoke.

49. "He whose *buddhi* is everywhere unattached, who is without
yearning, whose self is subdued, arrives by renunciation
at the supreme perfection of freedom-from-the-bondage-
50. of-activity (*naiṣkarmya*). Understand from me succinctly,
Son-of-Kuntī, how, having reached such perfection, he
reaches the holy power, which is the supreme culmination of
51. *jñāna*. Possessed of a completely pure *buddhi*, having con-
trolled his self with firmness[30], having relinquished the
various sense objects, having cast off passionate desire and
52. hate, / dwelling alone, eating lightly, with mind, body and
speech controlled, constantly given over to the disciplined
effort (*yoga*) of concentration[31], supported by dispassion, /
53. having forsaken ego, might, arrogance, desire, anger,
graspingness, without possessiveness and at peace, he is fit
54. for becoming the holy power. Become the holy power, calm
in self, he neither grieves nor desires; even-minded
amidst all beings, he reaches into the supreme devotion to
55. me. Through his devotion, he comes to perceive-and-

acknowledge in truth who I am and what my measure is[32].
Then having gained insight (*jñāna*) into me in truth, he
56. enters me at once. Ever doing all that he does cleaving to
me, by my grace he reaches the everlasting changeless abode.

57. "Having renounced all activity (*karman*) to me with your
mind, given over to me, relying on the disciplined-effort-
and-union (*yoga*) of *buddhi*, become constantly mindful of
*58. me ! Mindful of me, you will cross all difficulties-and-
dangers by my grace. But if, due to your ego, you will not
59. pay heed, you will be utterly lost. If, having sought asylum
in your ego, you think 'I will not fight', your 'resolve'[33]
60. will be in vain. Nature[34] will impel you. Tied to your own
work (*karman*) born of your own particular nature (*sva-
bhāva*), Son-of-Kuntī, you will do, although unwillingly,
61. that which due to delusion you do not want to do. The
Lord stands in the heart of all beings, Arjuna, by his
power (*māyā*) causing all beings, mounted on a wheel, to
62. revolve[35]. Go to him alone for refuge, Descendant-
of-Bharata, with all your being (*bhāva*)[36]. By his grace
you will attain supreme peace and an everlasting place-
63. and-standing. Thus has *jñāna*, more secret than any secret
been declared by me to you; having reflected fully on this,
do as you will.

64. "Hear once more my supreme word, most secret of all.
You are firmly beloved of me: therefore will I relate what
65. is good for you. Mindful of me, be devoted to me; sacri-
ficing to me, do me homage: you will come to me alone,
66. truly I promise you, you are dear to me. Having relin-
quished all *dharmas*[37], take refuge with me alone. I shall
make you released from all sins, do not grieve.

67. "This is never to be spoken by you to anyone who is not
possessed of austerity, not devoted, and not eager to listen;

68. and also, never to one who murmurs against me.[38] He who
will share this supreme secret with my devotees, having
supreme devotion to me, free of doubt he will come to me
69. alone.[39] None among men would do anything equally dear
to me, nor would there be another dearer to me on earth.
70. And he who goes over this *dharma*-possessed dialogue of
ours, should sacrifice to me by the *jñāna*-sacrifice: such is
71. my mind. The man who, unmurmuring and faithful, shall
even listen to it, shall be released (from sin); he shall gain
the fair worlds of those of meritorious action (*karman*).

72. "Son-of-Pṛthā, have you listened to this with your mind
one-pointed[40]? Wealth-winner, has the delusion belonging
to your lack of *jñāna* vanished?"

Arjuna said:

73. "Vanished is my delusion; by your grace, Unshakeable
One[41], I have gained remembrance[42]. I take my stand
firmly, with doubt dispelled; I will do your word."

Saṁjaya said:

74. Thus have I heard this marvellous hair-raising dialogue
75. of Vāsudeva and the Son-of-Pṛthā, of great self; / by the
grace of Vyāsa[43] I have heard this supreme secret, this dis-
cipline (*yoga*), related in person by Kṛṣṇa himself, Lord
76. of Magic-and-Discipline (*yoga*). O King, each time I recall
this marvellous holy dialogue of Fair-hair and Arjuna, I
77. am thrilled once again. And each time I recall that
exceedingly marvellous form of Hari, O King, my wonder
78. is great, and I am thrilled once again. Where Kṛṣṇa is,
Lord of Magic-and-Discipline (*yoga*), where the Son-of-
Pṛthā is, Bearer-of-the-Bow, there is fortune, victory, lasting
prosperity, wise conduct[44]: so it seems to me.

COMMENTARY

In my introductory remarks, I suggested that for a reader, and a Western reader in particular, the response which would put one into a position to grasp the teaching of the *Gītā* would be one attuned first and foremost to the drama, to the poetic world which one is being introduced into in the reading.[1] In the following commentary I would like to make a few remarks that would develop that suggestion by indicating how that drama within that world has come forth for me and how the teaching appears to me accordingly.

What is articulated most centrally, as the revelation in Chapter XI indicates, is time in its bearing upon human life as an active affair, an affair of commitment to activity in which there is something at stake. It is characteristic not simply of the *Gītā* but also of the Hindu tradition at large, to place this matter of temporality at the heart of an understanding of human beings and things at large. So far as concerns humanity, that has meant a focus upon human life as an affair of development and growth. Now in this regard a distinction is to be made. On the one hand there is the implication of the human being in the process of ageing, so that our participation in the movement of our lifetime from beginning to end brings us to be older. This ageing seems to show a natural pattern of phases through which human beings move, which may be pointed to by noting that birth leads into infancy, then childhood and adolescence, and on into adulthood, with its phases of middle age and old age ending naturally in death. On the other hand, there is something meant to occur within this movement and these phases, something that does not occur automatically as one ages but concerns a sort of qualitative upsurge which may succeed in varying degrees. We may or may not succeed in growing up adequately. No matter how long we actually live and into what age periods we enter in which we would be called "adult", we may end up merely immature adults: adults more or less defective in our realization of what it is to be a human being.

Characteristic of the Hindu's deeply engrained sense of life's movement is a conception of the movement of human growth as crucially centered in the development of those essential powers through which we are distinctively human beings. Through these powers we are meant to assume our lives in a reference to the real: nothing less than living and dwelling effectively with reality could constitute us grown-up human beings. It is against what was then apparently a widespread and influential conception of this movement and of how it could occur, that the drama of the *Gītā* articulates its contrasting notion. The view being contested delineates an ideal of phases, expressive of one's growth as a human being and indicating how such growth would bring one to the place where what is basically and from the first at stake in human life could actually be reached into. The development, conceived primordially to relate to a male of one of the higher castes, involves the following stages or *āśramas*: (1) that of the student or *brahmacārin*, which terminates childhood and involves educating the developing youth through religious and secular instruction which is to prepare him for the role he is to assume in society; (2) that of the householder or *gṛhastha* in which the young man is to produce a family, play his functional role in society, and practise the appropriate ritual and sacrifice; (3) that of the forest-dweller or *vānaprastha*, middle-age becoming the time for a movement beyond such active social involvement and for entry upon the effort to reach a deeper end than is apparent within such involvement, and making meditative and reflective efforts to form the core of one's active endeavor; (4) that of the wandering mendicant or *sannyāsin*, in which all social ties are cast off and effort is dedicated wholly toward final release through an enlightenment or illumination that reaches into the ultimate depths of the real.

Let us consider how the contrasting view which the *Gītā* offers becomes presented to us, first and foremost through the drama.

CHAPTER I

The very first verse points us toward two things, a place and an impending action. The place, the Field of the Kurus, is called by Dhṛtarāṣṭra a field of *dharma*. For it is to be the place of an action in which *dharma* is at stake. There are levels of meaning here. To begin with, the Field is a plain sacred to the Kurus and to their way of life. The latter is formed through *dharma* or (first and foremost) the fabric of standards which pervade and determine the social order involved in that way of life. Such a manifold articulation of norms and standards constrains and shapes one growing up within it, moulding the person's attitudes and fitting him appropriately in relation to things as he lives with them. Thereby *dharma* provides support and direction for one's acting and living, and the Field of the Kurus is a place in which the *dharma* of the Kurus has its roots.

Then again, the Field is now place of an impending action, a battle in which something basic is at stake, something which makes the struggle a life-and-death affair. Apparently what is at stake is the recovery of a kingdom, a matter of *dharma* in which basically the Pāṇḍavas stand in the right and the Kauravas in the wrong, given the way in which the battle has been brought on.

But finally, and most deeply, the Field is the place of an effort in which what is most deeply at stake in all human action becomes made explicit to one of the participants, Arjuna. That stake is contribution to the fulfillment of the impetus of creation that stems from Kṛṣṇa-Viṣṇu. Such contribution, and a share in that fulfillment, is what is ultimately meant to occur in action accordant with *dharma*; the whole of the *Gītā* is the gradual elicitation of this meaning to the struggle on the Field of the Kurus.

The beginnings of that elicitation are carefully constructed. The two armies have been drawn up face to face across the battlefield when Saṁjaya points us to the initial action. His pointer is to actions by Duryodhana and Arjuna that are counterpart to each other. First comes that of Duryodhana: looking over the army facing him, noting to Droṇa the composition and disparity of the two armies, he is poised for the battle, ready yet filled with a certain dismay. Then comes a transition: Bhīṣma sounds the call of battle to cheer him up, the return call from the Pāṇḍavas sends fear through Duryodhana and his brothers, and the whole world (heaven and earth) is brought to a focus in this tumultuous uproar. Finally comes the action of Arjuna that is counterpart to that of Duryodhana: looking over the army facing him, Arjuna asks Kṛṣṇa to draw his chariot up between the armies so that, drawing closer, he might survey more carefully the members of the opposing army. With this movement of the chariot Arjuna is brought spatially into the no-man's land in between the two armies. And thereby he is entered into a spatial and temporal present which has a peculiar force and character to it, and one which opens him out into the depths of time.

Who is Arjuna? By nature, by birth, and by up-bringing, he is a *kṣatriya*. By nature: for no human being is simply human, but by one's very nature one is a human being with a particular endowment, including what we in the West might refer to when we speak, for example, of temperament, natural aptitudes and talents, natural virtues, and the like. In the notion of things here involved, one with an inborn nature of the *kṣatriya* type would be someone for whom this particular nature was the fruit of past lives. And this would be so in such way that, due to the workings of the law of *karman* and the structure of Hindu society, he would be born into a family whose social status would enable his upbringing to be a matter of fitting him for a role in society which fitted the caste of the family into which he was born and which also fitted his inborn nature. By birth and upbringing: this educational process which would develop his inborn nature would accord with the *dharma* for a *kṣatriya* and thus fit him for a station defined by the function of a warrior and/or ruler. Thus he would be fitted for a life whose aims, roughly and generally, are primarily that of just and righteous accomplishment in endeavors of war and rule, and secondarily, that of pleasure in the form of simple enjoyment of the company of others of his kind, colored by accomplishments and by satisfaction in them.

In the actual course of his life up to the time of this battle, Arjuna has distinguished himself in these matters, particularly in his prowess in battle. Thus as he enters into the present in question, he takes his stand in the middle of the armies as a particular person whose present is defined for him within the terms of that way of life. As he surveys the armies, then, the present is charged with a future which, through the imminence of battle, holds the possibility of death and, even if not death, defeat. The present has, accordingly, an air of expectancy and an intensity to it, significant of a life-or-death matter whose eventual issue is unknown. The present is also charged with a past, which holds within itself in particular the occasion for the battle, the series of efforts to avert it, the failure of those efforts, and the gathering of the armies. Yet that past holds also the development of his inborn nature, of himself as a human being with that particular nature, his education in the use of capacities and powers and in the aims and proprieties of a certain way of life. Through that development as well, his past holds the growth of the attitude which is that of one at home in the kind of life and doings to which he has been moulded.

Thus Arjuna takes his stand there initially as one for whom that battle, that possible future, and that past series of events leading up to the battle, that actual past, are intelligible, falling within the scope of his orientation and understanding as a *kṣatriya*. Not only that, but the battle is a righteous one, one for which a *kṣatriya* is made and one to which he has committed himself as something required and significant. If he wins, he gains a share in a kingdom and both honor here and a place in heaven later; if he dies, but has fought righteously, he will be rewarded in heaven.

To this battle he has committed himself without apparent qualms. But as he comes to stand in that no-man's land, and to look attentively to the men around, Kṛṣṇa speaks: "O Son-of-Pṛthā, behold the assembled Kurus!" With that injunction the here and now which are Arjuna's alter in character. Having acted on an impulse to take one last look, he hears the command directing his attention to those who are assembled for battle. And looking to those others under the guidance of Kṛṣṇa he finds himself in that seeing drawn beyond his absorption in his commitment to the deed which is enjoined on him by *dharma*. He finds that, while he stands involved in *dharma* in some fashion, *dharma* no longer supports him in the way it did.

Kṛṣṇa's injunction has selected out certain warriors from among the assemblage gathered on both sides. These, Arjuna already knew were there; their presence was no surprise. Yet now, this presence comes home to him with peculiar force, and resonates with something which claims him, calls for his allegiance. Arjuna does not understand what that is; what is present and claims; he does not understand the significance of his dissociation from *dharma*. He does not understand that that presence and dissociation have explicitly opened him up to the possibility of entering into the culmination of creation, and that the claim is a call for him to act so as to move self-consciously in that direction. Instead, he finds himself thrust into an emptiness within which he is dissociated from himself in his socially-moulded *dharma*-supported side. It is in that emptiness that he becomes aware of others, who are present also beyond the pale of the *dharma* which had made the Kauravas evil and the enemy, and who are present—all of the Kurus—as intimately touching him. So thrust beyond what had been, he finds the previous moving forces for his action removed: *dharma* had been their supporting frame, but only so long as he could be immersed in the "social world" it defined. That immersion now broken, he is at first cognizant of nothing to stand in the stead of *dharma* as a supporting presence that would move him to carry through the battle. Or better: given his nature and upbringing, given the formation of his attention in the situation, there is nothing that he can immediately recognize as offering support. He finds himself at sea.

Thus, shaken in his resolve to fight, his orientation as a whole brought into question, he responds at first in the manner of giving up. He loses heart in that momentary listlessness introduced by his being thrust beyond *dharma*, and responds in the direction of resignation, abdication, retreat. In that response, he clutches at an explanation and justification for his retreat. In incomprehension amidst that strange emptiness, cognizant only that things are no longer what they were, he clutches at what he can comprehend of those others whom he has come to see in altered presence. The terms of this comprehension come from his past; through them, he grasps at something which he had known all along, something which does not touch the real nature of the presence but which nevertheless takes him into the only dimension he had known other than the social-and-public as defined by his *dharma*. He clutches at the personal-and-natural (in the form of kinship) which is implicated in *dharma* as underlying the social.

Holding to the fact that these men are his own kinsmen, Arjuna attempts to rationalize his refusal to fight. Thereby he reverses the terms he had known : what had been primary becomes now secondary (achievement in righteous war), and what secondary, primary (enjoyment of life with his own kind). And yet, in this rationalization, he is attempting to render intelligible what has happened, that for the moment there is something in the presence of these men that claims him in a way that transcends *dharma* as this ordains him to a just war against others whoever they be. But unable as yet to grasp what this is, he speaks of it as kinship—as, in a sense, it is, but not in the sense he understands.

His rationalization of his retreat from battle and from its unavoidable slaughter and destruction, involves a mixture of matters having to do with the personal and natural (family and kinship). What stands on the surface of his questions and words is the alleged primacy of a kinship relation for a significant life, with *dharma* important only as connective link with kin (dead and to come), only as family or clan *dharma*. In his confusion, then, Arjuna is placing in primacy the "my own" (*sva-*) : himself and his kinsmen, his happiness or punishment in hell. In this way he speaks in a certain recognition that it is human beings that basically count, not causes, not abstract aims like kingdom and pleasure, not even right and wrong in abstract form. Yet who is this that says these things? Who is this self, who those others?

In all that he says Arjuna speaks a grain of truth, but he does not really reach to the heart of the matter. Underlying all that he says—truth and untruth—is a self-pity, a failure to endure in that emptiness into which he has entered and to move through it, and instead, an effort to escape it and its initial incomprehensible oppressiveness for him by retreat. This failure to recognize himself and others, to reach into the reality of his situation and to find the place of action in that reality, is a failure to recognize and endure the emptiness and listlessness in their true significance, as characteristic of the initial phase of a transformation in his condition as an active center intrinsically involved in growth. Letting the oppressiveness get him down, he seeks to resign from action altogether, in the implicit presumption that, because the action he was about to undertake seems now to have no sense in ordinary terms, there is no point to it that could make itself felt for him.

Nevertheless, no matter how much his interpretation and response fail to reach to the point, they do suffice to halt his unhesitating commitment and plunge into action. With his floundering the question of action has its natural emergence: the "why" and the "what to do" arise. And an exploration of that question is possible. That exploration takes the form of the teaching by Kṛṣṇa-Viṣṇu of the import of what Arjuna is here in the midst of becoming explicitly aware of: the positive import of action in the midst of creation.

CHAPTER II

Something has happened to Arjuna. Resolute and capable warrior, entering upon battle without qualm, knowing right was on his side and confident in his ability and in that of his army, he found, suddenly, that the men who faced him came home in their presence to him beyond the confines of *dharma* through which they had been taken in previously as wrong-doers and enemies. Somehow in that presence, something took hold of him, something about them called for an allegiance on his part which, though he did not understand it, brought into question for him what he was doing in this act he was committing himself to.

Whatever else may have been involved in such an amplified awareness, there was at least a discovery of himself and others as human beings and a discovery of such sort as made it clear that it is human beings that count. And yet, what are human beings, and how is it that they count? In this altered presence and this dissociation from *dharma* as supporting and guiding force for his commitment to battle, Arjuna responds in a way that mistakes the significance of the disclosure, mistakes what men are and how it is that they count. For there is confusion naturally attendant upon this initial entry into the expanded awareness that is matrix for the effort self-consciously to assume the full human estate upon oneself. And in that confusion there is naturally a tendency to seek to make one's way, to find orientation, in the terms that have been known to one in the past.

Thus finding that *dharma* in its direction of effort within the social world no longer effectively claims him for battle, he interprets the experience as disclosing that the personal is the sphere of true humanity and true life: true humaneness, true human feeling, would lead him to renounce fighting. But in so interpreting the matter, Arjuna has taken man to be *less* than man-claimed-by-*dharma* rather than *more* than this. His pity and self-pity are egoistic, and he is moving in the opposite direction from that in which he is being called to move in that disclosive experience. Human beings count, but not as one's kin and relation, not as centers of personal life, any more than as centers of righteousness. Human beings must be seen and understood more deeply, must be seen as involved in a movement through which they are eventually to become more than all this. And the depth which opens up when one initially enters into the explicit awareness of oneself and others as so involved and so counting, is that into which Arjuna has been plunged. His initial response has been inadequate so far as it has involved a misinterpretation of what has claimed him and of what it calls him to.

It is to an Arjuna in this condition that, at the beginning of Chapter II, we find Kṛṣṇa speaking. He speaks here, and throughout the rest of the dialogue, in a way that is adjusted to Arjuna in his current (and changing) condition, and in a way that is adjusted so as to accomplish something in particular.

What is Arjuna's condition? He stands on the verge of that phase of growth which, in the account of the *āśramas*, would involve his movement from householder to forest-dweller; only that phase is here conceived in rather different terms. What is still at issue, ultimately, is growth toward release (*mokṣa*), only release conceived as a condition of adequate participation in the culmination of creation. For this to occur, Arjuna must grow as active participant and that requires development in his *buddhi* or that complex power which defines Arjuna in his common humanity. This power, through which he takes active part in the interplay that constitutes the created world, is one of judgment and decision operative within awareness, attention, and interpretation. In his life up to now, this power has been developed in its function of bringing his distinctive *kṣatriya* nature into play, but that development has involved inescapably an obliviousness to the deeper side to himself and the corresponding sides to the selves of others. Thus his *buddhi* has been formed so as to be held within a delusion concerning the actual and the real, within which his education of himself as human has made primary the terms he has assimilated in his socialization. Such learning has had its positivity: Arjuna has developed to a certain perfection in his particular nature. But it has had a negativity, reflective of the incompleteness in the functioning of his *buddhi* such that he has not been aware of the depths, and hence has been unable to be active responsively to the depths *and* the surfaces. Unable to discover himself in his active side as anything more than *kṣatriya*, he can not see his life and action to have a point in deeper terms, and unable to find others in terms deeper than their particular natures, he can not see the essential humanity of himself and others in its fulness. He can only see *buddhi* as it is confined in its outworking by the diverse or kindred particular natures and roles of men. The motivational forces, attitudes, ways of acting, and interpretations of the meaning of action and life he has so far formed, then, are appropriate at best to one side of his active being. Yet he is under the delusion that for him to think and to act as himself, and as the human being he is, is to think and to act simply as *kṣatriya*.

The initial and initiating step in the movement which is to take him beyond this delusion, has been the tentative and partial entry of himself into what is for him an unprecedented mode of being explicitly aware of himself and others. To complete the initiating movement, Arjuna must endure amidst the emptiness into which he has been plunged, and must deepen his entry into it. And this deepening must retain the positivity of his *kṣatriya* nature and its social development, while releasing his *buddhi* into itself as his central power. This latter can happen only as his current confused and misinterpreted awareness of the depths becomes a clear and distinct awareness, consolidated in understanding and made effective in his being and deeds. Then he will find himself creature and human being living and acting in effective union of inactive and active sides of himself and in effective responsiveness to all creatures as likewise dual-sided.

If this is Arjuna's condition, if he is in the midst of such a transformation, and is responding mistakenly within the confusion naturally attendant upon the first step in that transformation, then he is in need of coming out of that mistaken response in such way as to gather himself up into that active effort, which can bring him on the way toward the culminating issue of the transformation begun. It is in adjustment to this need, that Kṛṣṇa speaks. For though he initially appears to Arjuna as merely a human being, he is the creative and supporting power which is at work so as to help initiate Arjuna into the transformation, and to aid him in taking the needed first step properly. Thus the speech and revelation through which he makes his presence felt to Arjuna, are educational in a distinctly practical vein. Kṛṣṇa means to help Arjuna to bring himself into action, and in particular, into the action at hand, and to bring himself there in such way as can effectively start him on the way to his maturely responsible assumption of his active role in creation. This aim, Kṛṣṇa seeks to achieve by making his presence felt in various ways, altering the way as Arjuna's condition and responsiveness alter.

Thus, for the most part, he speaks, but at the proper moment—one preceded and succeeded by speech—he reveals his ultimate nature.

Then again, his speech itself varies. Most often, he attempts to make articulate for Arjuna the nature of things and of action as these emerge from Kṛṣṇa's own being as source, sustainer and destroyer in one. Thus he speaks in the indicative mood of what it is that Arjuna has become confusedly and partially aware of and must eventually become more deeply and clearly aware of—and not merely aware of, but cognizant of and responsive to in its nature and import. Since Arjuna stands at the moment in confusion and mistaken interpretation of such tentative and initial awareness as is his, the teaching is phrased and rephrased so as to drive its essence home.

Yet his speech, while centrally indicative, has a prevailingly imperative mood to it. Even in his very attempts to make articulate the nature of things, this is so, for he speaks of a creation which includes Arjuna as center having something to do and having something of creation at stake in his doing. The factors of which Kṛṣṇa speaks, then, are factors which Arjuna must come to heed—not just be aware of, but since in that awareness they bear on him and claim his attention and response in some fashion or other, to assess and heed within that awareness. Thus his characterization of the nature of things as well as of action is meant to illuminate Arjuna's condition as active amidst factors which, already in a confused and partial way, have come into his awareness and made a claim to which he is responding mistakenly. Thus Kṛṣṇa seeks to show, for example, that that presence of the Kurus which has layed hold of Arjuna in some basic way, is not the presence of factors which deprive active effort of all point (as Arjuna is initially disposed to think), but of factors that call him forth into action and sustain him in action if he heeds them properly, and does not cut himself off from their claim by withdrawal and mistaken interpretation.

Occasionally Kṛṣṇa goes even further in making explicit the imperative mood of the ground of creation, as it bears on the active side of creation, for he directly enjoins Arjuna to "arise and act !" Sometimes this call to a determinate deed is addressed to Arjuna in relation to the egoistic moving factors still confining his *kṣatriya* nature. For the *kṣatriya* side must be brought into play, its further development has a positive place, its directionality and outworking a legitimacy if in the course of that play it can be released from egoistic distortion and subordinated to something deeper. But normally this injunction is addressed to Arjuna in respect of his new-found awareness as it opens to him explicitly something more fundamental in the way of a moving factor. For that awareness is of the oneness of himself and others at bottom, and of the neediness of all in respect of entry into an establishment of that oneness *in concreto*, in their active being and their deeds.

In these ways Kṛṣṇa aims to reach Arjuna in his capacity to respond and heed, and to help him into a responsive effort in which he begins to do what needs to be done, that is, acts (in this case, fights) out of a free and witting allegiance to what claims him out of the heart of things. Seen from this perspective the major share of the dialogue in the poem is medium for the gradual effective strengthening of that resolve to act which had collapsed in Arjuna's initial entry into emptiness. In that strengthening Arjuna is not being restored to what he was, but is being brought into a movement forward which, if carried through, will bring him to grow beyond what he was by bringing him into his active efforts in an altered form. The dramatic movement of the dialogue, so seen, is the basis on which the poem is structured and its teaching articulated. Let me attempt to indicate how this is so, step by step, beginning with Chapter II.

Kṛṣṇa's initial words to Arjuna (II. 2-3) seem meant to make Arjuna's condition explicit and to confirm that the striking presence of the Kurus has momentarily brought him effectively beyond the support and direction that *dharma* had been providing. This confirmation Kṛṣṇa accomplishes by appealing to the egoistic but *dharma*-conditioned motivational factors pertinent to a *kṣatriya*. But given his current awareness and his interpretation of the import of what he is aware of, Arjuna is unable to respond to a call which is addressed to him in regard to that side of his ego which he feels to be challenged and undermined now. Instead he reiterates his confusion, his inability to see any point to going through with the deed. He is even drawn to suggest that begging might be better: withdrawal from the social order is apparently on his mind. In any case in his confusion he asks for help, placing himself in the hands of Kṛṣṇa as a pupil to be taught. As the very words in Sanskrit convey[2] this means more than to be given advice; it means to be chastised, chastened, that is, educated in a way that involves being brought back from out of error. Though the teaching and learning in question are focussed upon determination of what ought to be done in a particular situation, in fact the education concerns the matter of *being* human, the matter of how to take one's stand within the sense that something matters in life and action and thus amidst the competing claims upon one's responsive capacity. Education in this crucially involves, among other things, intellect, but it is neither an affair itself of intellect (a theoretical matter, for example) nor of the practical application of intellectual learning. In this critical situation Arjuna's entrusting of himself to Kṛṣṇa carries with it, then, some recognition that what is at issue is a matter of his becoming, a matter in which his whole being and way of life are under challenge and in which he is in need of removal from an unfitting condition and restoration to one that befits a human being, is befitting to the human being he is.

And yet, this recognition is unclear, for it is expressed in terms of a certain interpretation of himself and of his condition which does not, and cannot, do justice to what is at issue. Thus Arjuna speaks of his paralyzing sadness and pity as a fault in someone with his particular nature; judging himself under the standard of *dharma* still, he grasps himself as a *kṣatriya* who is failing. And thus too he asks Kṛṣṇa to clear up his confusion about *dharma* by telling him what he should do : which would be better, to go through with the deed or not? In so speaking Arjuna's recognition that something essential for him, something fundamental, is at issue, is expressed in the terms that are familiar to him but whose adequacy is in fact under challenge. For as he uses them at least, those terms signify and mean something to him only within his unwitting identification of himself with the *kṣatriya* side of his nature, and of *dharma* with certain things to be done and others not to be done. For it is only within such identification that the question of proper action in a situation could be a matter of judgment to be settled by appeal to a course of action which, given the circumstances and situation, could be seen to be regulated by *dharma*. It is given such a notion of proper action as rule-guided and proper judgment as rule-application, together with his sense of himself as unable to discern grounds within *dharma* as he knows it for resolving the conflict of a righteous war and slaying of kin, that it seems to Arjuna that if Kṛṣṇa would just tell him what really is the right course now, he could then proceed to "do the right thing" by following that prescribed course.

But what Arjuna has to learn now—and this would seem to be the very heart of Kṛṣṇa's teaching concerning action—is that in so grasping himself as active being, in so understanding his judgment and his engagement in action, he is under a delusion and confined by a too restricted notion of the matters in question. Speaking to an Arjuna already in a certain condition, Kṛṣṇa urges that the ultimate meaning of what is happening to Arjuna is the opening out for him in that condition of the possibility—and need—for participation in the fulness of action. And that means, for taking part in action in non-attachment to good and evil both, that is, in transcendence of *dharma*. Care must be used in interpreting this latter phrase. *Dharma* is that articulation of the normative which is meant, for so long as one is not ready to pass beyond delusion, to provide the ultimate guide in reference to which one is to channel one's energies in action.

But this guide is meant to be left behind eventually, transcended, and this, in the sense that ultimately one's awareness is to reach into depths so as to span the inactive and active sides of things and oneself and thereby allow one to form his efforts not by reference to rules and regulations as *ultimate* guides but in responsive heedfulness to the divine presence which is ground of such *dharma*. Such presence calls one into action whose meaning lies beyond the three worldly ends ordained through *dharma*. The heedfulness in question involves, first and foremost, a responsive cleaving to the Lord as Himself the ultimate imperative and directive factor within the whole. Thus action in the concrete is to take shape in a following out of the directive call of *this* factor within presence, and one acts as released from confinement in *dharma* as if *dharma* were *of itself* the locus of what is imperative on one. But such cleaving also involves an acknowledgement of one's creatureliness which signifies, in principle, the transcendence of egoistic grounds for participation in action and the entry upon action as agent of the Lord. Thus the heedfulness in question involves, secondly, such gathering up of one's particular powers of action as brings them into the effort of service which effectuates, so far as possible, what the Lord calls for and that means, contributes concretely toward the emergence of the unity of creatures in which creation finds its culmination. In that regard, what is called for concretely expresses and accords with *dharma*, but is not something undertaken merely on the strength of the (implicitly egoistic) reference to *dharma* as regulatory. There is an altered responsiveness at work in action now, even though *dharma* may be said still to point out the right and fitting, the wrong and unfitting, in relation to one's particular nature and situation.

This is what Arjuna is ready for: to take his stand in response to the Lord in His presence, to recognize the common humanity which defines himself and other human beings as creatures, to gather up his particular nature into particular action that is relevant to the situation and is medium for his movement along a path which gradually will purify him of egoistic distortion to his humanity, and eventually will enter him into the full responsibility of human participation in existence. If it is in responsive effort of such sort that Arjuna must now bé engaged, then Kṛṣṇa cannot respond to Arjuna's appeal for help and answer Arjuna's question simply by saying: "this is the right thing to do". He must rather work within the awareness Arjuna already has and seek to educate him in the import of what is disclosed within that awareness. And he must do this in such a way as enables Arjuna sufficiently to understand the import of what claims him that he is both confirmed in his entrusting of himself to that presence in his decision and action and is enabled to decide and to respond appropriately in the concrete. Arjuna is already cleaving to the presence but under a mistaken interpretation of its directive import. Kṛṣṇa is to help him become sufficiently cognizant of its directive thrust that he can gather up his particular powers into a decision and action that follow that thrust out wittingly and willingly in the concrete.

Arjuna has turned to Kṛṣṇa as a man, asking for guidance; and initially the latter responds as such, drawing upon traditional views and through them addressing himself to an Arjuna who had claimed wisdom to be on his side (I. 38-39). But as Chapter III (3) and Chapter IV (1-3) indicate, these views as they are found embedded in tradition as Arjuna would know it are in fact degenerate forms of an original teaching made long ago within the series of ages by Kṛṣṇa as the Lord. Thus the restatement of that original teaching (Chapters III-VI, primarily, with the change in the character of Kṛṣṇa, who is becoming increasingly disclosed as Lord and not merely man) places the initial teaching in Chapter II in perspective as basically provisional. The beginning with tradition, however, not only fits in dramatically with the character of the two men as human beings, but it also enables Kṛṣṇa initially to contest Arjuna's appeal to the wisdom of not fighting in a way that is appropriate to persons in a traditional culture, namely, by a counter-appeal to ways of thought which are inherent in the tradition but which would contend that Arjuna is misunderstanding his situation and rather than not fight should engage in battle.

Kṛṣṇa's words in Verse 39 and Arjuna's question in Verse 54 articulate the initial and provisional teaching into three phases. In Verses 11-38, Kṛṣṇa appeals to Sāṁkhya notions to clarify Arjuna's situation; in Verses 39-53, he appeals to Yoga notions. And then, responding to Arjuna's question concerning the kind of man both teachings hold forth as a human being at his finest, Kṛṣṇa draws on both teachings.

The Sāṁkhya to which Kṛṣṇa is appealing in Verses 11-38 seems to be an early form of what probably was originally a non-Vedic mode of thought but was gradually assimilated into the Vedic stream in close connection with the Upaniṣads.[3] As it came to developed form, it was a way of thinking which involved a sharp separation of what is called *puruṣa* (Spirit) or *ātman* (Self) from all else (called *prakṛti* or Nature). Taking as ultimate a multiplicity of Spirits and (so it seems) not recognizing a *creator* God, it conceives the universe to be endlessly involved in a sort of evolution and devolution (a cyclical process) within time, in function of an association of Spirit and Nature in which Spirit is deluded. Thus as deluded, Spirit becomes embodied and, mistaking its body for itself, thinks *it* is *doer*. Thereby an endless round of births-and-deaths is its lot, until a release is effectuated in an enlightened awareness of the absolute difference of Spirit from Nature. Since there is no point to be found *within* this associational existence, all effort is to be put into gaining enlightenment. In this effort a discipline—that of knowledge—defines a path leading there, but entry upon this discipline presupposes a moral perfection gained by way of action in the social order. Given such moral perfection, one can—and should—withdraw from the social order, since action inherently binds and all effort should now be put into the discipline of *buddhi* in its cognitive side. With the attainment of enlightenment, a Spirit is finally separated from embodied existence, to maintain itself in an ultimate aloneness (*kaivalya*).

This form of Sāṁkhya is not what Kṛṣṇa teaches as his own view. Speaking as a distinguished *kṣatriya*, he is here using the then extant form of this view in order to counteract Arjuna's pretense to wisdom by pointing to one important element in the tradition to which Arjuna belongs and saying, "This element would teach precisely the opposite of what you take to be the teaching of wisdom, Arjuna". Presumably, an important part of the reason for this appeal is because Kṛṣṇa thinks Arjuna must act, and the Sāṁkhya would support him in this. But the grounds for the Sāṁkhya urging would be somewhat different from the grounds Kṛṣṇa would have, as becomes clear in the course of the dialogue.

Kṛṣṇa's voicing of the Sāṁkhya teaching in its relevance to Arjuna is articulated into three phases, which involve three different levels of thought. The first phase—Verses 11-25—begins with the contention that "you grieve for those who are not to be grieved for, yet you speak words about wisdom" (11). Such grief, and the consequent desire to withdraw from battle, rest on a mistaking of the nature of things. For in things there is a fundamental duality. Kṛṣṇa avoids the Sāṁkhya terminology to mark this duality, presumably because at the heart of his own view he has other meanings for the terms, *ātman* in particular. Instead he formulates the duality by speaking of the embodied one in contrast with its embodiments. This embodied one is our basic side, and is that alone which is worthy of being called our reality (according to Sāṁkhya). Time-antecedent, it is nonetheless caught up over and over again in one embodiment or another that is temporal (finite, mortal, coming and going). Still it remains ever itself, unchanging and inactive, quite untouched by the changes and the recurrent but different embodiments, and untouched too by all activity and active conditions. But Arjuna believes that by fighting and killing he is going to injure others in their reality. This is mistaken: at best he can touch on their current embodiment and actuality.

In this first phase of Kṛṣṇa's use of Sāṁkhya, he is merely directing himself to the unfoundedness of Arjuna's grief and grief-inspired abdication. According to the Sāṁkhya, these are rooted in a misinterpretation of the realities of his situation and of the possible effect of his doing upon those realities. In fact, if he had a clear and distinct awareness of that of which he has so far become only confusedly aware, he would recognize the basic duality within each and all, and would not grieve. The use of Sāṁkhya so far, then, is merely negative. There is as yet no suggestion of a positive reason for acting, a reason which would be rooted in the differentiation of the embodied one from its embodiments.

The second phase of Kṛṣṇa's use of Sāṁkhya—Verses 26-30—is likewise negative. According to the Sāṁkhya the embodied one not only takes on many bodies but has a shadow, so to speak, which accompanies it throughout. For there is a carry-over from bodily existence to bodily existence, which takes the form of an enduring living principle (*jīva*) which persists throughout the alternations of birth and death and carries with it the inheritance from previous existences. Since this *jīva* enters into the succession of bodies which embody the embodied one, it is itself subject to perpetual birth and death in a way in which the embodied one is not. For it is temporal, although in contrast with the bodies which are temporal but transient, it perpetually endures. Now there would be no reason for Arjuna to grieve and withdraw even if this were the reality of beings (instead of the embodied one). For this persistent *jiva* is, by nature, meant to pass through death and birth: death is certain, but so is rebirth. In respect to the unavoidable, in respect to what in this fashion is natural and inevitable and a part of the order of things, there would be no legitimate ground for grief and sorrow. The *jiva* will endure, that is its nature; any particular life, body, existence, has a beginning and an end, that is its nature. What is there in this for lamentation?

It is only with the final phase of Kṛṣṇa's use of Sāṁkhya—Verses 31-38—that he introduces what the Sāṁkhya could offer in the way of a positive reason for action, hence for Arjuna to fight. In the Sāṁkhya there is no positive place for (social) action as itself a means to enlightenment. The only means is withdrawal, and entry upon the path of reflection. Yet (social) action is accorded a place as preparing a human being morally and readying him for the time when he is to withdraw from such action and seek enlightenment. Action, then, has its significance only within delusion. There it has an important preparatory function so long as it takes shape within the framework of *dharma*, even though it is egoistically participated in due to delusion. Thus in this phase Kṛṣṇa appeals to Arjuna's particular nature and particular *dharma* as *kṣatriya*, and appeals to them in terms of his old egoistic motivation. Arjuna's *dharma* calls for him to fight; to follow this out will bring happiness and (after this life) heaven, whereas failure to do so will bring sin and disgrace. The implication of Arjuna's grief and desire to retreat from action is, to the Sāṁkhya, that he is still morally imperfect, and therefore he must act in order to overcome this defect in himself. Until it is overcome, he is not ready to withdraw.

Such is Kṛṣṇa's use of an early form of Sāṁkhya, which he soon makes clear is a degenerate form of an original teaching which is his own as the Lord. Even in this degenerate form it contains a basic distinction which is integral to Kṛṣṇa's own teaching, that of a basic inactive factor within oneself in distinction from subordinate factors involved in its embodiment and active existence. Still, in this form, the distinction is not conceived in such way as to provide a positive import for action in the effort to achieve enlightenment or in the living of life to its end after gaining enlightenment. In contrast, Kṛṣṇa thinks action does have such a positive function, and this, because creation is (in his view) constituted somewhat differently from the way the Sāṁkhya envisages. Indeed, the point of existence is not to be found in the separation of the embodied one from embodiment (release into aloneness) but rather in a certain appropriate joining together of these sides to oneself. But more about this later.

Kṛṣṇa's appeal to Sāṁkhya is followed immediately by an appeal to Yoga (Verses 39-53). The Yoga school of thought, as it comes to develop and be formed in times after the *Gītā*, is in most respects like that which Kṛṣṇa here presents.[4] Originally a part of the non-Vedic tradition and even then linked closely with Sāṁkhya, it was later assimilated into the Vedic tradition along with Sāṁkhya. The connection between the two seems always to have been that Sāṁkhya provided most of the interpretation of the nature of things for both schools, whereas in regard to the path toward enlightenment, Yoga stood for a practical discipline as against the intellectual discipline of Sāṁkhya. Thus in its developed form Yoga accepts the Sāṁkhya distinction of Self or Spirit from Nature, accepts the need for eventual withdrawal from the social order in order to seek enlightenment, accepts the need for a preliminary moral purification before such withdrawal is proper, and accepts the gaining of release through enlightened awareness. What is added (or emphasized, at least) in Yoga is the conception of a god or Supreme Spirit, not a creator but the primary Self among Selves, itself never deluded. And this god is helper in man's search for enlightenment. That search, according to Yoga, involved utilization of an elaborate set of practices, which made its path toward enlightenment provide action of certain sorts a positive place, more so certainly than in Sāṁkhya.

Yoga in this form taught a disciplined form of action, in which the aim of discipline is to restrain the workings of *buddhi* so as eventually to achieve a release from the delusory identification of Self or Spirit with Nature (particularly, with *buddhi* itself). This disciplined effort involved manifold practices, leading through two important stages. The first stage is *kriyā-yoga*, or practical discipline, and is the needed preliminary for the second. It includes a manifold of moral regulations and of physical and mental exercises which are meant to enable one to develop a *buddhi* whose attention is no longer distracted by the outward influences that reach it through the senses and which is aware of its true relation to Self or Spirit. The second stage is *rāja-yoga*, or the royal discipline. Working by means of this relatively purified *buddhi*, one here seeks a concentration which poises the *buddhi* in secure balance and unites it with what is being concentrated upon. As such working proceeds one gradually removes from *buddhi* itself all traces of the false identification of Self or Spirit with Nature. And with the gaining of such purified awareness or enlightenment, Self or Spirit is released into its primal aloneness. In both stages of discipline, devotion to God is taken to be helpful to the success of one's effort to attain enlightenment. But the ultimate end, here as in Sāṁkhya, is aloneness of Self or Spirit, not e.g. absorption in God.

When in this Chapter, Kṛṣṇa avails himself of an early form of this Yoga view, he utilizes it for its emphasis on practice, and to begin with, on the undertaking of action within the social order. That is, *kriyā-yoga* or practical discipline is here primarily the disciplined undertaking of the actions called for by one's *dharma*. One does not have to withdraw in order to enter upon a path toward enlightenment, indeed one cannot withdraw to enter upon this path since it is the path of social and ritual action. What is different is simply that one undertakes this action in a different way, as part of a discipline of *buddhi* in which one seeks to act non-egoistically.

At the heart of its relevance to Arjuna is Yoga's view that *buddhi* is the power through which we enter upon and undertake any action as human beings. So long as this undertaking involves an egoistic orientation, so long our action is binding: we are attached to its fruit, we are building up dispositions to act again in this way, and we are committing ourselves to further existence and action thereby. But action need not be undertaken in this fashion, provided that one has come into the amplified awareness that Arjuna has reached into. For with this expansion in the awareness side of *buddhi*, a different motivation is possible. That *buddhi* which is capable of bringing one into action in a non-binding fashion, is spoken of by Yoga as a resolute *buddhi*. And in contrast *buddhi* still caught up in delusion (antecedent to this expansion of awareness) is called irresolute. What do these terms mean?

When Arjuna had come into battle to begin with, he had

apparently been "resolute" in his decision: he "knew" the situation, he "knew" what he was going to do, he was "determined" to do it, and the like. Yet as Chapter I unfolded and he lost that resoluteness, we discover that his resoluteness had been merely apparent, that he had not been judging and deciding in a way rooted in the realities of his situation: not simply in this case, but at any time previously. For he had, in all his decisions before, made up his mind and decided as he had in obliviousness to the depths. In this sense Arjuna's *buddhi* had been irresolute consistently unable to form a resolve which was adequately responsive to the realities of his situation. But now Arjuna's amplified awareness has placed him in the position where he can—for the first time—make a resolute decision. For having become aware of the depths of his situation and having been claimed by an imperative presence from out of those depths, he could now interpret and judge so as to decide upon what he is to do in consonance with reality. If he did this instead of what he is doing, and if he did it persistently, he would eventually strengthen and purify his *buddhi* so that, in any and every situation, it could be resolute in its decisions. That is, it could always bring him to act in a way adequately responsive to his situation. This would constitute a certain perfection of himself as active creature.

Now according to Yoga such a resolute *buddhi*—one purified of all traces of delusion and always capable of deciding so that one acts in the way mentioned—would be "unitary", whereas the irresolute *buddhi* is "many-branched and endless". What do these characterizations refer to? An irresolute *buddhi* is at work in action undertaken out of one of manifold desires and in reference to manifold things and persons in one's situation, and in action which through *dharma* (so far as it is assimilated), is to be guided by a manifold of rules and principles. Such a *buddhi*, then, must operate amidst the multiplicity of ramifications within the active side of existence, which have (for such a *buddhi*) only one ultimate reference point, the ego. But since the ego is itself only constituted by a multiplicity of desires and powers, there is inherently a complexity which must mark a *buddhi* that is irresolute. Not only that: the ego involves one in an unavoidable restlessness. It can never finally be gratified, it exists only in a continual striving for further gratification. And there is no end to this striving; *buddhi* cannot bring one to a resting place so far as it operates within delusion. *Buddhi* is "many-branched", then, through *dharma* and desires, and "endless" through the restlessness of the ego. What might it mean to speak of the resolute *buddhi*, in contrast, as unitary?

The resolute *buddhi* is one into which an ultimate simplicity has entered. What this means can be seen if one considers Arjuna again. In his current condition his *buddhi* has, in its awareness side, opened up the possibility of resolute decision to him, and eventually of a resoluteness to itself. And more than that: he has already become attentive to the claiming factor disclosed in his awareness, and has responded to this with a cleaving to it that acknowledges its greater authority over him as against even *dharma*. But he is not cleaving to that factor as what it is, namely, a factor calling him to something to be reached eventually in and through action.

According to Yoga he must cleave to that factor as engaging him in action, that is, he must hold to it under a proper interpretation of its motivational import. And he must cleave to it as engaging him in action on the strength of *its own* force as motivation, *its own* inspirational power, hence as engaging him in action undertaken in relinquishment of attachment. And finally, he must cleave to it while acting as it calls him to act, that is, he must judge and decide so as to bring himself in his whole active being into action which *dharma* points out as right given his particular nature. What I have just been calling a "cleaving to", Kṛṣṇa speaks of as a yoking oneself to, a joining oneself to, a uniting oneself with. It is fundamentally a paying attention to and heeding in such way as to hold in mind that which one is heeding as one responds to its call. Such an attentional heeding and holding in mind need not, of course, relate to a factor that is kept in the explicit focus of attention; indeed, for the most part, what is being responded to in this way is held at the back of the focussing of attention, so to speak.

In any case, action as Arjuna is to enter upon it now is disciplined action in that in it his capacities are harnessed into action in response to the directive factor, but it is also yoked action in that in so acting one is all the while inwardly joined to a factor which also inwardly supports one as one acts. And more, such action is non-egoistic in that the motivation to such action as is called for is merely that it *is* called for by that which one is heeding as authoritative. It is in this regard that Arjuna is currently failing: he does feel the claim of that factor, he is seeking to cleave to it, but he is not responding appropriately to its motivational force. Instead he is still taking himself as active center to be ego; and as ego, taken as basic and underived, he is distorting the motivational power which he feels the presence to have by his delusion that whatever he is to do must gratify his ego. He feels himself thrust beyond *dharma* and called to respond somehow to the presence of the Kurus; but he mistakes the call and, seeing that no gratification is likely to come from engaging in battle, he is tempted to withdraw, as if ego-gratification were what ultimately mattered.

In the Yoga view, however, Arjuna is at a place in life where he can no longer lay rightful claim to the fruits of activity, that is, to results that could confirm his ego. Instead he is at a place where he can—and must—begin to discover that he is not ego (that is not his reality) and that what truly matters in his action is not ego-gratification but his participation in enlightenment and release. These are to be reached through action: he has a right to action, therefore, but to action now only as part of a path, not to action as vehicle for ego-gratification. And not only has he a right to action in this vein: he must undertake it in that way now, moved to do what this presence calls him to do without ego-concern. If he is not to let the fruit of activity impel him any longer, so also he is not now to be impelled to avoid action (withdraw from it) out of attachment. This is, in the Yoga view, what Arjuna is about to do: he is egoistically attaching himself to inaction by refusing to fight, as if he had a right now to withdraw from *dharma*-accordant action just because it does not seem that his ego would be gratified by carrying it through.

If Arjuna now enters upon action as he should—if he responds to the claiming presence out of understanding that it calls him to enter upon a path toward enlightenment by engaging in battle —he will enter upon battle out of a resolute decision, one formed in awareness and attention and understanding and judging which issue in decision and heedful action grounded in the realities of his situation. That would be a first step only: his *buddhi* would not be itself resolute except after much more effort, many more steps of that kind. But gradually with such steps he would find himself given steady support within (balance, equilibrium) and would find action (as disciplined and yoked) to be an effective medium for effectuating release. In the end he would come into a condition in which, in the midst of acting, he would stand unmoved, immovable: self-possessed. It is along this path that Arjuna's *buddhi* will lose its "many-branched" and "endless" characters. For along this path Arjuna will have been enabled to transcend egoism and to transcend *dharma* and desire; the former means losing the "endless" character, the latter means losing the "many-branched" character. Thus he will have become enabled constantly to take his stand in the truly essential and real, with a *buddhi* which is "unitary".

This "unitary" character of *buddhi*, introduced through such discipline, involves a certain simplifying, I said before. What that means can now become clear. Along the path of disciplined effort, *buddhi* forms decision in one basic movement, that of cleaving in union to the ultimate claiming presence as one engages in action in each and every situation. Along that path *buddhi* thus forms decision in response ultimately to one and the same presence calling always to one and the same end, and calling in each situation for one and the same sort of action (a responsively undertaken effort that accords with *dharma*). A *buddhi* which is thus purified of egoism and all that goes with it will be unitary because one in its mode of operation, one in its support and aim, and one or inwardly united due to its purity. That is, such a *buddhi* will be wholly integrated and harmonious in its operation, which is always basically the same in its manner, in what supports and directs it, and in what it is eventually to culminate in.

Such is the way Kṛṣṇa initially uses the Yoga teaching of the tradition known to Arjuna. But as with the Sāṁkhya so here: that teaching is a distorted version of the original Yoga he taught at an earlier age. That original Yoga contains much that is found here, but gives it a somewhat different meaning than it otherwise might have because the original Yoga introduces the Lord into the very heart of things. Thus, for example, the negative ends of this traditional Yoga will soon be removed, so that release will signify not aloneness but a unity in which disciplined union is central.

These first two stages of Kṛṣṇa's initial teaching help him to indicate to Arjuna that his grief and refusal to fight rest in a misinterpretation of the true nature of his situation, and that his real need (given the truth of his situation) is to fight. Together they affirm that a proper understanding of the situation would involve a recognition of a duality in things, together with the recognition that the ultimate aim of human effort is reached into only with a clear and steady awareness of that duality. It is such an enlightened awareness that Arjuna must eventually reach, and whatever he is to do now must be seen as amplifying what he is beginning here so as somehow to contribute to his eventual achievement of this awareness. The third and final stage of Kṛṣṇa's initial teaching (Verses 55-72) speaks of this terminal condition eventually to be reached on earth, voicing the conception of it common to both Sāṁkhya and Yoga.

Arjuna asks (Verse 54), how is one to recognize this man that I am supposed eventually to become according to Sāṁkhya and Yoga ? Kṛṣṇa replies that there are no outward marks or signs, what distinguishes him is not how he walks or sits or talks, what is distinctive is his inner condition. What is that condition ?

In asking the question Arjuna has used terms that relate to what Kṛṣṇa has just been saying about *buddhi*, and through those terms we are pointed to the basic character of the condition being asked about. It is a condition of ingatheredness under the supporting presence of what is ultimately imperative (the supreme), and a condition of ingatheredness in which there is present both a *prajñā* and a *dhī*. Both of these terms refer to conditions of *buddhi*, and here, to settled conditions, enduring qualifications of this power through which a human being enters upon action in human fashion. And more, they qualify a mature form of human capacity, potency, capability, in regard to *buddhi*. As such they refer to factors integral to our effective capacity to participate in what is at stake in human existence. Indeed *prajñā*, a term with a wide variety of meanings, carries with it throughout that variety (like *sophia* in Greek and "wisdom" in English) an implication of know-how, of capability in regard to human affairs, as well as the presupposition of experience (as in a "man of experience"). Perhaps the relevant meaning of *prajñā* here, however, would be something like "clear-sightedness", where this refers to *buddhi* primarily in its awareness side. *Dhī*, in contrast, probably means something like "understanding", as a qualification of *buddhi* in its intentional side or in regard to thought as a matter of putting one's mind on something, paying attention to and concentrating on so as to understand. Again, *dhi* has a reference to know-how in regard to human affairs, as in a "man of understanding", but with the connotation of an understanding which fathoms the human within a religious dimension.

Since *buddhi* is that power through which the particular nature in a man is gathered up and entered into action, Arjuna's question about the man who is stably clear-sighted and understanding is answered by Kṛṣṇa with reference to the presence and functioning in his condition of certain important factors that are part of the particular nature of each and every man. The first four verses (55-58) thus speak of desire, feeling, and the senses. These are present in the enlightened human being, but because of the elimination of egoism, they have been transfigured from the character that they have in one whose condition is deluded. Thus desire persists, a legitimate natural (and socially inflected) spur to action; but cravings have vanished, unnatural and merely egoistic desires are gone. Again, feeling persists, but clarified feeling, its turbulence and troubling character removed, its character as e-motion gone (no "anger", "passion", "fear", and the like: these are forms of feeling that do not arise except within egoism). Pleasure and pain are present, so far as these are naturally attendant upon physical existence, but they come and go within a deeper feeling of content and peace and rejoicing in one's self. This feeling is constant, so that nothing in the way of emotional upset or disturbance occurs through pleasure and pain. And finally, the senses persist, where the senses include not merely our powers of projecting outward to take an impression from what we encounter but as well the register of such impressions on feeling (particularly pleasure and pain) and the disposition to react built up in this way and touched off in the sensible presence of things again.

In this broad and active sense, the senses are powers through which we take a certain cognizance of others, and inwardly, of ourselves as others affect us and as we function in effort that relates to them. But these powers function in our action only as, through *buddhi*, we attend to and interpret the impressions we are gaining, so as to respond to what we take them to signify. Thus the senses are initially brought to function (like desire and feeling) within the constraints of egoism. And because of this we use them and take ourselves to be opened out onto the real world through them; yet not only are we mistaking the real but we are also missing things in their actual sensible character. For our sensing is not only a selective perception (which it always is) but a perception whose selectiveness is egoistically guided. Things are taken in and register on us in their sensible presence only through the dulling and obscuring and distorting haze of our egoistic anxieties and preoccupations, which do not let us normally perceive things clearly in their actual sensible presence. It is only with the removal of the egoistic attitude and orientation that we take things in through the senses with a genuine openness to their sensible character.

In the next verses (59-68) Kṛṣṇa speaks of this matter of the senses at some length. We go out to things which the senses open us to and we take such things in. But this is normally done in such way that we feed upon such things: we taste and relish them, draw nourishment from them, feed our egos (egoistic desires and feelings) through them. Thus becoming intent on certain things, we can grow fond of them, attached to them: they offer what nourishes our ego, we like them, and we grow used to them and tied to them almost without noticing it. This fondness and attachment can strengthen into a grasping relation: we can desire to have and hold them, to possess them. Such is what is implied in passionate love and its desire (*kāma*). But if this desire is thwarted in some way, anger can arise. If we remember ourselves, if we do not forget ourselves, that is, if what we have learned and identified ourselves with in the way of *dharma* can suffice to constrain us to act properly (according to "ourselves" as it defines us), then we can perhaps resist anger.

But the strength of frustrated desire and anger can bring such turmoil—such deluding confusion—that *dharma* is forgotten. And with this we are lost: we act not simply irresolutely but out of impulse unrestrained by *dharma*. Having lost our capacity to judge and decide intelligently, guided by *dharma*, we can be led to transgress *dharma*. This all attests one possibility—one possible unfolding of our initially innocent attentiveness to what presents itself sensuously. There are many others; the point here is merely to indicate in one way how, given an immature *buddhi*, we can fasten ourselves to sensible things, can lay ourselves open to passion and turmoil and thence to the possibility of impulsive action contrary to *dharma*.

However, simply to abstain from things of sense (what we are fond of), that is, to try to avoid temptation, so to speak, does not get to the root of the matter. For into that abstention we carry still our ego and our egoistically formed attachments. What alone gets to the roots of the matter is whatever brings us beyond egoism, hence brings us beyond that sort of going-out-to and taking-in so as to feed-upon which is the root of the trouble. We can move beyond egoism through such experience as Arjuna has entered upon, if in it we really gain some cognizance of the depths and can adequately respond to the imperative presence we find there. This imperative presence alone gives us the possibility of forsaking egoism, hence genuinely forsaking unnatural cravings, emotional disturbance, sensuous attachment and the like. A single glimpse into the depths, however, is not enough to effect this forsaking. At best our initial response on the strength of that glimpse can begin the process that effects it. But this beginning needs to be carried through resolutely, that is, in a discipline in which all one's powers (the senses included) are harnessed into effort that is based in the cleaving to this imperative factor found in the depths.

As such discipline leads to its culmination in enlightenment one gains inner calm, freedom from agitation, out of which one moves amidst things of sense and perceives them with senses that are free from egoistic feelings (passion, hatred) and desires. The condition is not one in which the senses are not functioning (suppressed or eliminated), but one in which they come into their own because they are no longer being used to subserve egoism.[5] They are, indeed, "controlled". For they function within a man whose *buddhi* is resolute, and they subserve his efforts to act responsively to what is more than sensible. But this is no distortion of them, merely the role they are meant to play by their nature.

The initial teaching which Kṛṣṇa gives to Arjuna ends (Verses 69-72) with a summary indication of the man Arjuna is eventually to become. The enlightened man is awake to depths that are dark to men confined in delusion, and is at peace. Yet he still has desires: without egoism, however, so that he does not cherish them but has left them behind. Having reached this condition while alive on earth, and enduring in it up to death, such a man is not reborn in any form : he becomes extinct in his creaturely side. But according to Sāṁkhya and Yoga, this means that his Self or Spirit would gain aloneness. Kṛṣṇa here says, however, that such a one comes to extinction in the holy power. With this we are ready for the emergence of Kṛṣṇa himself into disclosure as the Lord and author of a more encompassing teaching than that offered by the traditional Sāṁkhya and Yoga.

CHAPTERS III-VI

The conversation in Chapter II took its crucial direction from out of a happening in which the involvement of Arjuna in action had unexpectedly altered. Arjuna spoke to this alteration in a way that recognized it as fundamental, yet anticipated a resolution which would emerge with the delineation by Kṛṣṇa of a course which he would be able to take and take with honor in the situation at hand. Kṛṣṇa's response has not answered to the expectation implicit in Arjuna's request. He has indeed urged Arjuna not to withdraw from battle, but he has done so by drawing on teachings which do not focus upon the differentiation of one course of action from another as the important matter but which focus instead on the nature and meaning of action generally for a human being. In using these teachings in this way Kṛṣṇa has initiated a shift in attention that will persist as he develops his own teaching concerning action in these Chapters, III through VI.

These four Chapters unfold dialogically from out of Arjuna's response to Kṛṣṇa's initial educative effort. Arjuna has not understood it. For he has been listening with the hope of hearing what would confirm him in his refusal to fight. And thus it is Kṛṣṇa's reference to Sāṁkhya that catches his ear, for with this reference there seems to be confirmation of his desire to withdraw. Yet he has also heard Kṛṣṇa enjoining him to fight. So he asks for clarification: you say the discipline of *buddhi* is superior to action, then why must I act? That is, you say that the teaching of Sāṁkhya is right, that men must withdraw from action and engage in a discipline of their *buddhi* in its side of understanding within awareness; then why am I supposed to act instead of taking this path of knowledge? Kṛṣṇa's initial answer to this, in the rest of Chapter III and in Chapter IV, speaks of ritual (sacrificial) and social action in connection with bondage and develops a notion of inward sacrifice culminating in *jñāna*; but it leaves Arjuna unclear as to which is indeed better, according to Kṛṣṇa, the renunciation of action or its disciplined undertaking. And with his asking of this question at the start of Chapter V, Kṛṣṇa is drawn into a further two-Chapter clarification of his teaching, which speaks of the condition of perfection in action and of the place of meditation in the disciplined undertaking of the way of action.

In the course of this beautifully articulated conversational interplay, that mode of speech which, in Verse 61 of Chapter II, betrayed Kṛṣṇa to be something more than a man—though Arjuna did not seem to catch this—becomes explained by Kṛṣṇa himself. For he comes to declare himself to be an avatāra (incarnation) of the Lord, and in that form to be proclaiming that teaching of a two-fold form of devoted effort which is the original form of the two traditional modes of thought to which he had appealed in Chapter II. As he offers this account of two major paths fitted to be taken by the two major types of men (men of action and men of thought) and fitted to lead the men taking them to the same perfection and fulfillment of release, his own presence as the Lord becomes more forceful. While Kṛṣṇa is disclosing himself as more than human and providing a clarification of the initial teaching by placing it into the perspective of an original teaching uttered long ago by Kṛṣṇa as the Lord, Arjuna is attentive and, in his effort to understand, is being drawn out and into what is being said. Thus by the end of Chapter VI Kṛṣṇa has offered a teaching about action and its point which, while it suggests these without any full and direct clarification of the encompassing conditions of action, provides Arjuna with a certain orientation even though his bewilderment remains.

Already with Chapter II and the account of a traditional form of Sāṁkhya and Yoga Kṛṣṇa has brought in a central notion for his own teaching, that of a differentiation between Spirit or Self and nature. Within the Sāṁkhya and Yoga of that Chapter, however, the ultimate bearing of this distinction for us in our ongoing existence is an eventuation in aloneness, in disjunction. Kṛṣṇa's own view runs in the opposite direction. Thus although there is a continuation of a kind of emphasis and viewing of things expressed in Chapter II, there is also a development which places what is continued in altered light. There is, for example, a deepening and complicating of the emphasis of Chapter II on the inward conditions of action, upon the dimension of effort that concerns one's involvement in action, the way one engages in action.

It is in reference to this dimension that the limitations upon courses of action and the determination of one course rather than another gains its basic intelligibility. For it does make a difference what one undertakes, but the difference that it makes pertains ultimately to what is to come to pass in the concrete interconnection of beings from out of the inwardness within which each acts and lives. But this deepening and complicating, this continuing, of Sāṁkhya and Yoga is given a reversed direction in the measure in which it is suggested that what is to come to pass in this interconnection is a kind of unification of diversity which has its vital center in the inwardness in question. What is important is a kind of integration, unification, the emergence of a kind of uni-verse, not a disjunction and aloneness. With this in mind, let me attempt to formulate certain important facets of the teaching that emerges in these Chapters, bringing them to focus around the notions of action on a path and of freedom.

ACTION ON A PATH

To the center of the teaching is the question, what is action? And involved in the answer is a denial of a traditional thesis that tends to identify "action" with overt social-and-ritual practice. Instead Kṛṣṇa views action broadly, as the engagement in effort which brings one's active being into play whether in overt action of one sort or another, or in overt inaction but in more subtle and hidden forms of inward effort. And given this broad view he understands creatures to be so constituted as to be unable to help being engaged in some sort of activity all the time. What is important, then, concerns the kind of action and the manner of engagement in it. And between these two it is the latter that is most crucial for Kṛṣṇa here.

In his understanding of the manner in which we are involved in active effort Kṛṣṇa retains the triadicity involved in the Sāṁkhya-Yoga conception of the being of things: the differentiation within a human being, for example, of the inactive from the active sides to the self, and within the active, of *buddhi* as the essential and common power from the powers which provide a particularity beyond this commonality which *buddhi* gives to human nature. Thus he conceives different human beings to be fitted for different sorts of activity by their different natures. But though a human being enter upon the actions that he is fitted for by his particular nature and that express concretely the definiteness of his particular and differentiating nature, he does this through *buddhi*, and thus through the functioning of a power which brings the powers of his particular nature into play humanly, in a way that involves and expresses his essential and common human nature. Since the particular natures of different human beings fit them for different kinds of activity, each human being takes his stand as human in the doing of particular deeds which all express, more or less adequately and with greater or lesser emphasis upon one side of his nature in contrast with another, both his particular nature and his essential human nature.

Now *buddhi* is a developing power, and the functioning of it as such is medium for a growth in human being. Since Kṛṣṇa is addressing Arjuna as someone who has just entered upon the inadvertent amplification of his *buddhi's* power of awareness which marks the initial phase of the transformation from immaturity to maturity in the capacity to enter upon action humanly, he concerns himself centrally with what this amplification signifies and what the import is of the presence that has taken hold of Arjuna. Speaking now his own mind, and with increasing explicitness to Arjuna this is the mind of the Lord Himself, Kṛṣṇa indicates that what Arjuna has become aware of is ultimately the imperative presence of Himself as Lord, and within this, the presence of himself and others as creatures involved in a movement that is meant to be carried forward toward a certain kind of concrete unity. Although Arjuna is misinterpreting the presence which has claimed his allegiance in his inadvertent opened-outness into the depths, that presence of the Lord is nonetheless imperative upon him toward a responsive effort which, holding as its end the fulfillment of creation to which Kṛṣṇa is pointing, will place him effectively on the path toward his own fullest contribution to the realization of that end and thus his own fulfillment as a being within the uni-verse.

A possibility has been opened up to Arjuna, which he must himself make good on in a responsive engagement of his whole being. In Kṛṣṇa's teaching there are a variety of paths of such responsive effort appropriate to a variety of men: Arjuna's, the path of action, is only one. But each path, as a path, is the same with every other in certain basic regards. The following three regards would seem to be the most important in Kṛṣṇa's teaching here.

First, the taking of any path is a devotional affair involving the Lord's immediate presence. Devotion to the Lord, in this sense, is that responsive offering of oneself in which one gives allegiance to the Lord in His presence (however adequately he be recognized in that presence for what He is). Thus faith, as the faithful adherence to that presence, lies at the basis of whatever particular efforts one engages in. And so too does sacrifice, in that devotion signifies an inwardly sacrificial entry upon effort in which, cleaving to the Lord in acknowledgement of one's creatureliness, one offers up his capacities for action to be purified and strengthened in service animated by His directive presence. Thus entry upon maturity occurs in a renunciation of ego. It is devotion with such faith and inward sacrifice intrinsic to it, that constitutes the appropriate responsive movement at the core of a creature's adequate responsiveness to the moving force provided by the imperative presence of the creator.

Second, the taking of any path is an affair of devotion in another sense. For the Lord commands, but not directly to any action in particular, instead to one's active movement toward the fullest possible contribution from himself to the fulfillment of creation. Since that fulfillment lies in a concrete unity which is established in and through active effort, and since one stands at the time in question in a relative incapacity to contribute toward that unity, adequate response to the Lord's command involves a devotion to concrete effort which not only subserves such unity so far as possible now but is discipline in both a negative and a positive sense.

It is discipline in the negative sense in that it is an ingathered effort in which one's active being—and one's *buddhi* first and foremost—is being purified and released from egoism and the distortions—attachment, graspingness, willful purpose, and the like—which pertain to effort as merely egoisitc doing. It is discipline in the positive sense in that it is an ingathered effort in which one's nature is being released into concrete effort that amplifies and consolidates one's capacity to engage effectively in the action that fulfills creaturely existence. Both sides of discipline involve a gathering together and functioning of energies and capacities in which one's education in what it is to be a human being is being shaped toward fulness. Both center in the education of *buddhi* in regard to how to bring one into action as agent, how to attend and interpret and assess and judge and decide and act as sustained by a directive presence inwardly cleaved to. That devotion to effort which is counterpart to devotion to the Lord, then, is a harnessing of capacities into such ongoing contribution as one can make concretely to the unity at stake in the guiding directive and a concomitant learning which is educative of one's capacity to contribute and which strengthens it in the course of one's venturing.

A third element of sameness lies in the end to which every path leads, the agent's effective participation in the culmination of creation as a fully mature human being. What is involved here is a unity brought to focus in the ongoing existence of a creature, but a unity which integrates a whole more deeply conceived than in any conception which makes the differentiation of Lord and creature ultimate. Along the way of whatever particular practice is involved on a path, one's effort is supported by the Lord in His presence. But as one's particular nature is brought into play in and through a *buddhi* which is becoming gradually purified of egoism, one's power of awareness becomes opened to something deeper in the nature of things than the Lord, something included in that of which the Lord is the unitary or simple but inclusive spiritual expression. For one becomes aware of that basic side to one's own self which is integral to what is the very self of the Lord and which is deeper than Himself as creator.

In Kṛṣṇa's characterization of this deeper side of our own self, he speaks of a presence which, sun-like, both burns and illuminates, and he calls it *jñāna* (this is only one of the meanings of this term). This inactive and time-antecedent side to one's self was not only hidden when one was deluded (hidden by the fire and smoke of desire and anger), but it remained hidden in the confusion attendant on the initial amplification of awareness and entry onto the path. At first it was the Lord alone, and the Lord as imperative factor out of the depths, that was effectively present. With purification, however, the "light" of this basic side to one's self begins to shine effectively into one's *buddhi* and its "fire" begins to purify one also.

The culmination to which this co-operative effort of Lord and creature is leading, is a complex condition of unity. To begin with, in the creature it is a condition of integration, centered in a *buddhi* which is pure, its awareness clear and steady amidst the light of the basic side of one's self, its understanding and attention and judgment and decisional power fully (within their limits) responsive to creatures and Lord out of openness to the deepest reaches to their selves. Thus one's particular nature is integrated as functioning out of one's ingatheredness in such a condition of *buddhi*; and one's basic and inactive side is integrated as illuminating presence entered into the responsiveness of *buddhi*. But this integration inward to the creature is a condition in which an active life is lived *with* others, and these others enter into the unity in question concretely as those with whom one dwells in ties of care. It is something about these ties of care, that receives the greatest emphasis in Kṛṣṇa's teaching, even greater, perhaps, than the contention that to enter upon and dwell within such release of capacity brings (with death) the final termination of involvement in the cycles of creaturely existence for the self in question. That this termination takes place, is due to the ultimate unreality of the creaturely, so that creation receiving its culmination in any being, the ultimate reality of that being—the basic side to its self—alone "remains", and "remains" as what it always has been and will be, element in the ultimate ground within the whole, in the basic side to the self of the Lord, in the sole reality.

What it is that is rendered emphatic in regard to those ties of care, might be best approached by speaking not of the elements of sameness to each and every path but of the elements of difference. Such elements lead Kṛṣṇa to speak, for example, of two basic paths for the devotional and devoted effort that culminates in enlightened participation in creation. These different paths—the path of knowledge and the path of action—reflect that in their particular natures men may be conceived roughly to be "doers" or "thinkers". Since the path toward enlightenment involves devotion to such work as brings one's particular nature into play, these basic differences in nature lead to the formation of the two outwardly different paths, so as to give appropriate scope for the play of the particular powers of the men in question. More than this crude difference is involved, of course, in the differences in particular nature; the order formed under *dharma* involves a manifold of differentiations social in nature but accordant in meaning with the manifold variety in natures. Still the broad differentiation, crude though it is, encompasses these differences and signifies that in all but a very few cases—those of the nature of "thinkers"—proper scope is provided for their particular natures *only within* the social order determined by *dharma*. Such is Kṛṣṇa's teaching: withdrawal from the social order in order to seek enlightenment is inappropriate for almost all men, and in particular, of course, for Arjuna.

One can see at least an important part of the reason for this emphasis, which ran counter to the then dominant idea within Hinduism that only withdrawal could provide the conditions of a proper seeking for enlightenment and release, if one recognizes that part of what it is to enter upon a path at all is to find what Arjuna in some measure found in the strange presence of the Kurus. And that is, that human beings count, that one *cares* for other men in a way that is integral to what it is to be a mature human being. Human beings who live within a social order which is formed with some acknowledgement that ultimately there is something deeper in life than comes into the purview of those active in the social order itself under its governing social aims, will be peculiarly influenced by the way those human beings who are supposed to be on a path toward that deeper issue—or who are supposed to have reached the goal—comport themselves. Such "superior" human beings will serve—regardless of their desires—as an example for ordinary mortals.

And in particular, ordinary human beings will draw their own conclusions from what they can see of such persons, as to whether the effort in which they are themselves engaged can ever amount to anything in the end. Ordinarily human beings are attached to action and unable to grasp—out of their own experience—what it might mean to act in any other way. There is, however, one recognizable contrast for them, that of duty vs inclination. For there is, for them, *dharma*—a constraining definiteness, one which makes demands and which moulds one properly only if one can identify with it and follow its guidance; and there is inclination, a factor which pulls downward in contrast with the upward and constraining pull of *dharma*, and which constitutes the easy way to take. For *dharma* often requires a certain restraint and constraint, and one which normally runs against the grain of inclination—not against one's nature, but against inclination, which (in one's delusion) one is liable to identify with one's nature. Such discipline as *dharma* involves can be accepted and entered upon if one can believe in its efficacy for bringing one to a significant participation in life. But to one caught up in egoism, this will be thought of as "happiness" and imaged most easily as a condition of gratification in which there is no restraint such as *dharma* represents. This is a mistake: the enlightened condition is not one of amorality or immorality but one in which one is *more* than merely moral. Still, what can be the effect on such a person, so conceiving things in the only way he really is able, when he finds the ultimate condition he is supposed eventually to reach to be imaged for him by the human being who has withdrawn from the social order (the forest-dweller and the wandering beggar, for example)? Will he not conceive them, from out of what his experience allows him to feel and see, to be men free from *dharma* and its restrictions, and (perhaps) to be free to make their way as they are inclined (with license even)?

However grossly unjust such a conception might be, it is appearance to the unenlightened that here counts. And Kṛṣṇa seems to think that such "superior" men, by their appearance in this social-but-asocial form, tend to reinforce in deluded men the tendency to give in to inclination and to give up the moral effort (which often can be a struggle) whereby one's nature is alone formed and shaped toward fulness. This demoralizing effect of "socially inactive" but "enlightened" men within society will be all the greater if it is combined with the implication that enlightenment can only be achieved by withdrawal and the discipline of knowledge. For since very few people are suited for this, hence could not in anticipation think of withdrawal as anything they could see themselves gaining from, most persons would have suggested to them by the wandering beggars, for example, the impossibility of their finding the fundamental point of life—at least, of finding it in this life without effort even more against the grain of their nature than moral effort is against the grain of the impulsive side of their makeup. For most human beings the ultimate fulfillment is to be found properly in and through participation in social-and-ritual action. And for all it is to be found only after a moral participation in such action has prepared them to transcend delusion and egoism.

If one cares for human beings, then, if the community of human beings in the closeness of their being creatures tied concretely into vital connection with each other has a claim upon one, then one should proceed on the path of action, not that of knowledge, provided of course that one's nature is fitted for the former path. For proceeding in this way can not only bring one to reach the goal oneself, but by the way in which it expresses, in a socially-adjusted form, the claim of community all along the way of the path, it can help others who are deluded. For if nothing else one is serving as an example that confirms the positive place of *dharma* in the movement of human life toward fulfillment and that therefore helps to strengthen in others their response to *dharma*.

Kṛṣṇa's emphasis on the path of action thus expresses the kind of unity which is at stake in the concrete fulfillment of the creation which emerges through his *māyā*. For that unity is a unity of the diverse, in which diversity is preserved but relieved of the insulating and self-enclosing features that distort the diverse with the emergence of delusion and egoism. As ingredient in unity as an affair of concreteness, diversity in many forms grows together in the unification and integration through which a uni-verse arises. So far as human beings are included in that diversity, they are included as not simply "identical" in the basic sides to their selves and as fairly diverse in their particular natures, but also as united through the commonality of their essential nature as active beings (*buddhi*). Integral to the communion and community that is distinctively possible among human beings, is the establishing and affirming of norms within the social dimension of human nature and the social ordering of human existence. In seeking to restore *dharma* to its efficacy among human beings, Kṛṣṇa is a conservative, critical of the current social order on the strength of its departure from standards of old. But he sees more deeply than that, and sees as a radical going to the roots; for what he seeks to restore is a factor—*dharma*—with manifold functions, the most fundamental of which is to help to shape diverse human beings in their growth and to shape them toward a liberation, a freedom, that involves its own transcendence. That means that Kṛṣṇa is seeking to foster a social order which assists human beings toward a community of themselves and a unity with all things, whose concreteness holds together all creatures on grounds much deeper than the social.

FREEDOM

The notion of freedom involved in these Chapters is a complex one. Through it Kṛṣṇa is able to speak of a center who is independent, yet who might be engaged with things in a way that involves it in dependence and bondage (indeed, often inescapably is so engaged), but who might also become released from these and enter into a freer engagement with things, eventually to stand in action as the independent center it is within the interdependence of things which are together dependent on a source. What is involved, then, is a notion of freedom as something in the capacity for which we alter and grow. That is the point which provides the perspective for understanding the notion of freedom, that we are beings on the move and that, as Arjuna images for us, we can move into times when we find ourselves ingathered and concentrated amidst an imperative presence accessible through *buddhi* and bearing on us with the force of a "must" that points our movement toward an end implicit in the animating and directive presence. It is to this can-and-must-move that our understanding of our freedom must be faithful. Yet it is not with such explicit presence and the light which it throws on our being, that we ourselves begin in our participation in freedom. We begin at the start of life, in an involvement in action in which the matter of ego is crucial, and in which we develop a notion of our freedom which is just as delusory as our notion of ego. Since the fuller entry into our freedom involves, among other things, a liberation from this inadequate notion, let me begin with the latter, and then move to the more adequate notion which we can gain only as we come more fully into freedom itself. As we gain this more adequate notion, we can come to understand what all along has been, and still is, involved in our freedom.

Ego represents an interpretative notion which arises in us and informs our effort in such way as makes effort form around what is ultimately a figment and a delusion, something without reality or actuality but merely seeming (to its fabricator) to exist and to constitute ourselves. It is formed in such way as to take into account the first-personal character of effort intrinsic to creaturely existence, and to take this into account in connection with the sense of such existence to the effect that for the active being there is in his action something at stake which concerns reality (his own included).

The formation of this fiction occurs and becomes established in us through the initial impotence in the powers through which we share in existence from birth onward. For to begin with we are—and can not help being—exclusively aware of and attentive to the display which greets us and to the centers displayed. Occupied with ourselves and others in this way it is desire which primordially educates us about ourselves and what is at stake in our existence in a world which apparently is all that is. Thus action, as a venture and a staking of ourselves which takes us out into the world and enters us into a having to do with others primordially at the behest of desire, is grasped as locus of our actuality. But it is locus of an actuality which we have in effort which, so far as we are aware and understand, has at stake in it the securing of something with which we have become identified through the desire that is moving us. In this mode of involvement in action the results matter not simply out of the neediness which desire attests but out of the identity that is at stake in the effort itself. To be ourselves as we are determining our identity, we *must* succeed, we must prove ourselves not simply doers in fact but doers in reality, doers of significance and power, doers who are *someone* for their capacity to have their way through action.

Thus out of a certain kind of identification with our own desires, we move into effort as creatures of desire mistakenly imposing on ourselves a "reality" which is to emerge for ourselves as a function of the success of our efforts in bringing ourselves what we desire. In such effort we develop a notion of freedom which, as explicit to ourselves, moves within the poles of the constraining limits of the environment on the one hand and our own capacity for obtaining our own way on the other. But unwittingly, in making effort into a doing whose significance is a matter of confirmation of ego, we have involved ourselves in an orientation that implicates us in other things that concern our freedom.

Thus there is an inescapable restlessness into which we are entered. We can not help being active, and we can not feel ourselves alive and real except as "doing" something which subserves desire and pride in ourselves as capable doers. And yet we are committed by our very mode of being active to the achievement of a "reality" for ourselves which is in fact unreal and thus incapable of providing any genuine resting place. Such restlessness is boundless, perpetual, and the effort pervaded by it knows no real measure. Then again, in this fabrication of an ego we involve ourselves in a dependence—a bondage and attachment—which rests in our intentness upon a "reality" which is "fruit" of our active accomplishment. For depending on something that action as doing is to bring in the way of confirmation of ego, we are handed over to the circumstances and factors which prevent or foster or allow this confirmation to occur: we become tied to that which is other than ourselves, as that which *must* work to *confirm us*. We are led, then, into insistence, aggression and force, ultimately, so as to "have my way".

That in this way I make the world center around myself as active, and more particularly, around an "I" whose "reality" is taken to be what is fundamentally at stake in my effort, reflects something that pertains to my actuality, but a something which is only partially or one-sidedly brought into awareness and is being interpreted within that awareness in a limited fashion. Thus consider more closely this matter of the freedom I attribute to myself. The ego appears as a center conscious of desires within itself as a whole, and is constituted through the center's identification of itself with at least certain of these. Ego appears primordially in "I want this-or-that". Then too, ego appears as a center conscious of standards which stem, in great measure, from its environment, and are gathered into itself in a socialization within which ego identifies with at least certain of these standards.

Thus the ego, as conscious center defining itself in identification with "I want this" referred in some fashion to "I ought to do or have that", appears as a center which is the ultimate source of effort and which can deliberate and decide and initiate action at the behest of desire as inclination (whether *dharma*-sanctioned or not). As conscious center so identifying and striving, ego appears as itself at stake in action and as asserted or denied in its reality according as action brings one result or another. Thus ego claims a right to the fruits of the action it initiates, under the presumption of being solely responsible for the initiation of the action which brings those results and thus of being rightfully claimant to them as its own. "I" then am "doer": "I" am active in the pursuit of "my" wants and under the constraint of standards "I" acknowledge, solely responsible for "my" conscious decision and the initiation of "my" action, rightfully claimant of the results of "my" action as "mine" when "I" intended and produced them.

And yet, consider this "freedom". Can "I" decide and do, for example, "what I want"? To answer this it is necessary to explore what it means to say "I want this-or-that". It would seem that "my" wants are "mine" only through an identification of myself with certain desires that emerge into the conscious side of effort. Emerging there, taken into *buddhi* consciously, their presence is an urgent one which presses on "me", which perhaps "I" can ignore or refuse to acknowledge as proper and which perhaps "I" can choose between. But they are "mine"—when they are taken into "me" as such—in a way that places them prior to "my" responsive acquiescence in them or refusal to acquiesce in them. Within this anteriority "I" am "free" to decide and act (or not to act) on their promptings.

But what about this thinking and deciding in which, given desires of one sort or another, I come to decide what I do? In a measure I can re-form my wants, play one off against the other. Yet not only do I stand at their mercy because of their anteriority, but through them I stand in dependence upon others, upon the world, as I cater (in some measure) to these wants. Thus I am layed open to suffering in manifold ways through the happenings in the world beyond "my" power to control. And then, if I look in retrospect at my deciding, I can occasionally discern the effective presence in it of factors which then I was not conscious of, even factors which "I" can not admit as part of "myself" really. Yet they were there, at work in "my" deciding, even occasionally driving "me" to do things "I" did not want to do.

Closer inspection makes me suspect that not only occasionally, but perhaps in some degree always, such factors are at work, surreptitiously bringing "me" to decide and act in one way rather than another, coming to "me" without (and sometimes despite) "my" attention and wish, compelling "me" sometimes—perhaps much more often that "I" would like to admit—to do one thing rather than another. Thus what "I" think and decide and do would seem to have many motivations which "I" do not accept or approve of or even know about (until later, perhaps), yet which "I" cannot escape so as to be able to do simply "what I want".

If this line of thought is pressed far enough in the direction in which it is heading, I would be led to say: "I" am not "free" at all, "compulsion" or determinism is the order of the day, even though "I" may go on thinking and deciding as if "I" were "free" to do what "I" want, indeed, even though "I" cannot avoid pre-supposing myself to be "free" in my active efforts.

In the light of what Kṛṣṇa is teaching, however, this conclusion would seem to be a mistaken one. For the notions of complete freedom, of complete determinism, and of partial freedom but partial determinism, *all* involve and presuppose a mistaken notion of the actual center who is active. For all presuppose the validity of a notion of "ego". But this notion is a fiction, delusory: "I" do not exist, acting is not "doing". What, then, of action engaged in within this mis-taking ? How is it to be understood? How is it "free"? And what of action and freedom beyond this delusion?

We *are centers*: that is what is being partially recognized in our egoistic notion of ourselves and our freedom. But what is being incompletely acknowledged is the *responsive* meaning of the power through which we actualize our freedom as centers, namely, *buddhi*. And this incomplete acknowledgement itself expresses something crucial to that power and to our freedom, that we grow into both only gradually, that we make them our own only gradually, in a movement from the incomplete to the complete. Arjuna stands in the midst of the time of transition from incomplete to complete, and thus in the course of the discovery that the freedom which pertains to ourselves in the constant functioning of ourselves as centers and initiators of active effort, is not a matter of having absolute power over others or ourselves, but a matter of having ultimate responsibility in a contribution of ourselves to a unity which we were meant as creatures to share in.

For a discovery such as Arjuna is making leads to the recognition of creatureliness made on the strength of the imperative presence of the power through whose working that creaturely existence which is one's own emerges into actuality. Responsiveness to this imperative presence leads the deepening self eventually to a further discovery, that of a side to one's own self which is real and antecedent even to the divine in its imperativeness. And then it is that this matter of being a center comes fully into the open for what it is. For then it appears as a matter of a responsive spontaneity through *buddhi*, whose meaning is to mediate participation in a unity which consummates the act of creation within which such a center emerges into being to begin with. That consummating unity integrates in fitting concrete fashion the disparate elements in the whole, down to the universal ground out of which all else stems.

Thus the temporal movement in which freedom comes into its own involves the constancy of initiation of effort as a center amidst a multiplicity of centers within the creaturely whole. And in this continual initiation one is ever taking up the manifold of particularity within and without; in responding to this particularity and entering it into some sort of ongoing unity of active existence, one is involved in two things at once. One is the process of responsive answering within the sense of something mattering, in which one changingly defines to oneself what matters. The other is a development and growth in one's capacities for (and toward) an integrated answering which would unfold out of powers and a center released from ego.

What is pointed to as the fulness of our freedom is the capacity to assume the independence of a creaturely center within the interconnected order of centers, and to assume this in a spontaneity which integrates into its responsive self-definition both what grounds the order of creatures and those creatures with whom the center has to do concretely in its care. Thus instead of an ego assertive of its ultimate independence but, through its very assertiveness, both bound and confined on the one hand and isolated on the other, one is to find eventually a simplicity of self reposing in itself. In that response such a self is supported by that divine presence which animates its effort; and so supported in its independence, such a self can move in equanimity amidst all circumstances, not resting on others in order to be itself but being itself as tied to others in care that stems directly out of the integrity of its own being. But even more: so supported by that universal divine presence, such a self moves cognizant of the deepest reaches of self in and through which the freedom harbored for a center through the very act of creation is seen as definitive for an integrated being who, through its deepest side, is ultimate, is not merely creature and center of freedom and thus merely derivative, but is the peculiar unity of the underived and the derived.

Kṛṣṇa puts this point in a particular way: one who is participant in action whole recognizes that in this involvement in action "*guṇas* are concerned with *guṇas*" (III.28). This is not fate, but precisely the opposite, namely, the recognition of a destiny significant for a center which, responsive within the differentiations which *buddhi* introduces, is entered into an existential order in which each and all else is complicit in its character with such destiny and complicit with a destiny which is to be worked out concretely. In that working out it is all who are at work together, each out of itself in inter-action with others. The *guṇas*, then, pervade the existential whole and constitute its characterization in a reference to such *centers*, so that every element is fraught with significance for the forming of effort in such centers.

But where effort is formed through *buddhi*, where the *māyā*-founded activating or influencing function of things bears upon a human center, this working is effective only as the factors are responsively taken into the formation of action. And such formation does not define itself mechanically, as if the *guṇas* meant qualitative characterizations of force which resulted in decision and action in an automatic fashion; nor does it define itself in function of a free will, as if ultimately all influence removed freedom and freedom meant merely absolute and arbitrary determination.

It is in one who has "transcended" the *guṇas* that this recognition emerges (that *guṇas* are concerned with *guṇas*). That is, this recognition emerges in a self whose judging and deciding and acting, into which are integrated the manifold and multiplicity of particularity, are effectively responsive to the divine presence which, amid the concentration and ingatheredness of the self, is ultimate ground for that integration. This is only what can and must eventuate, however. We begin within a rather different condition, working out of an endowment and within an order but working with a developing essential power which is continual medium for the responsive integration of particularity as our existence is defined concretely. And within the incompleteness of our essential condition we work our way by way of imperfections (such as that of ego, for example), only eventually to emerge where Arjuna is, opened into some measure of cognizance of a destiny which, to an ego which is insistent upon its own "independence", may appear a fate but which to a creature underway toward the fulness of its spontaneity and freedom forms a task to be entered upon. What has been the case all along, has been effort stemming from an actual center, who initiates it in a way for which nothing else is directly responsible. But though the meaning of the responsive character of this initiation is not apparent from the start, so that effort involves one in the fabrication of an ego or a guiding interpretation of ourselves as centers that exercise powers with no source and authority for such exercise but ourselves as independent (underived) centers, that meaning is nonetheless effective from the start.

And even with the emergence into the condition of Arjuna and beyond, it is still a responsive initiation within the sense of something mattering that has entered one into bondage and given shape to oneself as creature bound in multiple ways and directions. So also through such initiation that, though one is now entered upon an ampler responsive effort that would answer as it must, one may be "compelled": one may find that one's unpurified responsiveness subjects one to effective compulsion. This does not remove the freedom of spontaneity, but presupposes it. And not only that: it presupposes an antecedent pretense to a non-responsive freedom by a center whose nature opens it only to being responsively spontaneous. Not until, with full purification, one is released from the burden of such limited and mistaken involvement in the past, is one enabled to act and be and live with full freedom in the unity that securely holds the manifold and multiple into an integration founded in what is ultimately real. Then it is that freedom has grown into the fulness of itself, to bring release.

CHAPTERS VII-X

The conversation of Kṛṣṇa and Arjuna has so far defined itself in a movement that concerns not only the direction of the focus of word and thought but the very character and inter-relation of the conversants. The central conversation began out of a happening in which Arjuna turned to Kṛṣṇa for help, as pupil turning to teacher. Initially Kṛṣṇa responded as the trusted elder whom Arjuna had turned to for counsel, and recalled tradition in its bearing on the matter in question. But as the conversation developed, and Arjuna asked for clarification of what Kṛṣṇa has been saying, the dialogue took a turn. The focus was still upon the question that was preoccupying Arjuna, the question of action, and Kṛṣṇa continued to conceive this as a question to be answered ultimately through recognition of the reference of action to the real.

But in his conversing Kṛṣṇa altered in his presence to Arjuna, shifting from being a man voicing tradition to being a man voicing the presence of the Lord and uttering a teaching which he declared to be that of the Lord Himself. This teaching, developed on the background of this disclosure, was purportedly the original teaching underlying the human tradition to which Kṛṣṇa had earlier referred. At the end of this phase of the conversation, then, we find the two men engaged in changes as men conversing with each other: Arjuna, originally confused and shattered, seeking clarity but becoming bewildered as he attended to Kṛṣṇa, and finally gaining some comprehension of what he was being told; and Kṛṣṇa, originally simply man, now become god-man. And we find, too, that a teaching about action has been rendered in connected but somewhat repetitive fashion, but rendered on the as yet undeveloped background of an assertion of divinity.

Chapters VII-X continue these changes in the conversants, and bring the matter of divinity into the focus of conversation. Thereby Kṛṣṇa seeks to bring Arjuna to some understanding of the divine as it bears on him by indicating the discriminations which, if and when Arjuna finally comes to gain clear awareness and understanding for himself, would constitute the adequate interpretative rendering of the divine in its manifold facets as Arjuna would then discover it to be. In this phase of the teaching Kṛṣṇa takes the lead, Arjuna being mainly silent, asking once for a clarification of certain terms and (toward the end) for a more ample account of a matter Kṛṣṇa has touched on.

This change in the manner of participation in the conversation by both seems not merely to reflect what is being talked about but, more deeply, to signify the increasingly effective reaching out of the Lord in his descent to man, which correlates with the responsive movement of Arjuna out of his depression. For these underlie the shift in focus of the conversation also. Thus the increasing disclosure of the Lord in and through Kṛṣṇa's speech is working by way of Arjuna's ingatheredness and concentration to integrate him inwardly and to kindle in him a certain joy and eagerness.

Considered dialogically, then, these Chapters gather the participants into an upward movement and a drawing together whose culmination is to come in the revelation of Chapter XI.

And through the more ample teaching they involve, concerning Kṛṣṇa as ultimate source and as a ground for human effort, who is to be held to by man in devotion, they bring to word what is being enacted in the conversation as well: namely, that devotion lies at the heart of the aspirational movement which brings man eventually into the clear presence of the creator.

The teaching involved in these Chapters is best expressed in brief by the phrase "Vāsudeva is all" (VII. 19). Although it is difficult to determine with any precision and assurance what this phrase means, it seems clear nonetheless that involved in its meaning is the development of the question of action, which already in Chapters II-VI had become a question of an integration of the diversity into an ongoing condition that is firmly established in the real. This development brings the question of action into the question of the unity of the multiplicity (including active centers in an important way) within the whole. With this suggestion in mind, that the unity expressed in the phrase is one that crucially includes active centers, I proceed to suggest one possible understanding of the matter. This suggestion will be more easily comprehended, if it is kept in mind that a unity which is conceived dynamically, is one that requires diversity of some sort to be involved in that unity, rather than excludes diversity.

The initial direction for gaining a sense of the dynamic unity which is being pointed to in Kṛṣṇa's teaching can come by reference to the etymology of the term he uses for what is crucial to the unity (because it is alone ultimately real), namely, *brahman*. *Bṛh* is a verbal root whose meaning is "to grow great or strong, to burst forth", and on the strength of that, the noun *brahman* means (most basically) "expansion" (evolution, development, growth). Kṛṣṇa's use of the term *brahman* preserves this etymological suggestion of dynamism, so that he offers a conception of the mysterious power, which is the sole reality which grasps that power as intrinsically magical.

That is, the dynamic of the being of the sole power and reality means that that reality harbors a creaturely diversity within itself which does not introduce an ultimate duality into the real (for the creaturely is unreal), but which does (and must) exist and enter into the unity that characterizes the whole as a uni-verse. That whole, the unity of the real and the unreal, is intrinsic to the being of the sole reality, although it is not itself real any more than the creaturely is. It is in this intelligible emergence of the unreal and intelligible interweaving of the real and unreal that the magic intrinsic to the mysterious reality is expressed.

The terms with which such a magical uni-verse is to be grasped in its intelligibility are those which grasp the being-turned-into-one of the universe in focus around an act of creation. Thus the holy power which is alone real is "imperishable and supreme" (VIII.3), yet such as inherently to hold within itself (IX.4-6), under the condition of time, an unreal creation. To make this "holding" intelligible, Kṛṣṇa speaks (in these Chapters) of the very self (IX.5) of the holy power—that nature (*bhāva*: VIII.3) through which it is creative—as a nature (*prakṛti*: VII. 4-5) which is inwardly diversified. Thus there is a higher nature (VII. 5) which is an unmanifest (VIII. 20-22) but life-endowed spirit (the supreme divine spirit: VIII. 8). And there is a lower nature (VII. 4) which is a potency which, alternating under the cyclical rhythm of time between manifest and unmanifest expressions of itself, and is itself intrinsically diversified by those expressions into a world of creatures. This world and those creatures are entered into a perishable existence which, because temporal, is unreal, and yet is inward to the reality which alone is (VIII. 4).

And the time-conditioned sending forth of active and living creatures into manifest existence, supporting of them in a manifest world which stands over against the unmanifest spiritual nature of the Lord (VIII. 4), and drawing creatures (and the world, eventually) back into unmanifest existence, is the work of the lower nature in the presence of the higher and under the witnessing (VIII. 9) and governing (VIII. 9) function of that spiritual presence (IX. 7-10).

The unreal creatures which are harbored intrinsically within the real as expressions of its lower nature, exist under time and thus are ever involved in process. Their perishable temporal existence involves (as a whole and for each creature) a multiplicity of temporal rhythms, from that of Brahmā days and nights on down, so that each and all exist in finite and periodic fashion. What partakes of such temporal creaturely existence is first and foremost centers of activity, and these gain, from their source and as intrinsic to the lower nature of the divine which they inflect, the elemental determinations which constitute temporal existence to be active existence. Thus, for example, there is the differentiation of the essential in a center from its body, with the factors of *manas*, *buddhi* and ego, pertaining to the essential, and the five elements pertaining to body (physical existence) (VII. 4). But also, such centers are marked by the qualifying factors (*guṇas*) that give all existential conditions whatever an activity-referent determinateness which, within the presence of the Lord in his spiritual nature, works consonantly with the centricity of the centers (VII. 12). And in the measure in which the *guṇas* do not simply characterize creaturely existence but so ordain it, that the divine is veiled to the creaturely centers in question (VII. 27), those factors express the divine so as to constitute the delusive facet within the whole (VII. 13-15). But however that may be, all creaturely factors not only inflect the lower nature of the divine but constitute expressions of the higher nature, presumably in the sense of being more or less permeable to its splendor: thus the numerous indications by Kṛṣṇa that "I am......" (VII. 8-11; IX. 16-19; X. 20-42).

The brief suggestion of such terms of intelligibility which is being made in Chapters VII-X. can be profitably supplemented here by certain notions found in later Chapters which express more fully what is only mentioned in these Chapters. Thus, for one thing, there is the suggestion that in itsex pansive being the holy power has a definiteness, which functions as the ultimate factor in the universe, a basic or primordial uni-versal determinateness to spirit. This determinateness is the indivisible unity of the infinite factors of definiteness which, through the creational efficacy inherent in the divine nature, become in their diversity the basic sides to the selves of the creatures which express that nature (XIII. 16 and 30; XV. 7). Then, for a second thing, there is the indication that this uni-versal definiteness is characterizable in its presence through the image of the sun, so that it constitutes a uni-versal *jñāna* which radiates to illumine and heat the infinite multiplicity of creatures (XI. 17-19; XIII. 2 and 33). As such a radiating splendor in its presence, the spirit in the divine nature is "seer" (VIII. 9) and "witness" (IX. 18) who "knows by its own self" (X.15) and whose illumination makes it the "supreme purifier" (X. 12) when it comes into the cognizance of active creatures. And finally, for a third thing, the higher and lower natures through which the divine is what it is, are—in an image—father and mother through which creatures exist within the divine (IX. 17). The higher or paternal nature is the living spirit through which the creative action is overseen and on the strength of whose presence to the lower nature that action goes on. What it activates by its presence is the lower or maternal nature, the ultimate (unmanifest) potency which, persisting through the temporal rhythm of manifest and unmanifest which pertains to the creaturely expressions of this potency, is the womb into which the father places the seed which determines that creatures exist (XIV. 3-4). The seed in question (IX. 18; VII. 10) is the multiplicity of factors in the uni-versal definiteness of spirit, but endowed with life as diverse and not themselves the uni-versal spiritual life which is the father (XV. 7). This seed or living nucleus of the infinite creaturely diversity is the ultimate side in the selves of beings which, due to the contribution of the mother, are in their creaturely side active centers.

From the view of things as so far expressed, then, it would seem clear that there is, to begin with, a unity that pertains to the divine power in its reality (a unity of an inwardly inflected sort, but itself entering into the constitution of the sole reality); and there is, secondly, a unity that pertains to the universe which, presupposing that what is unitary in the first case functions as creative of the unreal, itself is constituted in a conjunction of creator and creature that is marked by derivation and permeation. But there is a further and culminating unity, which develops the second in the direction of the first. For the act of creation involves more than merely bringing creatures into manifest existence, supporting them there for a while, and then drawing them back. It involves the introduction of creatures into a manifest temporal existence in which there is a point to be found by them, immanent in such existence due to the very nature of the holy power itself. For the expansiveness of that power is directional, toward such unity of the unreal and the real as arises when the unreal comes to function so as to take into itself the light of the real and to become completely irradiated, permeated, transformed. Thus the temporal movement of creaturely existence involves a drama, with an issue at stake in the action and an end or culmination that is to come to pass.

In the working out of the creaturely movement upon the background presence of the Lord, and within the creaturely world that is more or less permeated by the divine presence, a creature is meant eventually to come into an interacting with other creatures which brings its participation in the movement into such a pass that the constant shining presence of the Lord can come to some sort of explicit notice in his existence. And from out of this beginning, emerges the possibility of movement on a path toward enlightened existence, in which Kṛṣṇa offers his version of the responsive interplay between divine and human. The devotional effort through which man moves on a path toward release leads to a unity that involves creaturely agency, the guiding and supporting presence of the creator, and the discovery and concrete appropriation by a being of an ultimacy to itself which is beyond the creaturely and which is integral to the real.

The suggestion of Kṛṣṇa's teaching, then, is that the universe or whole is constituted by a unity in and through a creational movement which is intrinsically formed in the holy power which constitutes the reality of the universe or whole. Creation takes shape out of a beginning, and with an ending, in the ultimate uni-versal definiteness intrinsic to the spiritual side of the holy power. For through the co-working of higher and lower natures in the holy power, a world of creatures is periodically brought forth into manifest existence. And these creatures are active centers, to the selves of each of which there is a side that is ingredient in the ultimate spiritual definiteness of the divine. The emergence of the creaturely in this fashion has an intrinsic directionality toward a consummation in which this whole uni-versal definiteness comes into an integration in an active center which has become transparent and purified to the divine presence. In such consummation the expansive action of creation has given rise to a creational amplification of the original uni-versality of the ground for the creaturely whole, so that that ground now permeates effectively the unreal actuality in question, and through it, is radiated out into the creaturely whole in which that center is involved. With the achievement of such a transformation in a creaturely center, the creative act reaches its end for the distinct element in the uni-versal definiteness which is immediate ground for the creature in question.

Thus, the creaturely having been fulfilled in its being through this joining together in the creature of the real and unreal and this concrete integration into the creature of the creaturely whole in which he exists, the creaturely side to the being in question lapses, and the movement of creation reaches full circle, with the return of the distinct element to its simple inclusion in the universal definiteness of the spiritual side of the holy power. In such a creational movement, there is no point *to* creation, as if there might have been no creatures, or they might have been otherwise (say, if the external purpose or end for the sake of which they were created had been otherwise). But there is a point *in* such creation to be found by creatures as they contribute—within the medium of the "could-be-otherwise" that being a center involves—to the consummation of creation in a unity of real and unreal, of time-antecedent and temporal: a unity which is eternal, though not everlasting.

Such seems the deeper teaching about the real and the one, which Kṛṣṇa claims underlies the traditional Sāṁkhya and Yoga, and which provides to action a meaning and an intrinsic place in the universe which those traditional teachings fail to see. It is a teaching of a unity of the diverse, which, when the dynamic character of the unity becomes lost, degenerates into teachings of duality and aloneness. In the fact of Himself disclosing all this to Arjuna, Vāsudeva—as man-god—bears witness, by His own presence and working, to the meaning of which He speaks.

CHAPTER XI

In the conversation of this Chapter the dramatic interplay of conversants that has been present from the start reaches its peak. For here the unity of a conversational movement which both speaks about an interplay of divine and human and incarnates that interplay so as to make it dramatically visible in its responsive character, is expressed in brief compass amidst dramatic events complexly recounted. Let me consider the Chapter, then, in two stages; first by simply following through its movement, and then by considering how that movement is itself intelligible in accordance with the general teaching of the dialogue as a whole.

At the beginning of the Chapter Arjuna has taken the initiative once again. What Kṛṣṇa has been declaring in the way of a notion that the whole is a creational one has finally lifted his delusion. And after expressing this to Kṛṣṇa, Arjuna goes on to voice his desire to "see" and not merely hear about this lordly form which makes the whole what it is. For the conceptual clarification has obtained in one whose "vision" or awareness is still quite obscure and confused, even though it is now open to the depths. But it has also emerged for one who, in his attentiveness to Kṛṣṇa, has been drawing closer and closer to Him, more deeply and effectively absorbed in his presence, so that the desire to "see" arises as a quite natural development within his responsiveness to that presence.

Acceding to this request (by His grace, as Kṛṣṇa later puts it) Kṛṣṇa also brings forth in Arjuna the supernatural visual capacity which must be added to Arjuna's current nature for such beholding to be possible. And then he calls upon Arjuna to "Behold...... !" At that point Saṁjaya speaks in his own person for the first time since the beginning of Chapter II. So speaking he places the dialogue of Kṛṣṇa and Arjuna explicitly back into its context as something being seen and heard at a distance, and he does so in a way that directs us to listen to the dialogue in a particular way. For having just recounted the words of Kṛṣṇa which anticipate the revelation, and are directive for Arjuna's eager attention, Saṁjaya goes on to provide us with his own account of what in fact comes to be shown to Arjuna. Since Arjuna was enjoined to behold certain things and "whatever else you desire", and was thus given a certain leeway to attend to what is presented in a way reflective of himself and his condition, we are enabled by Saṁjaya's account to assess what happens in Arjuna's own responsive beholding.

Saṁjaya's account of what was shown conforms with what Kṛṣṇa had anticipated for us, but his account of Arjuna's speech to Kṛṣṇa makes clear also that while Arjuna was indeed witness to such a presence certain things in particular solicited his attention from out of the richness presented and dominated his awareness of the whole. For while Arjuna begins by declaring his awareness of things already anticipated for us (Verses 15-18), he moves from there (Verses 19-23) to an indication of the way in which he sees the pervading presence being responded to, first by the variety of divine beings (who respond differently depending on their character) and then by "the worlds". And this leads him (end of Verse 23-Verse 25) into a characterization of his own response as the particular worldly being he is, and with this we discover that that presence is for Arjuna dreadful, terrifying, upsetting. Out of his own current condition Arjuna finds the wondrousness of the Lord's form, indeed, but finds the form impressive in a way that also unsettles him. In the face of certain aspects of it he finds himself unsupported and unprotected, exposed and without landmark to give him bearing: in short, at sea.

In that condition certain things come to the fore from out of the world around him, only now as held within this vision and, more specifically, as held within the vision of mouths open and dreadful, tusk-filled mouths like to the flames of time (Verses 26-30). Thus Arjuna sees "yonder sons of Dhṛtarāṣṭra" and the other Kurus assembled on the battlefield all rushing into those mouths. The presence of the Kurus, already brought into altered form with Kṛṣṇa's injunction in Chapter I, now gains further inflection. The Kurus are seen in reference to the divine heart of the whole, as this is looming large for Arjuna in a certain way. That mode of presence of the divine bewilders Arjuna (Verse 31): who are you in this guise, tell me the secret of your appearance here in this manifestation of yourself, he requests. And with Kṛṣṇa's answer the progressive disclosure of Kṛṣṇa as the Lord culminates in the declaration of himself to be, in that manifestation, time.

In the universe as Kṛṣṇa is creator in it, time constitutes the mediating factor between creator and creature, not only in that the creaturely exists in a time-grounded being brought forth, being sustained, and being taken back out of manifest existence, but also in that in the course of ongoing existence it is in the depth of the ongoing present that the creature can meet its creator and enter into the final phase of its movement toward the culmination implied for it in the act of creation. Thus when the creator becomes present for Arjuna and looms forth "visually" to him on the battlefield, it is as that time which mediates the Lord's creational working that he impresses Himself on Arjuna most strongly.

And more particularly, it is in that aspect of time which Śiva the destroyer normally represents. For Arjuna stands on the battlefield, and stands there brought momentarily to halt in his entry into battle by the implication which such a battle seems to hold in regard to the death of his kinsmen. Time in its destructive aspect has impressed itself on him, even to the extent that initially it has seemed to him to remove all reason for engaging in battle.

However, when Kṛṣṇa's speech explains how the destructive aspect of time manifests Himself as Lord, that aspect is made visible in an alleviating context, and Arjuna's initial response is not supported.

Thus Kṛṣṇa speaks of "all those warriors standing over against" Arjuna as going to cease to be even without Arjuna. For time in its creational character and function implies for each creature an inevitable end to its current existence, and this, as part of the meaning of its condition as creature. This inevitability of an end, this perishable character of creaturely existence, holds quite regardless of any particular "how" of the coming of the end. In particular, and in the case at hand, it holds quite regardless of whether Arjuna is instrumental in the coming to an end or whether he is not. What is being expressed here is, thus, no fate and pre-ordainment of things to a particular end for which Arjuna is helplessly fated to be cause, but the recognition of the intrinsic finitude of creaturely existence which makes simple enduring in existence nothing unconditional in value. What is of significance in such existence lies deeper than continuation: "therefore" enter into battle, gain the (worldly) ends which *dharma* sanctions, and be at most the occasion for the death of those who are already handed over to death because they are temporal in their being, because they are "already slain" by reason of "me who am time".

To understand the full force of this "therefore" one must only keep in mind that it is the Lord in His imperative presence that is voicing Himself here as time and speaking to Arjuna *ad hominem in situ*. What he says hearkens back to Chapter II, where in using Sāṁkhya notions Kṛṣṇa spoke of the differentiation of the embodied one and his embodiments. But now two things that are of the essence of Kṛṣṇa's own teaching come to the fore, to place this differentiation in a different light. One is the Lord Himself, speaking, and the other is the time to which he gives voice, the time which differentiates yet unites the embodied one and his bodies within the Lord's creation. Given these two things the differentiation of embodied one and embodiments is placed in a universe in which active and temporal existence has a stake that bears on creation itself and that accords to existence and action within time a point, a meaning, a positive significance.

Thus in this speech Arjuna is being addressed by his creator from out of that termination that is inherent in creaturely existence. And he is being spoken to as a man standing before that termination at a time when he must move in the path of action toward the culmination ordained for creaturely existence. In the ongoing effort which Arjuna is to make now, death and destruction will inevitably have a large place; and positive future earthly conditions (glory and kingdom through victory in a righteous cause) will have their place. But that effort is neither justified by those future goods, nor rendered unjustified by the destruction involved.

The significance of the effort—its justifying reason—lies deeper than the future in its worldly dimension (negative or positive); it lies in the direction of the depths of time. For it is the meaning of what it is to be a human being, to be entered into a movement whose culmination requires gathering up effort in the temporal dimension of the ongoing and transient into aspiration for an end which is more than temporal in that dimension: which is more than ongoing, which involves the union of the temporally ongoing with what lies in the temporal depths. And it is the meaning of *dharma* to be that factor through which alone human beings are prepared for making such effort, and to be a factor through which most (if not all) human beings are meant to make the effort when their time comes.

And finally, it is the meaning of Arjuna's discovery of the Kurus pressing in on him in his amplified awareness at the beginning of the dialogue, that he is now being summoned out of the depths to begin the task of purification that will eventuate in his own participation in the fulfillment of creaturely being. At such a time a human being must act on that summons, and act in a way that accords with the unity of human beings on the move toward that end. Then it is not enough to be a relation, or even to be a *dharma-moulded* person: one must be more, without denying either. To Kṛṣṇa's mind that means, for Arjuna: your time has now come, the way is open, you must enter upon it through participation in this *dharma-accordant* battle. And so, speaking as that time which gathers back worlds, which ends the ongoing existence of creatures with a limited future, Kṛṣṇa enjoins Arjuna to move into the future on the side of the positive rather than the negative worldly factors: but *not* for worldly reasons.

What Kṛṣṇa is saying to Arjuna, then, is that the latter is mistaken in seeing the relation of kinship to outweigh the claim of *dharma* when an action impends that is fraught with death. *Dharma* has precedence, but not such precedence as denies humanity, only such precedence as prepares the way for a genuinely full human existence to be entered into and for the full meaning of what it is to be a human being to be realized. All human beings will have their time eventually, and will have it in and through their own efforts as those have become moulded within commitment to *dharma*. Others may not be ready now, but they never will become ready until their commitment to *dharma* is sufficient. Arjuna is ready, and his readiness needs to be expressed in a way that accords with *dharma*. If that means for him his commitment to battle on the side of *dharma*, on the side of that commitment to which alone can ready human beings, then the death and destruction that are likely to come, touching on human beings whatever their active condition, and whatever the direction of their current movement as expressed in their own efforts, have to be endured.

But endured not for an egoistic end, not as occasion for Arjuna's taking a step toward an enlightenment which has claim upon him for its promise of gratifying his ego, but rather for the sustaining of the surge toward that fulfillment in himself and others which is ordained by the Lord and which he is called upon to subserve in the very heart of destruction. What is ultimately at issue in the battle on the Field of the Kurus, then, and what makes it a field of *dharma*, is not the matter of killing or not killing, not even simply the preservation of *dharma* through action upon it, indeed not anything taken like these in the abstract, but rather the function of *dharma* to promote the movement of human life toward its creationally-ordained fulfillment. It is concretely to affirm his ultimate allegiance to the divine source which calls human beings into this movement, and to affirm that allegiance in a way that promotes such movement within himself and in others, that Arjuna must fight and fight in the responsively undertaken fashion that Kṛṣṇa calls him to.

After Kṛṣṇa's brief explanation of his manifestation, the dialogue brings us back to Saṁjaya (Verse 35), who recounts how the revelation was terminated through the request of Arjuna and through Kṛṣṇa's acceding to that request (Verses 36-51). And the Chapter then comes to its close in verses (52-55) which reiterate the devotional theme which Kṛṣṇa has sounded just before restoring his human form as Arjuna had requested. For while to see Kṛṣṇa in that lordly form which Arjuna has just glimpsed is impossible through meritorious (but egoistic) effort of any sort, nonetheless, to see and know and enter into that form is central to the culmination of creation called for. But that culmination, reachable by sustained devotional effort, will bring Arjuna back into a seeing and knowing of a rather different sort from the current ones. For they will be a seeing and knowing out of a purified and unified condition, so that the fearful side of the Lord will have subsided for attention.

Such is the movement of the conversation in the Chapter, considered step by step. That movement expresses in particularly emphatic fashion the character of the responsive interplay of divine and human which Kṛṣṇa places at the heart of the culminating phase of human existence. That interplay involves two partners, one of which is changeless, the other of which is changing. But an inter*play* is possible because of the peculiar character of the two. On the one hand, the holy power is "dynamic" in such way as "radiates" into the ongoing now of all temporal creatures, and in particular, in such way as "approaches" man as "living" but changeless Lord constant in His imperative presence. On the other hand, the human is inherently active and is involved in process in such way as, through the responsive character of the power through which man participates in active existence, to be involved in a reference to (among other things) this presence. But this reference reflects concretely a developing and altering responsiveness within the present, so that although the changeless Lord does not change, there are manifold variations in the way in which the Lord enters into the current so as to be at work within the ongoing formation of human effort. Thus in reference to the actuality of its effective working, the manner of that working, and the character of its received presence, the divine reaches variably into the present of temporal human existence in this sense, that according as what is taking shape temporally is more or less responsively permeable to (and permeated by) this constant presence, and according as response is more or less fully devotional in its assimilation of and answer to that presence, so the constant presence is inflected variably in the relation that is being established concretely.

Consider in this light the interplay between the Lord and Arjuna in this dialogue. To begin with, it arises through the figure of Kṛṣṇa as a human avatāra of the Lord. This "descent" occurs not because of any change in the Lord, but because the temporal unfolding of the creational whole has reached a certain time and state. That is, within the creational rhythm men have fallen away from the impetus which a communally-supported *dharma* gives to life and efforts; and which is necessary if men are to reach the fulfillment which is the constant care of the Lord. In expression of that constant care in these extreme circumstances, a man appears—Kṛṣṇa—who, as if in counterbalance to the downward pull currently effective upon the many, enters so effectively into the responsive aspiration which the Lord enjoins and supports that he "incarnates" the Lord for the men of his time.

Then again, it presupposes the drawing closer of the Lord to Arjuna through this incarnation. Just as the Lord's appearance as Kṛṣṇa was occasioned by the larger whole within which Arjuna has a place, so his approach toward Arjuna through Kṛṣṇa is occasioned by the hidden readiness in Arjuna for the movement in growth into which at the very beginning of the dialogue he is entered. In this way the emergence of the conversation in which the Lord gradually discloses Himself through Kṛṣṇa is occasioned through the working of the particularity assumed by the Lord. For through this Arjuna, in his ongoing effort, is brought to find in the depths an imperative presence which speaks explicitly to him. Arjuna was ready; in his antecedent growing he had unknowingly been defining an altering relation to the underlying constant which has become explicit in its presence now that the concrete working of changing particularities has enabled the movement of his growth to flower in deepened explicit awareness.

Then finally there is the actual course of the dialogue itself, in which the Lord—as and through Kṛṣṇa—alters in the explicitness and fulness of his presence. This also involves no change in the Lord, but in the particularity of Kṛṣṇa the man and, most importantly, in the responsive formation of Arjuna's own efforts. The initial awareness is only a beginning. Within it, Arjuna at first seeks to resign, yet not without confirmation from Kṛṣṇa as to the propriety of this; thus turning to Kṛṣṇa and attending to him and his speech, Arjuna finds that the initial claiming presence gains altered (and more apt) hold over him as he is drawn out by the audible presence of what is authoritative for him.

Thus within the explicit awareness within which Arjuna begins, confused though that awareness is, he takes his stand in a responsive forming of effort; in a forming which is intrinsically an affair of effort, of making an effort, but of making an effort within a receptivity such that, quite beyond what is or could be deliberately commanded in the making of that effort, that making involves a strengthening, reinforcing, fostering, which can peculiarly implement the bearing of presence in the effort and can hiddenly alter thus the forming and the effort being formed. By way of the particularity of Kṛṣṇa, Arjuna has gained access to the constant presence of the Lord, which has such character to it that it lends itself to being more deeply and effectively entered into by one who can respond appropriately, and lends itself as itself reinforcing such response when begun. Thus the dialogue develops, mediated by action and words, and in its course the constant presence of the Lord varies in its inflection, in its "working" in and upon the forming of Arjuna's effort, in its "lending" and "reinforcing", in its "leading" and "disclosing"—none of which signify alteration in itself, but rather alteration in the way **it** is held within effort which, more deeply responsive than before, open and attentive for the first time to the deeper sides to the whole, pays it attention.

There is magic in this interplay, intelligible magic, the intelligible magic of presence and the freedom of concrete responsive effort. And this magic it is, which the interplay of Chapter XI most forcefully portrays. Right up into and beyond the revelation, in the interplay of request and response, granting of visual power and emergence into view, receptivity to presence and request for its termination, response to this request and return to the conversational mode of presence, the Lord is "reaching out" to Arjuna *ad hominem in situ*, and Arjuna is responsively engaged with things in a way that reflects his condition and situation, his need and capacity, his readiness and unreadiness.

That engagement involves a conscious working at its focus, but through the concentration and ingatheredness of Arjuna the whole of himself as active center is entered into that working. And it is as that whole enters into the working and enables that which enters into concrete presence to come to work there too, that the essential shifts are enabled to take place. Even the disclosive vision—perhaps especially the disclosive vision—attests the concreteness of the magic.

In this dramatic dimension in the conversation, then, Kṛṣṇa is educating Arjuna first-hand in the co-operation that is to obtain within the gracious and compassionate presence of the Lord to any man who devotes himself to Him in the taking of any path toward enlightenment. It is the "co-operation" of a constant presence radiating directively and imperatively and coming to explicitness for an actual changing temporal effort which is continually but alteringly taking into itself particularity as it becomes present, which is deepened in its awareness through the working of such particularity, and which is enabled thereby to define itself within the entry of such constant presence into the conscious working which focalizes the ingathered active center engaged in effort. The initial—and recurrent—mode of such entry is inadvertent, beyond the power deliberately to command and produce; yet with its occurrence comes the possibility of a developing dialogue, itself graciously sustained in complicity with devoted and faithful effort that is free but also cannot force the matter, cannot command and produce that sustaining and developing any more than it could that beginning. Through this grace-ful and faith-ful interplay it is, that what is meant to happen by way of the fulfillment of creation can eventually come to pass.

CHAPTERS XII-XVII

The vision of Chapter XI is a peak in the dramatic movement of the dialogue between Kṛṣṇa and Arjuna. This peak is by no means the end, however, either to the dramatic movement of the conversation or to the transfigurational movement into which Arjuna is entering. The vision is rather a transient affair, in need of being assimilated and responded upon so that, in regard to the movement of transfiguration, Arjuna is started on the way toward that culmination of his movement as creature and human being in which he regains something like this vision and becomes constant in the awareness it presages. In order that such a start may be made, there is immediate need for a conversational relief of the tension and intensity introduced by the vision. Time must be given for Arjuna to recover, for the immediacy of the vision not simply to go but now to reverberate in an Arjuna whose condition has once more become "normal", hence appropriate for making the decision he must make. This release of tension is the dramatic function of these Chapters, whose development is ordered in a way that accords with the restoration of Arjuna's condition that is occurring during its course.

In their overall movement, these Chapters begin from Arjuna's question, itself growing out of the end of Chapter XI and bringing to the fore the character of the response needed: it must be devotional, but what path is Arjuna's devotion to take? Which path is best? Then in a series of Chapters the teaching proceeds in descent from the revelation, and in terms of focus, the series has the reverse order to the focus in the ascent that led to the revelation. For first come three Chapters (XIII-XV) which relate primarily to the encompassing conditions of action (God and world—like Chapters VII-X). Then come two Chapters (XVI-XVII) which relate to the diversity of men and of factors involved in action on earth (like Chapters II-VI). These Chapters all amplify and illuminate Kṛṣṇa's teaching, but mainly by way of filling in details and making fuller appropriation of traditional views within the framework already set forth.[6]

CHAPTER XVIII

The movement of Chapters XII through XVII takes Arjuna from the heights of revelation down into the depths of the demonic, and then brings him into the variety of expressions of the religious nerve of human existence. And thus we are brought quite naturally into Chapter XVIII, and that gathering together of the teaching of all the preceding Chapters which places Arjuna in thought back into the place where he finds himself in actuality and which leads into Arjuna's response to what has been happening to him, into his assumption of responsibility in the moment of decision.

In its dialogical movement this Chapter begins with a request by Arjuna which, like many of his earlier questions and requests, is directed toward the matter of action as this is something which Kṛṣṇa is urging him to partake in in a certain spirit. The request is for clarification of two terms, *saṁnyāsa* and *tyāga*, the former of which had figured in Arjuna's question at the beginning of Chapter V. What is renunciation, what is relinquishment? From a beginning of this sort, Kṛṣṇa gradually brings his teaching concerning action into final focus for, and upon, Arjuna. Let me follow the development through.

In contrast with the account of renunciation and relinquishment which some men give, Kṛṣṇa's account involves the notion that each man has his allotted *karman*—the works, the achievements, the deeds, the directions for the outworking of his energies, which he is fitted for by his nature and which he is meant to undertake and effect as media of his participation in creation. Included in such allotted tasks are works of sacrifice, charity, and austerity, incumbent on all men. One is not to renounce them either but to partake of them. Renunciation, in the sense of giving up the doing of certain things, pertains only to works which are beyond the allotted ones, and which are done only because of egoistic motivation. In the doing of what is allotted, however, there is to be, inwardly, a relinquishment of any claim to fruit—a sattvic relinquishment (Verses 2-12).

The rationale behind this briefly suggested teaching lies in the conception of *karman* which it involves. To this Kṛṣṇa turns, to speak of it in two stages: first, Verses 13-17, then Verses 18-39. The first stage draws on the Sāṁkhya teaching which was extant in the *kṛta* age and was as yet uncorrupted into the Sāṁkhya of tradition to which Kṛṣṇa had appealed in Chapter II. According to that teaching, the accomplishing of *karman* always involves five factors, which are together at work in the forming and execution of *karman* in the world. Thus threre is the physical body, the seat of such active effort; and given that this is a living body, there are the manifold functions without which it would not be the seat it is (the functions of the life-breaths, for example). But the body is simply the mediating dwelling-place for the active center itself, which is center of efforts that draw upon and utilize powers, which are instrumental to the accomplishing of what effort aims at. And finally, such an embodied center finds itself operative within the world at large, which enters into the forming of effort and effects the execution of action; and this environing factor, which is supported in the divine and ordained by the divine to enter intrinsically into the determination of the action of a center, is a fifth factor in the determination of all action. But although all five factors are involved in every *karman* undertaken by man through his body, mind, and power of speech, one of them tends to be taken as exclusive factor of responsibility by any center whose *buddhi* is immature; and that factor is the center itself as center of effort, which is thus taken as "doer", in a mistaking not only of the total self of the being involved but of the active side to that self as well. For that active side is responsible, in the measure in which it is, only within the working of all five factors together. With the maturation of *buddhi*, however, comes such participation in action as is free from that delusion and as involves the engagement in action self-conscious to the responsively-working cooperation of all factors in the action in question.

The second stage in the conception of *karman* amplifies this crude contrast in mode of participation in action through a consideration of further factors involved in *karman*. Thus human action involves a deciding and initiating which take shape within a cognizance—an awareness and an interpreting; that is, human action is formed within an apprehension of something by someone, within the awareness and interpretation of *buddhi* which brings the actualities of the situation into some interpretation-mediated presence through which they bear on the decision made by a center. And thus, in respect of the active human center acting by way of the exercise of his powers, there is cognizance to be considered, there is the center who has such cognizance, there is the power through which such a center cognizes and decides, there is the attentive steadiness and firmness with which a center decides and acts, and there is the happiness which emerges in issue of effort: there are all these factors involved crucially in human action. And since action is always colored by the *guṇas*, Kṛṣṇa sketches out certain variations which are significant in relation to all these factors, using the schema of the three *guṇas* to do this. Thus expressive of *sattva* is a man who participates in action out of an ultimate release: freed of egoism, with a *buddhi* that is open in clear awareness to the ultimate unitary ground within the whole, that is knowing with respect to *dharma* and the matter of bondage and release, and that is firmly in charge of the workings of the lesser functions of mind and breath and sense, such a man engages in works allotted for him and knows a happiness that is like to the finest nectar. In contrast there are men whose participation in action is still confined within delusion. As one suggestion, expressive of *rajas*, Kṛṣṇa speaks of a man who is passionate and dynamic and grasping, with a *buddhi* that is open only to the multiplicity, that indeed knows *dharma* but only as blind duty and obligation, and that is firm in its attachment to worldly goals alone; such a man engages in allotted action as in something laborious and knows only the poisonous happiness of the union of sense with sense-objects. As a second suggestion expressive of *tamas*, Kṛṣṇa speaks of a man who resists the upward pull of *dharma* in a variety of ways, with a *buddhi* that is blind not only to ultimate unity but to the diversity of factors involved in the determination of action and that leads him to cling to himself as center in a mistaking of responsibility, with a *buddhi* also which mistakes *dharma* altogether and which refuses to give up its refuge in factors that pull the man downward; such a man enters into action heedless of the situation and his own capacities, and knows only the delusory happiness of a condition of moral paralysis. Clearly these sketches are only suggestive and certainly not exhaustive classifications; what is central to them is their power to indicate in suggestive fashion what sorts of difference are involved in the way men become defined in their inescapable participation in action.

These two stages not only amplify and clarify the initial teaching concerning relinquishment and renunciation but bring Kṛṣṇa back to that very matter again, and thereby to the suggestion of the consummation and perfection of their active being which is open to the diversity of men (Verses 40-56). For the *guṇas* permeate the active side of human being in such way as to differentiate the particular natures of men into four main groupings. Thus men are in general diversely fitted in their natures for works and for the achievement of conditions in their active being. It is these works and conditions that the *dharma* relevant to each nature seeks to foster. And this fostering is meant to develop the particular nature of each in such way as prepares each man for the perfection of active life as he is to participate in this. What is involved in this perfection is something which retains but transcends the differentiation in natures and works, namely, a devoting of oneself to his own work which is devotional, a responsive worshipping of the Lord. This dual devotion brings perfection to active existence by bringing freedom from the bondage of *karman*, though the release involved in such freedom does not mean the empowering of a man to do everything perfectly: the perfection concerns devotion, not outcomes and results. And it in turn leads into the final release into the holy power, entry into Kṛṣṇa's ultimate nature-and-being, accomplished with the help of *rāja-yoga.*

With this fairly well-rounded reformulation of his teaching as it concerns action, Kṛṣṇa is ready to bring out for the final time its implication for Arjuna (Verses 57-72). In doing so he speaks to this effect: you, likewise, Arjuna, in your condition and situation, renounce all your actions to me, enter into the disciplined effort through which, mindful of me, you will eventually reach such a culmination, with the aid of my grace. If, out of your understanding of yourself as ego, you will not pay heed, you will be lost, die to be reborn again. And not only that: if, seeking your support in ego, you seek to do as you have said ("I will not fight"), if you try to rest in this self-pity that is still under the sway of egoistic delusion, you will find that this "resolution" of yours not to fight will not stand up against the bent of your nature and the strength of the dispositions developed in you in the growth of that nature in the past. Instead, these will compel "you" to fight. You—you in your actuality as creaturely center—*can* rise above this compulsiveness, *if* you rise responsively above this egoistic pretense and its pretension to a non-responsive "freedom". You can so rise if, with all your nature and being, you take shelter in the Lord—the Lord through whose creational working you and all creatures are entered into the revolving cycle of temporal creaturely existence. Then, with the help of his grace, you can make your way. The beginning is here and how: with your particular (inborn and developed) nature brought into play in an effort of fighting which is responsively entered upon as initial answering to the Lord's imperative presence, you can set yourself on the path that brings you to the consummation, in which you share in and realize the point and meaning of active existence. Your actual alternatives, then, are to respond in allegiance to me and to fight out of that allegiance, or to seek refuge in ego and be compelled nonetheless to fight, from out of the strength of the force of your own nature.

"Thus has *jñāna,* more secret than any secret, been declared by me to you; having reflected fully on this, do as you will!" (Verse 63). "Have you listened to this with your mind one-pointed? Has the delusion belonging to your lack of *jñāna* vanished?" (Verse 72). In these last questions the function of Kṛṣṇa's speaking to Arjuna is indicated. The deepening of Arjuna's awareness is presupposed in that speaking; and his turning to Kṛṣṇa as pupil to teacher involves a certain giving of himself over to an attentive listening. Thus the speaking—as well as the vision—through which Kṛṣṇa has sought both to clarify interpretatively for Arjuna that of which he is as yet only confusedly aware first-hand and to confirm this clarification in a moment of immediacy, has had the function of removing that misinterpretation of what he is aware of confusedly which holds him back from the needed effort of response to that which claimed him in that initial being thrust beyond *dharma*. But this removal of misinterpretation can work as it does only in presupposition of Arjuna's attention, his being brought into a concentrated and ingathered condition in the effort to listen. Within that listening, Kṛṣṇa's speaking can clarify in its import what Arjuna has become aware of, and from out of that ingatheredness that is now not only claimed by what before claimed him but is marked by the removal of the misunderstanding that had threatened to prevent his appropriate response, he can come to do what he must.

And thus Arjuna replies: my delusion is vanished, by your grace I have been recalled to myself and what I am meant to be doing as *kṣatriya* here on this battlefield, with my hesitation and doubt gone I will act upon your commanding presence and in accordance with your clarifying word.

With the final words of Saṁjaya to Dhṛtarāṣṭra, we are recalled to the mode of our access to the hair-raising dialogue of Kṛṣṇa and Arjuna; it is the extraordinary sight and hearing bestowed on Saṁjaya by Vyāsa that has enabled us to have an account, through Saṁjaya's voice, of the conversation which expressed this "supreme secret", this "*yoga*", and of the vision that marked its high-point.

Such is the dialogue which is the *Bhagavad Gītā*. It is a dramatic whole which takes shape in the initial phase of that movement of Arjuna's growing awareness and understanding which is meant to bring him eventually into the fulfillment of his life and existence. Within itself its own movement begins with an Arjuna apparently firm and resolute, and ends with an Arjuna again apparently firm and resolute. Outwardly there is perhaps no noticeable difference; but inwardly, an eternity has passed—the eternity of one of those moments which, fleeting and brief in its ongoing temporal measure, seems nonetheless to last and last in the experience of it, so that one seems drawn out within it into an expanse and depth which it will take more than a lifetime to fathom.

For Arjuna the intervening time has been shattering and renewing. His initial "resoluteness" had rested upon a delusion; his sudden emergence beyond that immersion in things which had been intrinsic to his self-confidence, shook him to the roots. Confused, seeking to retreat, yet turning to Kṛṣṇa to help him find the way he must take, Arjuna listens, asks, and gradually becomes renewed in his will, transformed in his understanding, and instated once again in a readiness for battle which is substantially different from that which was his at the beginning. But he has yet really to embark upon the needed effort: the movement from confusion and bewilderment, through a high-point of momentary penetrating awareness of what is yet to be reckoned with and worked within as supporting ground of effort, and into a clarified understanding and renewed will, may be for Arjuna merely transient. There is a genuine resoluteness now in Arjuna, but there is much still within him that lays him open to the possibility of becoming swallowed back up into his former life. A way has been opened up for his taking, a step is in the process of being taken; but the *Gītā* leaves the reader in that suspense of the ongoing movement of freedom which is continually his own condition, and leaves him there to ponder the meaning of the drama and its relevance to the reader himself.

Notes to the Introduction

1. 100,000 verses, as contrasted with an original of, say, 24,000 (or 20,000, or 9,000); in comparison, the Iliad has 15,693 lines.

2. According to E. Washburn Hopkins, pp. 230-1 in Chapter XI of Volume I, *The Cambridge History of India* (Indian Reprint in 1955 by S. Chand & Co., Delhi). Thomas J. Hopkins, *The Hindu Religious Tradition* (Dickenson Publishing Co.; California, 1971), says the core "may well date back to pre-Buddhist times" and the poem reached "its more or less final form" "by around A.D. 200" (p. 87). Similarly, Vincent Smith, p. 57, *The Oxford History of India* (Oxford University Press; Oxford, 1958).

3. Cf. T. Hopkins, pp. 87-89. Also Lionel D. Barnett, *Bhagavadgītā or The Lord's Song* (Beacon Press; Boston, 1951), with a slightly different account (pp. 59-60).

4. W. Douglas P. Hill, *The Bhagavadgītā* (Oxford Press; London, 1966), pp. 23-24. In previous pages (1-18) Hill has developed the thesis that the Kṛṣṇa Vāsudeva cult developed around a *kṣatriya* warrior who fought at Kurukṣetra, who received mystical and moral teaching from Ghora Āṅgirasa, who taught followers to worship the Sun and who in the course of centuries became the object in turn of their worship. At first a demigod, he became a supreme god (by the second century B.C.) and identified with Viṣṇu, probably out of "a natural sectarian desire to claim supremacy for the sectarian god by making him one with a deity already regarded by many as supreme", and out of "a wish to conciliate the more orthodox Brāhmans, who looked with jealousy and distrust upon the spreading cult" (p. 16). At this stage, a member of the sect composed the *Gītā*, "to insist on the absolute supremacy of Kṛṣṇa Vāsudeva, and at the same time to conciliate the enemies of his cult" (p. 21). Barnett (Sections 43-46, Introduction) provides another account of this cult parallel to Hill's, but his subsequent account of the Vāsudevic school and its ideas (Sections 47-51) presupposes that later conceptions are adequate to understand the thoughts in the *Gītā* which reflect this cult.

5. Hill suggests: "The Bhagavadgītā, as we have seen, presents us with the first clear statement in Hindu literature of the doctrine of *avatāra*; it is not, then, surprising that a poem in which not only the personality of God but his descent among men for gracious purposes is taught should seize on love as a vital element in that way of life that leads to liberation, enlisting for its sectarian purpose the aid of an emotion to which the best religious natures would rapidly respond. One of the Gītā's strongest claims to fame, one of the chief causes of its age-long popularity, is the fact that after centuries of pent-up emotion it presented the worshipper with a visible object of devotion and taught the value of pure, disinterested love in the religious life" (p. 66). Franklin Edgerton, in *The Bhagavad Gītā* (Harper and Row; New York, 1964), suggests: "...Kṛṣṇa... was apparently a deified local chieftain, the head of the Vṛṣṇi clan. Indeed, he appears as such, in strictly human guise, in the greater part of the Mahābhārata.

In the Gitā he is still both god and man; an incarnation of the Deity in human form. We know nothing of the process by which he attained divine honors, nor of his earlier history as a god, before the Bhagavad Gītā, which is probably the earliest work preserved to us in which he appears as such. In this work he has all the attributes of a full-fledged monotheistic deity, and at the same time, as we shall see, the attributes of the Upaniṣadic Absolute. In other words, the popular God is philosophized into a figure who can appeal to both the higher and the lower circles of the population. Therein lies the strength of Kṛṣṇaism in later India; it is many-sided enough to satisfy the religious requirements of almost any man, whatever his intellectual or social status may be" (pp. 132-3).

6. The translation closest to my own is that of Eliot Deutsch (*Bhagavad Gītā*: Holt, Rinehart and Winston, 1968). His supplementary essays involve an interpretation somewhat different from my own, and a number of differences in translation reflect this divergence in approach and understanding.

7. Swami Prabhavananda and Christopher Isherwood, *The Song of God* (The New American Library; New York, 1958).

8. Hill, *op. cit.*

9. Annie Besant and Bhagavan Das, *Bhagavad Gītā* (Theosophical Publishing House; Adyar, Madras, 1962).

10. S(arvepalli) Radhakrishnan, *The Bhagavadgītā* (George Allen & Unwin Ltd; London, 1958).

11. Mahadev Desai, *The Gita according to Gandhi* (Navajivan Publishing House; Ahmedabad, 1951).

12. R. C. Zaehner, *The Bhagavad-Gītā* (Oxford University Press; London 1969).

13. There are translations into English, such as *The Bhagavad-Gītā (with the commentary of Śrī Śaṅkarāchārya)*, translated by A. Mahādeva Sāstri (Madras, 1961), and *The Gitabhashya of Ramanuja*, translated by M. R. Sampatkumaran (Madras, 1969).

14. Sri Aurobindo, *The Message of the Gita* (George Allen & Unwin Ltd; London, 1946); also *Essays on the Gita* (E. P. Dutton; N. Y., 1953).

15. See Ftnts. 4, 10, 12, and 3 respectively.

16. Bharata was a King, the grandfather of Kuru, and the ancestor from whom the main figures in the core story of the epic descend.

17. Pāṇḍu and Dhṛtarāṣṭra descend from Bharata through Kuru.

18. Actually, Kuntī was mother only of the three oldest, with Pāṇḍu's consent and by way of an incantation becoming mother of Yudhiṣṭhira by the god Dharma, of Bhīma by the god Vāyu, and of Arjuna by the god Indra. Nakula and Sahadeva have Mādrī for mother.

19. When the caste system is conceived on its broadest scale, a *brāhmaṇa* represents a member of the highest caste, and is often a priest; the second caste, *kṣatriya*, is that of kings and warriors; the third, *vaiśya*, is that of men of trade and agriculture, while the fourth and lowest, *śūdra*, is that of men who served the members of the three upper castes.

20. As a man Kṛṣṇa is a *kṣatriya*, head of the Vṛṣṇi clan, a cousin to the Pāṇḍavas (though not a son of Dhṛtarāṣṭra), and the brother-in-law of Arjuna.

21. Cf. note 15 under Notes Concerning Text, Chapter I.

Notes to the Translation

CHAPTER I

1. I.1: the use of the term *dharma* in the *Gītā* is manifold, but the core usage would seem to make it stand for the divinely-grounded and socially-expressed projection of ideals and goals, proprieties and directions of effort, that governs life in a Hindu society.

2. I.3: the teacher is Droṇa, son of Bhāradvāja and teacher of the art of war to both the Kaurava and the Pāṇḍava princes.

3. I.3: the five are Yudhiṣṭhira, Bhīma, Arjuna, Nakula and Sahadeva.

4. I.3: Dhṛṣṭadyumna; Drupada is King of Pañcāla.

5. I.4: Kṛṣṇa's charioteer (also called Sātyaki).

6. I.4: King of the Matsyas, at whose court the Pāṇḍavas had lived in disguise for a while.

7. I.5: King of the Cedis, and brother-in-law of Nakula.

8. I.5: a famous warrior.

9. I.5: Kāśī is the modern Banaras (Vārāṇasī).

10. I.5: two brothers.

11. I.6: two men known only as chieftains in the Pāṇḍava army.

12. I.6: Subhadrā, sister of Kṛṣṇa, was the wife of Arjuna; their son was Abhimanyu.

13. I.6: Draupadī is the daughter of Drupada whom Arjuna won in the contest; she married all the five Pāṇḍava princes, and had a son by each.

14. I.7: a *brāhmaṇa*, *kṣatriya* or *vaiśya* became "twice-born" when invested with the sacred thread, signifying initiation ("birth") into the study of the Vedas. Droṇa, though a teacher of military arts, was a *brāhmaṇa*, or "highest" of the twice-born.

15. I.8: an old sage-warrior, son of Śāntanu and the river-goddess Gaṅgā; step-brother to their father, he raised Dhṛtarāṣṭra and Pāṇḍu.

16. I.8: Kuntī's son before her marriage to Pāṇḍu, thus step-brother to Yudhiṣṭhira, Bhīma and Arjuna.

17. I.8: brother-in-law of Droṇa.

18. I.8: son of Droṇa.

19. I.8: the third of the hundred sons of Dhṛtarāṣṭra.

20. I.8: Somadatta was King of the Bāhīkas.

21. I.12: Bhīṣma.

22. I.14: Kṛṣṇa.

23. I.14: Arjuna.

24. I.15: Kṛṣṇa. The epithet could mean "having strong, or upstanding, hair", that is, "High-haired one".

25. I.15: his conch, made of the bone of the demon Pañcajana.

26. I.15: Arjuna.

27. I.15: his conch, literally, Gift of a God; Arjuna had received it from Indra, his divine father.

28. I.16: literally, Unending Victory.

29. I.16: literally, Sweet-toned and Gem-flowered, respectively.

30. I.20: literally, with weapons having begun to fly. So to translate it might make it more harmonious with XI. 26-27.

31. I.20: Arjuna.

32. I.20: *dṛṣṭvā*, the same word as in I. 2.

33. I.22: *nirīkṣe*: *nirīkṣ*, to behold, observe, look at, here, to take a good look at (a close look at).

34. I.23: *avekṣe*: *avekṣ*, to look at, behold, consider attentively, here, carefully to observe.

35. I.23: Duryodhana.

36. I.24: Arjuna. The epithet could mean "having his hair in a ball" ("having knotted hair"), or "Lord of Sleep".

37. I.24: Dhṛtarāṣṭra; Bharata was the grandfather of Kuru, who in turn was ancestor to both Pāṇḍu and Dhṛtarāṣṭra.

38. I.25: Arjuna; Pṛthā was another name for his mother, Kuntī. The name is derived from *pṛth* (to extend) and is connected with *pṛthivī* (earth).

39. I.25: *samavetān*, the same word as in Verse 1 (there translated "gathered together").

40. I.25: Kuru was an ancestor of both the Kauravas and the Pāṇḍavas, although only the former were normally still called by his name. Thus in this context "Kurus" has a significant ambiguity, referring to members of both sides, yet pre-eminently to members of one (that opposed to Arjuna).

41. I.27: *samīkṣya*: *samīkṣ*, to look at or inspect thoroughly, look at closely.

42. I.28; *kṛpayā*, compassion, or pity.

43. I.28: *viṣīdan*, literally, "sinking", but "in spirit" (as in the English "depressed"), hence here, "weighed down by his sorrow".

44. I.30: the bow given to Arjuna by Agni, god of fire.

45. I.31: Kṛṣṇa. The epithet could mean "Long-haired one", "Hairy one", or "having fine hair".

46. I.32: Kṛṣṇa. The epithet could mean "Cattle-finder", or "Lord of Herdsmen" ("Lord of Herds"), or even "Earth-finder". Also perhaps, "Giver of Enlightenment".

47. I.35: Kṛṣṇa; Madhu, here, is a demon.

48. I.35: the three worlds here are heaven (the world of gods), earth (the world of men), and either *pātāla* (the world of demons) or the region between heaven and earth (the world of semi-divine beings).

49. I.36: Kṛṣṇa. The epithet could mean "one who is entreated by the prayers of men"; or "troubler of men" (that is, of foes), "folk-disturbing", "destroyer of a people"; or "destroyer of a demon named Jana"; or "liberator of men".

50. I.39 : *jñeyam*, gerundive of *jñā* (to know).

51. I.39: *prapaśyadbhir*, ultimately from *prapaś*, to see before one's eyes, to see clearly.

52. I.40: that is, absence of *dharma*, the antithesis to *dharma*, or what is contrary to *dharma*.

53. I.41: Kṛṣṇa.

54. I.41: caste is here *varṇa*, referring only to the four main castes.

55. I.42: ancestor-worship takes the form of *śrāddha*, a ceremonious offering of water and rice-cakes to departed ancestors (*pitṛ*, Father) at stated intervals after their death. If these duties are neglected, the ancestors fall from higher to lower states.

56. I.43: the plural of *dharma*.

57. I.44: *niyataṁ*.

58. I.45: *vyavasitā*.

59. I.46: *kṣemataraṁ*.

60. I.47: *-saṁvigna-*, agitated with, or overwhelmed by.

CHAPTER II

1. II.1: *āviṣṭam*.

2. II.1: *kṛpayā*.

3. II.1: *viṣīdantam*.

4. II.3: Arjuna. As the epithet suggests, Kṛṣṇa is here addressing Arjuna not simply as an individual (Verse 2) and as a member of a certain family (beginning of Verse 3) but also as a member of a certain caste, the *kṣatriya*, with a certain ideal of nobility to which he is to live up.

5. II.7: nature which distinguishes him, his own nature as that of a *kṣatriya*, as that of this particular type of human being. "Nature" refers to native endowment entered into the process of development, with a certain assimilation of the social norms and standards of a *kṣatriya* being involved, so that Arjuna sees himself essentially in this light, as (here) failing to act "naturally" because of a certain fault (pity is not intrinsically such for a *kṣatriya*, it is such however in these circumstances).

6. II.7: pupil is *śiṣyas*, teach is *śādhi*. Both involve the root *śās*, which means (among other things) to teach, but whose initial meaning is to chastise or correct. That initial meaning should be kept in mind here, as also a particularization of that meaning in regard to adult and child. There is a "childish" element to Arjuna's response, enacted in his behavior as well as in his words. Cf. Verses 9 and 10, for example.

7. II.8: *prapaśyāmi*. Cf. I. 39, and the note to *prapaśyadbhir* (note 51).

8. II.10: *viṣīdantam*.

9. II.11: *prajñā-*. Cf. I. 39.

10. II.11: *paṇḍitāḥ*. There are numerous words in the Sanskrit which could in many contexts be translated adequately by the single word "wise" in English. Yet this would lose not only the sense of variety that the Sanskrit involves but also the different connotations which different Sanskrit words contain. Here "learned" is a rather unsatisfactory rendering, to avoid "wise" and to point to the connotation of the Sanskrit. Of course, the learning involved has noth-

ing to do with a university education, but concerns that sort of learning commensurate with the teaching Arjuna has just asked Kṛṣṇa to provide him. Cf. its use in IV. 19 and V. 4 and 18.

11. II.13: *dhīras* (II. 15: *dhīraṁ*). Alternatively, "the steadfast".

12. II.16: literally, "of *asat*, there is known no *bhāva*, of *sat*, there is known no *abhāva*". Cf. *Chāndogya Upaniṣad*, VI. 2. 1-3; yet also cf. *Taittirīya Upaniṣad*, II. 7 and *Chāndogya Upaniṣad*, III. 19. 1.

13. II.16: *antas*, limit, boundary-line.

14. II.16: *tattva-*.

15. II.18: literally, " 'end-possessing' are called these bodies..."

16. II.19: *vijānīto*, from *vijñā*, to understand.

17. For Verses 19-20, cf. *Kaṭha Upaniṣad*, I. 2. 18-19: "The knower of this is never born and never dies, he has not come to be someone from somewhere. Unborn, eternal, everlasting, primeval, he is not slain when the body is slain. Neither a slayer thinking he slays, nor the slain thinking himself slain, understands: this one neither slays nor is slain." There are numerous echoes of this Upaniṣad, or of a source common to it and the *Gītā*, in the latter.

18. II.29: this verse seems out of place, and perhaps is an interpolation. In any case, the author would seem here to be echoing *Kaṭha Upaniṣad*, I. 2. 7: "Of him even the hearing about whom is not given to many, and the knowing of whom is not given to many of those even who have heard, marvellous is the one who can tell and skillful the one who can find, marvellous the knower who has been skillfully instructed in the skills to find [or, marvellous is he who, skillfully instructed, knows Him] ."

19. II.31: *avekṣya*, gerund of *avekṣ* (cf. note 34 in Chapter I).

20. II.38: *yujyasva*, an imperative form of the verbal root *yuj*, from which the term *yoga* is derived. Its initial meaning is to yoke, to harness (cf. *yukte*, harnessed, in I. 14); here, a more generalized meaning is involved, namely, make yourself ready for.

21. II.39: *buddhir*. In the *Gītā*'s usage there are many meanings to this term *buddhi*. Derived from the verbal root *budh*, meaning (initially) to be awake, the noun can shift from meaning the power of understanding to the power of resolve or decision, to the understanding or the resolve itself; but the central usage seems to be for the essential power that makes a human being human. In this usage it is comparable to *nous* or *logos* or *ratio* or reason in the Western tradition. But normally this usage of *buddhi* lays weight on two things most importantly, the power of decision and the power to be enlightened. Hence the title for Gautama, the Buddha or Enlightened One. Thus there is a strong intuitive and purposive cast to the term, rather than an intellectual one. Cf. Notes, II.41 (Aurobindo's comment).

22. II.39: the Sāṁkhya was a school of thought apparently originally outside the Vedic stream, though gradually being assimilated into the latter. For further discussion, see Commentary, p. 84 ff.

23. II.39: *buddhir*; cf. note 21 above.

24. II.39: the Yoga was another school of thought, closely connected with the Sāṁkhya. Again, for further discussion, see Commentary, p. 88 ff.

25. II.39: *yukto*, past participle of *yuj*.

26. II.39: *buddhyā*, instrumental case form of *buddhi*. Cf. note 21 above.

27. II.39: *karman* has an almost bewildering variety of meanings in the *Gītā*'s usage. Since Kṛṣṇa's teaching involves an altered notion of *karman* from that of the tradition he was disputing, it is important that the basic meanings be clear. Seen schematically there are four ranges of reference that are important: (1) *karman* is ritual action, that involved in ceremony and sacrifice, involving reference to the gods (interplay, interaction, with them); (2) *karman* is social action, including ritual but also all that is part of one's duty or obligation as a certain member of society; (3) *karman* is any overt action that produces a result beyond itself; (4) *karman* is all effort, whether overt or inner, whether producing an overt result or not (thus thinking, perceiving, feeling, dreaming, and the like are action). Now each of these ranges of reference can be meant in one of three ways: (a) the *karman* may be being conceived in disregard of whether it involves bondage or not; (b) the *karman* may be being conceived as involving the doer in bondage; (c) the *karman* may be being conceived as free of bondage, and as such because of the way it is undertaken on a path toward enlightenment or out of a condition of enlightenment. The term *karman*, without qualifying words, can mean any one of these twelve things. Its most common meaning, one which Kṛṣṇa opposes but which is traditional, is that of 2b (social action, implicitly meant as bondage-producing); but Kṛṣṇa teaches *karman* in the meaning 4c (any active effort, as part of the path toward enlightenment or as expressive of enlightenment). But there are normally no indications but context to differentiate the twelve possible meanings in question, and what is more: *karman* can also take on the meaning of "work" or "working" or "function" or "functional character" or "character one ought to have due to one's ordained function". Thus, at the risk of belaboring a point, I have placed the term *karman* in parenthesis at almost every place of its occurrence (or that of its cognate verbal forms, when translation of these seemed better through the noun).

28. II.40: *dharmasya* (genitive of *dharma*).

29. II.40: the fear of death as something to be experienced endlessly, given rebirth and transmigration.

30. II.41: *vyavasāyātmikā*, literally, what has *vyavasāya* (resolve, resoluteness) as its very self. Cf. IX. 30-31, for another use of "resolute" (*vyavasito*) that may help clarify the meaning of its usage here.

31. II.41: *Kaṭha Upaniṣad* (II. 1. 14) speaks of the matter under a different image: "as water rained down on inaccessible rough ground runs off among the mountains, so seeing real things as separate, one precisely runs off after them."

32. II.42: *avipaścitaḥ*.

33. In regard to Verses 42-43, cf. *Muṇḍaka Upaniṣad*, I. 2. 8-10: "Abiding in the heart of ignorance (*avidyā*), to themselves wise (*dhīrāḥ*), thinking themselves learned (*paṇḍitam*), these fools afflicting themselves go about like blind men led by one who is himself blind. Childish, abiding manifoldly in ignorance (*avidyā*), they think, 'we have accomplished our aim'. But due to passionate attachment these doers-of-ritual-deeds do not see (truth), therefore when their worlds (those attained as fruit of meritorious action) are exhausted they sink down, wretched. These deluded men, regarding sacrifice and meritorious action as most important, do not know any other good. Having taken enjoy-

ment in the high place of heaven won by good deeds, they enter again this world or a still lower one." There are numerous echoes of this Upaniṣad, or of a source common to it and to the *Gītā*, in the latter. [*Muṇḍaka Upaniṣad* I. 2. 8=*Kaṭha Upaniṣad* I. 2. 5; the verse is also quoted in *Maitrī Upaniṣad* VII. 9. Cf. also *Īśā Upaniṣad*, 9.]

34. II.44: nowhere in the *Gītā* does *samādhi* seem used in its technical Yoga sense (the third and highest phase of *rāja-yoga* or meditation). It rather refers to an ingatheredness, an inward centeredness of *buddhi*, that underpins its concomitant outward-directed functioning. Cf. Notes, II. 65, II. 54, and II. 55 in Aurobindo's comments.

35. II.44: *vyavasāyātmikā* modifies *buddhi* here, as in verse 41, and yet seems to have a different meaning in this case, namely, "whose very self is making resolves (decisions)".

36. II.45: the *guṇas* are the three-fold qualitative power that constitutes all that is created and that qualifies it in such way as makes of it a single created world of active centers with activity-referent characteristics. Thus *sattva* is the power expressed in perfect purity and luminosity and serenity, in what is true and what is good, in what is essential and fully developed and perfected, and so on; *rajas* is the power expressed in imperfect purity and luminosity (in what is dusty or partially opaque), in energy and restlessness and passion and forcefulness, in movement and development, and so on; *tamas* is the power expressed in darkness and foul impurity, in inertia and heaviness and indifference, in slowness and stupidity, in the embryonic and undeveloped, and so on. Through these *guṇas* active centers are constituted as participants in a world-whole who hang together in their interaction as ordained toward an issue, a fulfillment that is more than *guṇa*-constituted. That issue is to be reached in a movement the beginning of which is characterized by delusion and bondage (imperfection, impotence, and the like). In this beginning, and as they move and develop, centers are confined within the *guṇas*; and as confined, they are characterizable in a way that expresses a hierarchy, at the head of which is what expresses *sattva*. (Cf. XIV. 5-8 especially, but also 9-18; and XVII. 4). Yet the ordering in question is toward a perfection that is not *guṇa-confined*, that involves transcendence of the *guṇas*. Thus the notion of the three-fold constitutive and qualifying power involves another ordering, in terms of which *sattva* represents the condition of one free from delusion and bondage (hence not merely perfect in a worldly sense, but now with a perfection permeated by the light and life of *sat* or the real beyond the world), in contrast with *rajas* and *tamas*. (Cf. XVIII. 18-39; also XVII. 8-22).

37. II.45: *sattva* here has a meaning only indirectly connected with its meaning as one of the *guṇas*. The emphasis is here upon what is essential in the being of a creaturely center; cf. XVI. 1 *sattva-saṁśuddhir* (and similarly, *Muṇḍaka Upaniṣad*, III. 1. 8; *viśuddha-sattvas*, purified essence). See also XVII. 3, *sattvānurūpā*, "conformably to his essence", where *sattva* signifies something like innermost nature (*sva-bhāva*).

38. II.45: *ātmavān*; *ātman* is the common reflexive pronoun in the Sanskrit of the *Gītā* (classical Sanskrit), and simply means "self" with no further or technical implications whatever. But early on, in a way that probably reflects its original meaning ("breath, life-breath": cf: *Ṛg-veda*), *ātman* came to gain

inflections of meaning through which it could stand for what is most real, most essential, in a thing, "its very self". And in extension, it has since gained a variety of technical meanings, in the Upaniṣads, for example, but in later philosophical usage as well. In the *Gītā* the term is used in a wide-ranging way, and not as a fixed technical term with a limited (and abstract) meaning.

39. II.47: *adhikāras*. This word could mean authority, sphere of authority, jurisdiction, prerogative, or—as I have translated it—right or claim (especially to perform sacrifices with benefit: although here, in the *Gītā's* thought, the benefit that is to arise can not be claimed as fruit).

40. II.48: *yoga* is one of the most common words in the *Gītā*, but its meaning, and that of its cognate verbal forms, varies with context. Apart from its being the name for a school of thought, *yoga* seems primarily to mean one of the following things: (a) union, conceived of normally as with the divine (the Lord) and as an issue of a disciplined effort; (b) the disciplined effort through which union is achieved, or such effort out of the achievement of such union; hence (in generalization) any discipline; (c) the meditational exercises which can be an important form of such disciplined effort but are not the only form, and to begin with, are not the important form. All of these meanings reflect the basic meaning of the verbal root *yuj*, to harness or yoke. Cf. Note to II. 48, and a suggestive account by Edgerton.

41. II.50: *-yukto*.

42. II.50: *yujyasva*. Cf. note 20 above (to II. 38). Notice the echo here (*yogāya yujyasva*) of *yuddhāya yujyasva* there, and the implications for Arjuna's taking part in the imminent battle.

43. II.51: *manīṣiṇaḥ*, those having *manīṣā*, thought or understanding; ultimately from the verbal root *man*, to think.

44. II.52: I have added "from the Vedas" in parenthesis, to make clear the meaning from the context; likewise in the next verse, 53. Cf. *Muṇḍaka Upaniṣad*, I. 2. 12, for a similar use of *nirveda* (indifference); compare, also, with *Bṛhad-āraṇyaka-upaniṣad* IV. 4. 21 ("having known him [the self] alone, let the wise [*dhīro*] *brāhmaṇa* practise *prajñāṁ* [the seeing through which wisdom is wisdom]; let him not reflect on many words, for this is mere weariness of speech."

45. II.54: *prajñā* means something like "wisdom" here and in the remainder of this Chapter, but with an emphasis upon the element of clear-sightedness involved (cf. Commentary, pp. 94-5). The term gives way to a related one, *jñāna*, as the dialogue unfolds; almost all of the occurrences of *prajñā* are to be found in Chapter II.

46. II.54: *-dhīḥ*. Cf. Commentary, p. 94, for a brief consideration of the term.

47. II.55: *kāmān*. The term *kāma*, when it means "desire", can be used in a sense that is free of any implications of egoism and bondage, but such connotations are often a part of the word. Cf. similarly *karman*, and also, the parallel with the term "pride" in a Christian context.

48. II.55: a similar verse ("when all the desires that have entered into his heart are cast off, then a mortal becomes immortal, right here he attains to the holy power") is to be found in *Bṛhad-āraṇyaka-upaniṣad*, IV. 4. 7, and *Kaṭha Upaniṣad*, II. 3. 14.

49. II.56: or, "is free of yearning for pleasure".

50. II.56: *munir. Muni* is a term used particularly of a recluse who has taken a vow of silence, but often, is used in general of any saint, sage, or ascetic.

51. II.58: for a similar notion of the senses, as powers that go forth to feed on sense-objects and whose going forth must therefore be restrained, cf. *Maitrī Upaniṣad*, VI. 31, for example.

52. II.63: *buddhi-*. This verse should be kept in mind when considering XVIII. 73. Cf. Commentary, pp. 96-97, for a brief consideration of verses 59-68.

53. II.64: *prasādam*, which has an implication also of "clarity" as well as tranquillity. Cf. Aurobindo's comments in Notes, II. 65.

54. II.64; *-viyuktais*, that is, unharnessed from, disjoined from; note the implication that normally the senses are harnessed to such emotional factors.

55. II.66: that is, no true power of judgment and decision, no power capable of resoluteness (Verse 41).

56. II.66: *bhāvanā*. This term could mean numerous things, but I take it here as the correlative to *buddhi* in the rhythm of action and meditation which Kṛṣṇa urges. Thus I translate it "contemplative steeping of oneself", thinking of the meditational coming into touch with deeper factors and the drawing of strength and energy, the being renewed, from those factors through that touch.

57. II.70: *kāmā*.

58. II.70: or, "he whom all desires enter as the waters enter a sea which is ever being filled yet ever stands fast immovable."

59. II.70: *kāmakāmī*.

60. II.72: *brāhmī sthitiḥ*.

61. II.72: *brahmanirvāṇam*. As to *brahma-*: the root of *brahman*, *bṛh*, means "to grow great or strong, to increase"; and *brahman* then etymologically means "growth, expansion, development", and in the particular meaning that is most relevant here, "swelling of the spirit or soul". For in its oldest meaning in a religious vein, *brahman* seems to have been "holy utterance", that is, utterance not simply concerned with the divine (addressing it, and—at least, often—about it) but also inspired by the divine, devotional in that fashion. This meaning occurs in the *Gītā* when, in following the tradition that takes the Vedas as inspired, Kṛṣṇa speaks of "holy utterance" and means the Vedas. But the most common meaning in the *Gītā* is the divine or holy power itself. Although the term developed in this direction early, and gained (for example, in the Upaniṣads) numerous technical connotations and references thereby, the *Gītā*'s usage, here as with *ātman*, seems free of confinement to a single determinant referent. Thus I have generally translated it simply "holy power". As to *-nirvāṇam*: see under Notes to II. 72.

CHAPTER III

1. III.1: Arjuna's misunderstanding here is partly grounded in the multiple meanings of certain key Sanskrit words Kṛṣṇa has been using. What Arjuna says here refers most directly to II. 49, where he has heard "*buddhi*" as the

power which Sāṁkhya seeks to discipline, has heard "*yoga*" as the discipline Sāṁkhya calls for upon withdrawal, and thus (hearing no transition within Sāṁkhya from theoretical to practical) has heard "*karman*" in a Sāṁkhya way, as something to be left behind. This "hearing" typifies his understanding of the teaching of Chapter II. For given that he is listening for a word that would confirm him in his sense that withdrawal is justifiable, the mention of Sāṁkhya seemingly confirms his hope, and makes Kṛṣṇa's urging him to fight a puzzle for him.

2. III.2: *buddhiṁ*.

3. III.3: *niṣṭhā*.

4. III.4: *siddhiṁ*. The perfection here in question is that in the capacity to engage in action free of bondage; it is not perfection in the capacity to produce results, nor the full perfection of man (which includes the meditative as well as the actional side of human capacity).

5. III.5: *prakṛti-*.

6. For thoughts similar to those involved in Verses 4-7, and indeed in Kṛṣṇa's *karma-yoga* generally, cf. *Īśā Upaniṣad*, 1-2: "All this, whatever moves in this moving world, is inhabited by the Lord; take your enjoyment in it as something relinquished, do not covet the wealth of another. May one desire to live a hundred years engaging thus in *karman* here on earth; if you live in no other way than this, *karman* will not pollute a man."

7. III.8: *niyataṁ*. Cf. XVIII. 45-46, *sva-karman*; and XVIII. 47, the *karman niyataṁ* by one's *sva-bhāva*; and XVIII. 48, the *karman* that is *sahajaṁ* (native to one). What is involved, first and foremost, is the work appointed to one along with his nature, and thus, along with his social station (since transmigration assures a correlation of social station and the works pertaining to this, with the inborn nature of the person). Cf. Hill, Introduction, Section 30.

8. III.10: there is no indication in the Sanskrit where the words attributed to the Lord of Creatures end; I have chosen the end of verse 12 as the most appropriate place.

9. III.13: according to Śaṁkara, these are the sins committed at the five places of animal-slaughter (the fireplace, the waterpot, the instruments for cutting, grinding, and sweeping).

10. III.15: *brahma-*. The Vedas seem what is meant.

11. III.16: *pravartitaṁ..anuvartayati*, literally, rolled forward..make roll after. The play on the verbal root *vṛt* (turn, roll, revolve) underlines the fitting together that is to be effected. The wheel-imagery is a common one in the Upaniṣads, but not in this specific and limited application.

12. III.17: for similar phraseology and thought, cf. *Chāndogya Upaniṣad*, VII. 25. 2; and *Muṇḍaka Upaniṣad*, III. 1. 4.

13. III.19: *kāryaṁ* (likewise in III. 17), gerundive of *kṛ*, to act. Cf. note 7 above (on *niyataṁ*).

14. III.20: Janaka is presumably the King of Mithilā, who was father of Sītā, the wife of Rāma.

15. III.25: *vidvāṁs*, in contrast with the *avidvāṁso*, those confined in *avidyā*. It is well to keep in mind that *vidyā* (knowledge, and especially, the triple knowledge of holy utterance) also means "magic". This is in keeping with the sense of the fullest insight into things as disclosing the universe to be at heart some-

thing magical, so that those confined within the lack of such knowledge take part in the world as in something prosaic, to be used and controlled rather than to be participated in.

16. III.26: *ajñānāṁ*.

17. III.27: *kriyamāṇāni*, are done by (present passive participle).

18. III.27: *ahaṁkāra-*, I-maker, ego-maker.

19. III.27: *kartā-*.

20. III.28: *-vibhāgayoḥ*; that is, the created world is, as such, ordained to activity, and it is through the three *guṇas* and their differentiation of agents and conditions that activity is made possible. Cf. IV. 13, and especially, XVIII. 42-44.

21. III.32: terminologically, *jñāna* begins to replace *prajñā* in Kṛṣṇa's account, and at times itself becomes linked with *vijñāna* (e. g., Verse 41 of this Chapter). All three go back to the same verbal root, *jñā*, to know; so far as that meaning is inflected through the prefixes, *prajñā* (as a verbal form, not the noun) seems to point in the direction of knowing one's way around, knowing how to proceed, whereas *vijñā* seems to point to knowing through distinctions, distinguishing and recognizing intellectually. But the nouns have overlapping meanings, and numerous meanings which are not reflective of their verbal roots. In the *Gītā*'s usage *jñāna* would seem to have several important meanings, the central one of which might be expressed as "wisdom"; as the English term suggests, what is involved antecedes any differentiation of intellectual from practical, but does so not as "wisdom" suggests (with a unity of the reflective and the practical) but with an emphasis upon an element of illumination and illuminated vision. Yet though it is these which lie at the heart of *jñāna*, the term can mean, also, not so much the vision belonging to wisdom itself (in cluding the vision initiating the possibility of wisdom) but the understanding which brings that vision to articulation. And even more, it can include the very conditions of such vision and articulation, conditions of character, for example.

22. III.34: *rāga-*.

23. III.35: cf. XVIII. 48.

24. III.37: *kāma*.

25. III.39: *kāmarūpeṇa*, protean, or, in the form of desire. Similarly at III. 43.

26. III.41: *-vijñāna-*. In this linking of *jñāna* and *vijñāna*, which is repeated in later places in the poem, the former would seem to refer to something that is a matter of direct experience and the latter to a matter of the articulation of such first-hand cognizance.

27. III.42: *parāṇy*. I take it to mean "superior to the things of sense", but it need not be taken comparatively; then it would mean "high".

28. III.43: *buddhvā*.

29. For Verses 42-43, compare *Kaṭha Upaniṣad*, I. 3. 10-11, and II. 3. 7-8, where in each case there is a series built up similarly to that in these verses.

CHAPTER IV

1. IV.1: Vivasvat is the sun, the father of (the seventh) Manu, who is

progenitor of the present human race. Ikṣvāku, born of Manu, was the first King of the Solar Dynasty.

2. IV.2: presumably, the Kings of the Solar Dynasty.

3. IV.2: *naṣṭaḥ.*

4. IV.3: *bhakto.*

5. IV.6: *adhiṣṭhāya.*

6. IV.6: *prakṛtiṁ.*

7. IV.6: *māyā* is the magic power, the mysterious power, through which creation occurs in a measuring out and revealing of finite temporal things and in an involving of them in delusion and in the possibility of release. I agree with Edgerton, who says: "This does not mean (in my opinion: some scholars take the contrary view) that the world outside of the self is illusory, without real existence, as the later Vedānta philosophy maintains; *māyā*, I think, is not used in the Vedāntic sense of 'world-illusion' until many centuries later" (pp. 117-18).

8. IV.13: *-vibhāgaśaḥ.* Cf. note 20 in Chapter III.

9. IV.13: *kartāram, akartāram.*

10. IV.14: *abhijānāti.*

11. IV.15: *jñātvā*, that is, having such *jñāna.*

12. IV.15: *kṛtaṁ karma*, literally, action (was) done (by the ancients who desired release). Then "you be active" is, literally, "do action" (*kuru karma*).

13. IV.16: *jñātvā.*

14. IV.17: *boddhavyaṁ*, from *budh.*

15. IV.17: *vikarman* could mean "modified activity", that is, the inward action of mind and heart, as contrasted with overt action.

16. IV.19: *budhāḥ.*

17. IV.19: *paṇḍitaṁ.*

18. IV.20: *karoti*, a present form of *kṛ*, the verbal root for *karman.*

19. IV.24: *-samādhinā.*

20. IV.26: I add this phrase, to bring out the implications of the context. The previous verse seems to name the two extremes, the most outward and the most inward forms of sacrifice, between which range a variety of other forms (Verses 26-30).

21. IV.26: presumably this means, endeavor not to allow sensuous things to come in contact with the senses at all, as in certain forms of meditation.

22. IV.26: presumably this means, endeavor to allow sensuous things to touch the senses but without allowing this touching to engender the movement of feeding on sensuous things (cf. II. 62-64).

23. IV.28: *tapo-*. *Tapas* here probably means ascetic practice concerned with the body, not the broader *tapas* that Kṛṣṇa speaks of in XVII. 14-16.

24. IV.31: *-amṛta-.*

25. IV.31: *yānti.* This could mean "go to, attain".

26. IV.32: this could mean, "set forth in holy utterance, in the Vedas", or, more likely, "established as gateway for reaching the holy power" (cf. the preceding verse). In any case, this phrase echoes III. 14-15, at a more inward level.

27. IV.33: *akhilaṁ*, complete, or, without exception (thus "All action without exception...").

28. IV.33: cf. *Maitrī Upaniṣad*, I.1: "A sacrifice to the holy power, indeed,

is the laying (of the sacrificial fires) of the ancients. Therefore let the sacrificer, laying these fires, meditate on the self. That sacrifice becomes fulfilled (*pūrṇaḥ*) indeed and truly entire (*avikalaḥ*). Who is he that is to be meditated upon ? He who is called life (*prāṇa-*). Of him there is the following story."

29. IV.34: cf. *Kaṭha Upaniṣad*, I. 2. 8-9: "Taught by an inferior man, he cannot be well understood (*suvijñeyo*), being conceived in manifold ways; unless taught by one who is not other (than he) [or, with no other teacher than that], there is no way there, for he is more subtle than the subtle, not to be reasoned out [or, inconceivably more subtle than what is of subtle nature]. Not by reasoning is this apprehension (*matir*) attainable, but dearest, taught by another he is well understood (*sujñānāya*). The steadfastness in truth which you have attained: ah, you are a marvel indeed ! May we find, Naciketas, an inquirer like you !"

30. IV.36: for the imagery, confer II. 67.

31. IV.37: for a similar thought, cf. *Chāndogya Upaniṣad*, V. 24. 1-3; also *Śvetāśvatara Upaniṣad*, II. 6-7. There are numerous echoes of this latter Upaniṣad, or of a source common to it and the *Gītā*, in the latter.

32. IV.39: *śraddhāvāṁl*, that is, having *śraddhā*. Here, believing in the possibility of release that has been opened up to one, or more directly, in the possibility of reaching in oneself the *jñāna* that is indispensable to achieving release. And since all this presumably concerns a man who finds himself already in that presence of Kṛṣṇa (whether understood as such or not) which opens the way toward release, also believing in Kṛṣṇa as supporting such a movement toward release.

33. IV.39: for a similar thought, cf. *Muṇḍaka Upaniṣad*, III. 1. 5; also *Praśna Upaniṣad*, I.2.

34. IV.40: *saṁśaya-*. This doubt is not an intellectual affair simply, or primarily, but a matter that concerns one's incapacity to respond with that commitment of self which would alone take one forward on the path toward release. Arjuna's current hesitation and doubt are one form of this, but only one.

CHAPTER V

1. V.4: *bālāḥ*.

2. V.4: *paṇḍitāḥ*.

3. V.5: *sthānaṁ*.

4. V.6: or, "is difficult to attain to without the disciplined-undertaking-of-action". In that case, the meaning is: the path of withdrawal is scarcely to be attained without *kriyā-yoga* or the kind of discipline that constitutes the first phase of the path of action. Yet there seems, too, a suggestion of how much easier and quicker the path of action is than that of renunciation of action.

5. V.7: for a similar phrase, see *Īśā Upaniṣad*, 7.

6. V.8: *yukto*. For the thought here (V. 8-9) and earlier (IV. 18), cf. *Bṛhadāraṇyaka-upaniṣad*, IV. 3. 23-30.

7. V.10: cf. III. 30. Also XII. 6, and XVIII. 57.

8. V.10: for the same image, cf. *Chāndogya Upaniṣad,* IV. 14. 3.

9. V.11: "bare" means "without egoistic distortion in terms of passion, hate, and the like"; cf. II. 64.

10. V.12: *-kāreṇa.*

11. V.13: that is, the body with its nine openings. For similar imagery, cf. *Śvetāśvatara Upaniṣad,* III. 18; also *Kaṭha Upaniṣad* II. 2. 1, and *Chāndogya Upaniṣad,* VIII.1.1.

12. V.14: the genitive here, "of the world", could be referred to the object rather than to the subject: "the presiding one does not create the world's...."

13. V.14: *sva-bhāvas.*

14. V.16: that is, *jñāna* as the sort of cognizance which is opening one to the depths not only dispels ignorance of oneself (bringing a deeper and deepening self-awareness) but gives rise also to a *jñāna* that shines into the darkness to bring the holy power also into the light of cognizance.

15. V.17: *-niṣṭhās.*

16. V.18: *paṇḍitāḥ.*

17. V.19: that is, birth and what it enters us into in the way of the illusion of duality (thus delusion and bondage: see VII. 27-28), and in the way of the (endless) round of birth-and-death, *saṁsāra.*

18. V.22: *budhaḥ.*

19. V.26: *-viyuktānāṁ.*

20. V.29: *jñātvā.*

CHAPTER VI

1. VI.1: in the traditional view the *saṁnyāsin* (man of renunciation) is the man who has withdrawn from the social order and who, as part of this, may perform no sacrifice or ceremonial act (indeed, may keep no fire even for the purpose of cooking food).

2. VI.2: or, a man of disciplined engagement in action, that is, a man on the path of action.

3. VI.3: *kāraṇam,* that is, medium, or perhaps, means.

4. VI.3: *muner* (that is, *muni*).

5. VI.7: or, "the superior (or best) self, belonging to...."

6. VI.7: *samāhitaḥ.*

7. VI.8: *-vijñāna-.*

8. VI.8: *yukta.*

9. VI.10: that is, day after day, at appointed times (but not, every minute of every day).

10. VI.15: or, which culminates in extinction. In connection with Verses 10-15 as a whole, compare with *Śvetāśvatara Upaniṣad,* II. 8-15.

11. VI.18: *yukta.*

12. VI.21: cf. *Kaṭha Upaniṣad,* I. 3. 12: "the self, hidden in all beings, does

not shine forth manifestly; but it is visible to subtle seers, through their proficiently attentive and subtle *buddhi*."

13. VI.23: *-viyogaṁ*.
14. VI.23: *-saṁyoga-*.
15. VI.25: *dhṛti-*. Steadiness, especially of will and attention; cf. XVIII.33.
16. VI.28: *-saṁsparśam*.
17. VI.29: *Īśā Upaniṣad*, 6-7 ("But he who sees all beings in his very self, and his self in all beings, does not desire to shrink away from them. When to one who knows [*vijānataḥ*] all beings have become his very self, then what delusion, what sorrow, [can there be] for him seeing oneness?"); also, the similar phrasing ("sees the self precisely in himself, sees all as self") in *Bṛhad-āraṇyaka-upaniṣad*, IV.4.23.
18. VI.31: *sarvathā vartamāno'pi*. I translate this with the etymology of *vṛt* (to turn) in mind, and with a view to emphasizing the movement-character of existence as Kṛṣṇa is conceiving it.
19. VI.35: *calam*.
20. VI.38: that is, fallen from the ordinary ritualistic path of the Vedas, leading to heaven, and from the path of action, leading to release.
21. VI.38: or, "bewildered and not firmly established in the path of the holy power".
22. VI.42: *dhīmatām*.
23. VI.43: *-saṁyogaṁ*. That is, he regains his former *buddhi's* internal integration and unity as a power of intelligent decision (a limited one, of course).
24. VI.44: *-abhyāsena*. Cf. Verse 35, above.
25. VI.44: *śabda-brahma-*.
26. VI.47: *yuktatamo*.

CHAPTER VII

1. VII.1: *jñāsyasi*.
2. VII.2: *-vijñānam*.
3. VII.2: *jñātavyam*, gerundive of *jñā*, to know.
4. VII.3: Taking an alternative reading, *yatatāṁ ca sahasrāṇāṁ*.
5. VII.4: mind, as the more limited power which connects the senses with *buddhi*; a sort of sixth sense (cf. X. 22).
6. VII.4: *prakṛtir*.
7. VII.4: this can be taken as a short-hand version for the more extended Sāṁkhya division of manifest nature into 23 factors, if the five elements are taken to stand for both gross and subtle elements, and if *manas* is taken also to stand for the (other) ten sense-powers (of perception and action).
8. VII.6: this dual nature, or this higher nature: either is grammatically possible.
9. VII.6: this dual-causation is very important; cf. VIII. 4, 16-20, IX. 7-10, 18, X. 20 and 32, and the revelation of Chapter XI.
10. VII.7: the image of a string comports well with the notion of the

creaturely as constituted by the three *guṇas* or strands of a rope. For another notion of the "string", cf. *Bṛhad-āraṇyaka-upaniṣad*, III. 7. 1-2 and III. 8.

11. VII.10: *buddhir.*

12. VII.10: *buddhimatām.*

13. VII.12: *bhāvā.*

14. VII.13: *bhāvair.*

15. VII.16: *jijñāsur.*

16. VII.21: *tanuṁ.*

17. VII.25: cf. *Kaṭha Upaniṣad*, I. 3.12 (see note 12 to Chapter VI above). Similarly, but with a different reference (to the "great passing-on" through which human beings are finally freed from re-birth), I. 2. 6 ("That passing-on does not shine out to the childish who, deceived by the illusion of wealth, throw themselves heedlessly into its enjoyment. Thinking 'this is the world, there is nothing beyond' [or, there is no other], such a one falls again and again into my [=Yama's] power."

18. VII.26: for a similar thought, cf. *Śvetāśvatara Upaniṣad*, III. 19.

19. VII.29-30: concerning the terms *-adhibhūta-*, *-adhidaivam*, and *adhyātmam*, see their usage in *Bṛhad-āraṇyaka-upaniṣad*, III. 7 (especially 14 and 15) and II. 3, also II. 5.1-15; and in reference to the last two terms, cf. *Chāndogya Upaniṣad*, III. 18. 1-2. For *adhidaivam* as "in relation to the manifest world at large", cf. the use of the term in the *Bṛhadāraṇyaka-upaniṣad* references, and Kṛṣṇa's replacement of the "gods" (become identified with the manifest world they were once conceived to support: e.g. *Praśna Upaniṣad*, II. 1) by "spirit" (VIII. 4). See also the textual note to VIII. 4, under Notes Concerning Text.

CHAPTER VIII

1. VIII.3: cf. *Kaṭha Upaniṣad*, II. 3. 13: "He is to be apprehended precisely in 'he is' and by his true nature (*tattva-bhāvena*) both; apprehended precisely in 'he is', his true nature becomes clear." Also, relate to *Gītā*, X. 11, but particularly to V. 13-14.

2. VIII.6: *bhāvaṁ.*

3. VIII.5-6: for similar thoughts, cf. *Chāndogya Upaniṣad*, III. 14. 1, and *Praśna Upaniṣad*, III. 10. Also *Bṛhad-āraṇyaka-upaniṣad*, IV. 4. 6.

4. VIII.9: *kaviṁ purāṇam.* Cf. *Īśā Upaniṣad*, 8 (*kavir*).

5. VIII.9: *anuśāsitāram.* Cf. *Śvetāśvatara Upaniṣad*, III. 1-2 (*īśata īśanībhiḥ*, rules with his ruling powers), and III. 18 (*vaśī*, controller).

6. VIII.9: *aṇor aṇīyāṁsam.* Cf. *Kaṭha Upaniṣad*, I. 2. 8 and 20, and *Śvetāśvatara Upaniṣad*, III. 20.

7. VIII.9: *dhātāram.* Cf. *Taittirīya Upaniṣad*, I. 4. 3 (*dhātar*) and *Maitrī Upaniṣad*, VII. 2 (*dhātā*).

8. VIII.9: *acintyarūpam.* Cf. *Muṇḍaka Upaniṣad*, III. 1. 7.

9. VIII.9: *ādityavarṇaṁ tamasaḥ parastāt.* Cf. *Śvetāśvatara Upaniṣad*, III. 8.

10. VIII.12: that is, the gates of the nine-gated city, the openings of the body, in short, the senses.

11. VIII.11-13: for similar thoughts, cf. *Kaṭha Upaniṣad,* I. 2. 15-16 ("That word [*padam*] which all the Vedas declare, which all the austerities proclaim, desiring which [men] live the life of a religious student, that word I shall tell to you in brief: it is *aum*. This syllable [*akṣaram*] is the imperishable [*akṣaram*] holy power, this syllable [*akṣaram*] is the imperishable [*akṣaram*] supreme. Knowing [*jñātvā*] this very *akṣaram* (syllable, but also imperishable), whatever he desires will be his.") Cf. also *Praśna Upaniṣad,* V. 5-7, and *Muṇḍaka Upaniṣad,* II. 2-4.

12. VIII.16: the realm of Brahmā is the highest of the created worlds.

13. VIII.17: A period of four *yugas* (ages) or one *mahāyuga* (great age), lasts for 4, 320,000 mortal years. One thousand *mahāyugas* are one day in the life of Brahmā, and his night is equally long. 360 such days and nights (*kalpas*) form one of Brahmā's years, and he lives for 100 years.

14. VIII.23-27. For the thought in these verses, cf. *Chāndogya Upaniṣad.* IV. 15. 5 and V. 10; also *Praśna Upaniṣad,* I. 9-10; *Muṇḍaka Upaniṣad,* I. 2. 11; *Bṛhad-āraṇyaka-upaniṣad,* VI. 2. 15-16.

CHAPTER IX

1. IX.1: "most secret" presumably because concerned with what is most ultimate and most deeply hidden; compare with *Kaṭha Upaniṣad,* I. 2. 12 (Bring to mind, through the practice of meditation [*yoga*] in regard to self, that god, ancient, hard to be seen, entered into a secret place, set in a cave and dwelling in the depths, the wise [*dhīro*] leaves behind both joy and sorrow.").

2. IX.1: *vijñāna-*.

3. IX.2: *pratyakṣāvagamaṁ*, literally, understood before the eyes, that is, directly and immediately apprehended.

4. IX.3: *dharmasya-*.

5. IX.7: *prakṛtiṁ*.

6. IX.8: *avaṣṭabhya*, to lean or rest on, but perhaps, to take hold of or seize.

7. IX.10: *-adhyakṣaṇa*. Cf. *Śvetāśvatara Upaniṣad,* VI. 11, for the one god hidden in all beings as *karmādhyakṣas*, overseeing or supervising *karman*.

8. IX.13: *jñātvā*.

9. IX.14: *-yuktā*.

10. IX.15: or, "and others also, sacrificing with the sacrifice of *jñāna*, attend upon me who face in all directions, attending with *jñāna* into my oneness, my distinctness (or separateness), and my manifoldness."

11. IX.16: compare with IV. 24.

12. IX.18: *sākṣī*. Cf. *Śvetāśvatara Upaniṣad,* VI. 11, and *Maitrī Upaniṣad,* VI. 16. Also *Praśna Upaniṣad,* VI. 5 (*paridraṣṭur*) and *Bṛhad-āraṇyaka-upaniṣad* IV. 3. 32 (*draṣṭā*).

13. IX.18: *prabhuḥ*. Cf. *Śvetāśvatara Upaniṣad,* III. 12 and 17. Also *Maitrī Upaniṣad,* III. 2 and VI. 16.

14. IX.18: *bhartā*. Cf. *Śvetāśvatara Upaniṣad,* I. 8.

15. IX.18: *gatir*. Cf. *Kaṭha Upaniṣad*, I. 3. 11. Also *Bṛhad-āraṇyaka-upaniṣad*, IV. 3. 32, and *Maitrī Upaniṣad*, I. 4 and VI. 24.

16. IX.18: cf. IV. 3 and V. 29.

17. IX.18: *śaraṇaṁ*. Cf. *Śvetāśvatara Upaniṣad*, III. 17.

18. IX.18: *nivāsaḥ*. Cf. *Śvetāśvatara Upaniṣad*, VI. 6 and *Muṇḍaka Upaniṣad*, III. 2. 1 (in these cases, the word is *dhāma*, not *nivāsa*).

19. IX.18: for the thought, cf. *Śvetāśvatara Upaniṣad*, III. 1-2; also *Muṇḍaka Upaniṣad*, II. 1. 1.

20. IX. 18: *nidhānaṁ*. Cf. *Muṇḍaka Upaniṣad*, III. 1. 6. Also *Śvetāśvatara Upaniṣad*, I.6 (*saṁsthā*).

21. IX.18: *bījam avyayam*. Cf. *Śvetāśvatara Upaniṣad*, VI. 12, and *Kaṭha Upaniṣad*, II.2. 12.

22. IX.19: for being and non-being, cf. *Chāndogya Upaniṣad*, III. 19, *Bṛhad-āraṇyaka-upaniṣad*, I. 2, and *Taittirīya Upaniṣad*, II. 7; also *Chāndogya Upaniṣad*, VI. 2, *Muṇḍaka Upaniṣad*, II. 2. 1, and *Praśna Upaniṣad*, II. 5. For a further meaning to the contrast, cf. *Bṛhad-āraṇyaka-upaniṣad*, I. 3. 28, and II. 3. 6.

23. IX.24: *prabhur*.

24. IX.24: that is, they return to worldly existence again when their enjoyment of merit in heaven is exhausted.

25. IX.30: *samyag vyavasito*.

26. IX.32: that is, born in low conditions (that of a woman, or the two lower castes) because of sins committed in former lives.

CHAPTER X

1. X.4: *buddhir*.

2. X.4: *jñānam*.

3. X.5: *bhāvā*.

4. X.6: there are various lists given, in the *Śatapatha Brāhmaṇa*, for example, and in the *Mahābhārata*.

5. X.6: the saints Sanatkumāra, Sanaka, Sanātana, and Sanandana.

6. X.6: Manu is the generic name for the fathers of the human race; there are fourteen Manus, each presiding over the world for a *manvantara* or period of 4,320,000 years. The first Manu was called Svāyaṁbhuva; the seventh, and ruler of the present age, is Vaivasvata (son of Vivasvat: cf. IV. 1).

7. X.7: *vibhūtiṁ*.

8. X.8: *budhā*.

9. X.9: compare with *Muṇḍaka Upaniṣad*, III. 1. 4 ("life is that which shines forth in all beings; knowing [*vijānan*] life, the knower [*vidvān*] does not talk of anything else. Sporting in self, delighting in self, performing action, this one is the greatest of the knowers of the holy power.").

10. X. 11: *ātmabhāvastho*, that is, standing over (or in) my own self's nature.

11. X.11: *ajñāna-*.

12. X.12: *dhāma*.

13. X.12: *vibhum.*

14. X.13: Nārada is a favorite figure in Hindu legend, especially connected with the *vīṇā* (lyre) and music and in later legend closely connected with Kṛṣṇa.

15. X.13: Vyāsa (whose name means "compiler", "arranger") is the reputed author of the *Mahābhārata* and the *Purāṇas*, as well as the compiler of the Veda in its present form.

16. X.21: the Ādityas are the sons of Aditi, a goddess of Vedic times; once six (or seven), they later became twelve, and were solar deities presiding over the months of the year.

17. X.21: the Maruts are sons of Rudra, a band of Vedic gods important particularly as Lords of wind and storm.

18. X.22: *cetanā.*

19. X.23: the Rudras, identified in the *Ṛg-veda* with the Maruts, are spirits of storm and destruction. Their leader, Rudra, became identified in post-Vedic times with Śiva (Śaṁkara), the destructive power in the trinity of Brahmā, Viṣṇu and Śiva, and often worshipped as the ultimate divinity.

20. X.23: the Yakṣas and Rākṣasas are lesser spirits, monsters or imps, ogres or goblins; Vitteśa, or Lord of Wealth, is Kubera, whose wealth the Yakṣas and Rākṣasas guard.

21. X.23: there are eight Vasus, divine powers of phenomena like wind and dawn and fire; their chief was Agni, or fire.

22. X.23: Meru is the mountain at the center of the earth; on its top live divine beings, and from its top flows the Ganges.

23. X.24: the chaplain and preceptor of the gods.

24. X.24: the son of Śiva, and god of war; also called Kārttikeya.

25. X.26: cf. XV. 1.

26. X.26: Citraratha is the leader of the Gandharvas, celestial beings of a sensual type (in the Vedas), but later, singers and musicians who attend divine feasts.

27. X.26: Kapila is the reputed founder of the Sāṁkhya philosophy.

28. X.27: the horse of Indra, who was among the things produced when the gods churned the ocean to secure nectar (the elixir of immortality).

29. X.27: the elephant of Indra, produced along with Uccaiḥśravas.

30. X.28: another product of the churning of the ocean: cf. III. 10.

31. X.28: a lord of the serpents.

32. X.29: the Nāgas are serpents with human heads, living in Pātāla; their leader is Ananta (or Śeṣa), the thousand-headed serpent on whose body Viṣṇu lies during his periodic sleep.

33. X.29: Once the Lord of Sky and Guardian of the order of things (*ṛta*) among the Vedic deities, Varuṇa later appears as Lord of the Waters.

34. X.29: chief of the Fathers (spirits of departed ancestors).

35. X.29: in the Veda, Yama and his sister Yamī are the first human pair. After death, Yama found the way to the other world, and the later dead have followed him. Thence he became lawgiver and judge of the dead.

36. X.30: the demons (Daityas) are descendants of Diti; Prahlāda, the son of the demon King, Hiraṇyakaśipu, became devoted to Viṣṇu and was saved by the latter when his father sought to kill him.

37. X.30: or, tiger.
38. X.30: the king of birds, on which Viṣṇu rides.
39. X.31: the hero of the *Rāmāyaṇa.*
40. X.33: *dhātā-.*
41. X.34: the corresponding Sanskrit nouns are all feminine in gender.
42. X.35: comparable to our late November-early December; the first month of the Hindu calendar.
43. X.36: *vyavasāyo-.*
44. X.36: or, of things good, the goodness.
45. X.37: Vṛṣṇi, son of Yadu, is the great-great-grandfather of Vasudeva, the father of Kṛṣṇa.
46. X.37: the son of Bhṛgu, and preceptor of the demons (Daityas). "Seer" is *kavi.*
47. X.41: *vibhūtimat,* possessed of *vibhūti.*
48. X.41: *śrīmad.*
49. X.41: *ūrjitam.*
50. X.42: *jñātena.*
51. X.42: or, "Abiding, I pervade this entire world with one portion (of myself)"; or, *viṣṭabhya,* "pervade", could mean "support" or "establish". Also, "of myself" might be "of my flaming splendor" (cf. X.41).

CHAPTER XI

1. XI.1: the reference is back to VII. 1-2, where Kṛṣṇa is promising to declare how Arjuna may gain full insight into him. That insight discloses Kṛṣṇa as more than mere mortal and as the changeless source of all transient things.
2. XI.6: twin Vedic deities, closely connected with Uṣas, the Dawn. They were celebrated as physicians and, generally, helpers in time of need.
3. XI.7: *icchasi.*
4. XI.9: a name for Viṣṇu.
5. XI.22: an inferior class of deity, connected with sacrificial rites and prayers, dwelling in an intermediate region between heaven and earth.
6. XI.22: a collective term for deities of an inferior order.
7. XI.22: a class of Fathers, or spirits of departed ancestors.
8. XI.22: originally a title applied to important gods, later the title came to stand for a class of anti-gods engaged in continual struggle with the gods.
9. XI.22: mortals who have gained perfection and dwell between earth and sun.
10. XI.27: recall that Arjuna is seated on his chariot in the no-man's land between the armies, and that, the call to battle having been sounded, the armies are on the verge of engaging each other, or indeed, have begun (cf. I. 20). Thus his vision here has this futural dimension, or, if the battle has already begun, this present dimension leading into the future of mutual destruction.
11. XI.31: *pravṛttim,* that is, your stepping forth in disclosure to me, that appearance of yours which dominates my attention now.

12. XI.31: *na....prajānāmi.*
13. XI.32: that is, "the time is ripe".
14. XI.32: *pravṛttaḥ.*
15. XI.34: he is King of Sindhu, and son-in-law of Dhṛtarāṣṭra.
16. XI.35: Arjuna.
17. XI.39: the Vedic god of wind.
18. XI.39: the moon.
19. XI.41: descendant of Yadu.
20. XI.43: compare with *Śvetāśvatara Upaniṣad*, VI. 8 ("..there is not seen his equal or his superior....").
21. XI.51: *prakṛtiṁ.*
22. XI.54: *jñātuṁ.*
23. XI.53-54: compare with *Muṇḍaka Upaniṣad*, III. 1. 8 ("He is not to be grasped by the eye nor also by speech and other sense-powers, nor by austerity nor by work [*karmaṇā*], but when one's essential being is purified by the light of *jñāna*, then alone, by meditating, one sees him who is without parts."); also, in the same Upaniṣad, III. 2. 3 (which is the same as *Kaṭha Upaniṣad*, I. 2. 23) ("This self cannot be attained by instruction nor by intellectual power, nor by much hearing-and-learning; he is to be attained by him alone whom this living-self chooses, to such a one does this living-self reveal its own self [*tanūṁ*].").

CHAPTER XII

1. XII.2: *-yuktā.*
2. XII.4: *samabuddhayaḥ*, with balanced *buddhi.*
3. XII.7: *-saṁsāra-.*
4. XII.9: *samādhātuṁ.*
5. XII.9: *abhyāsa-*; presumably this is the repeated effort to reach a steady concentration.
6. XII.8-11: these verses seem to mark, in reverse order, the phases in the development of the needed capacity in one who is moving along the path of action toward final release. There is the reaching to perfection in two stages, that of seeking to act in relinquishment of the fruit and that of giving over the action to Kṛṣṇa; then, with the reaching of perfection in action of this sort, there is possible the completion of the path, through two phases of meditation, one the practice aiming at steady concentration on Kṛṣṇa, the second the actuality of such concentration.
7. XII.12: this verse seems an interpolation, much in the way that II. 29 does. In both cases, a verse using words involved in the preceding context introduces an uncharacteristic shift and discordance of meaning. Here the words are *jñāna, abhyāsa,* and *dhyāna*. Cf. Hill, footnote 1, p. 170, for an indication of the problem of meaning and the efforts to deal with it; despite his valiant attempt, I agree with Barnett, who concludes his note on the verse (p. 203) with "v. 12 seems spurious".

8. XII.16: for undertakings as born of the predominance of *rajas*, cf. XIV. 12. The relinquishment here is toward enterprise as egoistic; put as Kṛṣṇa otherwise expresses it, one could utter the other side of the matter by "who has relinquished all undertakings to Me".

9. XII.20: *dharmyāmṛtam*. This could be translated also "*dharma*-accordant nectar", or even "*dharma*-accordant immortality". Cf. X. 18, and IX. 2.

CHAPTER XIII

1. Some manuscripts begin this Chapter with the following verse: "Arjuna said: Nature and Spirit, the field and the knower of the field, *jñāna* and what *jñāna* is of: these, Fair-hair, I desire to know." I have omitted it, in agreement with the tradition that it is a late interpolation. Cf. Hill, footnote 1, p. 173. In this connection, Zaehner comments on the character of the whole chapter (p. 336): "It is strange that after promising to give a brief account of the 'field' and the 'knower of the field' the author of the Gītā stops short after he has described the 'field'. He adds nothing to what he has said about the 'knower of the field' in verse 2, and the word does not appear again until verse 26. It is, then, quite possible that verses 7-25 are an interpolation introduced perhaps at the time when verse 0 which is missing in many MSS first became current. This seems all the more probable in that the definition of 'knowledge' in 7-11 is totally different from that in verses 2 and 34. There it is to know the 'field' and the 'knower of the field', that is to say, to know how to distinguish between them, whereas the 'knowledge' or 'wisdom' of 7-11 is simply a list of virtues and clearly is not at all what is meant by 'wisdom' in the rest of the Gītā, that is, a direct intuition of eternal Being."

2. XIII.1: in footnote 3, p. 173, Hill suggests (re the use of the term "field") that "perhaps the conception is that of an area where things grow and develop, then wither and die, and again come forth; a scene of continuous activity."

3. XIII.1: for other uses of this term, cf. *Śvetāśvatara Upaniṣad*, VI. 16, and *Maitrī Upaniṣad*, II. 5. Zaehner (pp. 333-4) refers to an earlier non-technical use of the term in a negative form (*a-kṣetra-jña*) in *Chāndogya Upaniṣad*, VIII. 3. 2. After quoting the passage ("just as [a group of people] who do not know the country [*a-kṣetra-jñā*] might wander about and pass over a hidden hoard of gold time and again without finding it, so too do all these creatures go on day after day without finding the Brahman-world within them, for they are led astray by unreality [*anṛta*]."), he continues: "The *kṣetra-jña*, then, is the 'man who knows the local country', the 'man who knows his own field' as we would say in English meaning the 'man who knows his own subject'. And it is interesting to note that in secular language this is precisely what *kṣetra-jña* means.... One's 'field', then, one's 'subject' is oneself as a psychosomatic complex, but under the field there is a 'hidden hoard of gold', the Brahman-world, which lies latent in the heart of all of us, and so one can only be said to be a true 'knower of the field' if one has discovered this treasure. The treasure is,

of course, the self; for as the Upaniṣad goes on to say: "Truly, this self is in the heart. . . . Then this deep serenity which, rising up from the body, attains the highest light, reveals itself in its own [true] form: this is the self. . This is the immortal, [this] freedom from fear: this is Brahman. And the name of Brahman is this—what-is-real-and-what-is-true."

4. XIII.4: *bahudhā*, many times, or, in many ways.

5. XIII.4: *viniścitaiḥ*, apparently, arrived at as settling deliberation and argument, hence conclusive, decisive, carrying conviction and assurance, considered.

6. XIII.4: probably passages ("strings" of verses) in the Upaniṣads and similar works in schools of the time (perhaps of the sort later systematized by Bādarāyaṇa).

7. XIII.5: earth, air, water, fire, and ether.

8. XIII.5: smell, touch, taste, form, and sound. The twenty-four factors mentioned in this verse as a whole constitute the Sāṁkhya enumeration of the factors of *prakṛti*.

9. XIII.6: *cetanā*.

10. XIII.7-11. *Jñāna* as the illuminated cognizance which opens the way to release, can not be gained except through a transformation in *buddhi* as a whole; since *buddhi* is not simply, or mainly, intellectual power, this means that *jñāna* must involve conditions of the person as a whole, expressing his way of taking life upon himself. For a similar contention, cf. *Muṇḍaka Upaniṣad*, III. 2.3-4.

11. XIII.13: this verse is the same as *Śvetāśvatara Upaniṣad*, III. 16. For the image, cf. also (same Upaniṣad) III. 3.

12. XIII.14: the first half of this verse is the same as the first half of *Śvetāśvatara Upaniṣad*, III. 17. Cf. also III. 19 (same Upaniṣad).

13. XIII.15: cf. *Īśā Upaniṣad*, 5 ("It moves and It moves not, It is far and It is near; It is within all this, and It is also outside all this."); also *Muṇḍaka Upaniṣad*, III. 1. 7 ("...farther than the far, yet here near at hand...").

14. XIII.17: cf. *Muṇḍaka Upaniṣad*, II. 2.10 ("light of lights"), and *Śvetāśvatara Upaniṣad*, III. 8 ("beyond darkness"); also *Bṛhad-āraṇyaka-upaniṣad*, IV. 4. 16 ("light of lights"), and *Maitrī Upaniṣad*, VI. 24 and 30 ("beyond darkness").

15. XIII.19: *prakṛtiṁ*.

16. XIII.22: *upadraṣṭā-*. See note 12 to Chapter IX above for relevant references.

17. XIII.22: for the image, cf. *Muṇḍaka Upaniṣad*, III. 1. 1-2 (same as *Śvetāśvatara Upaniṣad*, IV. 6-7).

18. XIII.22: *bhartā*. See note 14 to Chapter IX above for relevant references.

19. XIII.22: for the term (*bhoktā*), cf. *Śvetāśvatara Upaniṣad*, V.7 and I. 8; also *Kaṭha Upaniṣad*, I. 3. 4. and *Maitrī Upaniṣad*, VI. 10.

20. XIII.22: *maheśvaraḥ*. Cf. *Śvetāśvatara Upaniṣad*, IV. 10 and VI.7.

21. XIII.24: *dhyānena-*.

22. XIII.24: *sāṁkhyena*.

23. XIII.25: *atitaranty eva*. If *eva*, in emphasizing "they cross beyond death" ("indeed they do"), is taken as suggesting that they do so in the same sense as

the others, that is, as going to a condition of no return, this would be a significant departure from Kṛṣṇa's teaching otherwise, or it would represent an elliptical mode of speech omitting the intermediary steps (included in which would eventually be *jñāna*). But more likely, *eva* anticipates "taking refuge in what they have heard" (presumably, here, in revelation) and signifies that even men who do this can be said to cross beyond death ("indeed they do, that phrase can be used of them"), but in their own sense. That sense, then, would be, they go to the heavenly world; cf. *Kaṭha Upaniṣad*, I. 1. 12-19 (especially 12 and 18) for such a meaning. In any case, Verses 24-25 "appear to bear no relation whatever either to what precedes or to what follows" (Zaehner, p. 346); they might well represent an interpolation that should be excised.

24. XIII.30: *vistāraṁ*. Note how this image fits in with the sense of *brahman* involved in its etymology, as expansive. Cf. note 61 to Chapter II above; also Commentary, p. 117.

25. XIII.31: *nirguṇatvāt*. Cf. *Śvetāśvatara Upaniṣad*, VI. 11 (*nirguṇaḥ*). Also *Maitrī Upaniṣad*, VI. 10 (*nirguṇo bhoktā*) and VII. 1 (*nirguṇaḥ*).

26. XIII.33: cf. *Śvetāśvatara Upaniṣad*, V. 4: "As the sun shines, illumining all regions, above, below and across, so that one god, adorable Lord, stands over whatever creatures are born from a womb."

CHAPTER XIV

1. XIV.2: *sādharmyam*.

2. XIV.3: for a similar thought, cf. *Muṇḍaka Upaniṣad*, I. 1. 6 ("That which is invisible, ungraspable, without family or caste, without sight or hearing, without hands or feet, eternal, pervasive, omnipresent, exceedingly subtle: that is the Undecaying which the wise [*dhīrāḥ*] see as the womb of beings."). Also *Kaṭha Upaniṣad*, II. 2. 12, and *Śvetāśvatara Upaniṣad*, VI. 12, for the "seed".

3. XIV.8: *ajñāna-jaṁ*; I treat *jam* as *janam* and translate "gives birth to", in the light of Verses 9, 16, and 17 below. Otherwise, "is born of lack of *jñāna*".

4. XIV.10: reading *vardhate* instead of *bhavati*.

5. XIV.20: assuming the body here is the field (cf. Chapter XIII). If "body" be taken as the particular body, then the compound should be read as "giving rise to the body".

6. XIV.20: Zaehner, taking this to be "a reflection of the current Buddhist view that birth, old age, and death are the outward and visible signs that show that all phenomenal existence is 'suffering, pain, or ill' (*dukkha*)", reads the compound so as to translate: "from the sufferings of birth, death, and old age".

7. XIV.23: *udāsīnavad*, literally, like one seated apart.

8. XIV.25: cf. note 8 to Chapter XII.

9. XIV.27: *pratiṣṭhā-*, that is, as its incarnation I am the place where that power dwells (particularly, dwells for the purpose of approaching human beings and receiving worship and devotion from them).

10. XIV.27: *dharmasya*.

CHAPTER XV

1. XV.1: *aśvattham*. Cf. *Kaṭha Upaniṣad*, II. 3. 1, for another use of this same image.

2. XV.1-2: in the imagery there is a peculiarity ("roots above and branches below") that has led some commentators to take the *aśvattha* to be a banyan tree (whose branches descend to become new—secondary—roots) rather than a *pīpal* tree. Hill's footnote, pp. 185-6, is helpful here: "The *aśvattha* (probably derived from *aśva-sthā*—the tree under which horses stand) is the Ficus Religiosa, or *pīpal* tree, well known to those who live in India as a tree held in great reverence among Hindus. It does not, like its cousin the banyan, drop aerial rootlets to take fresh root in the earth. Why, then, is it said to have roots above and branches below? The formation of the tree is peculiar, in that its roots (which often stand in part above the ground) do not altogether, as in other trees, lose themselves in a central rounded trunk, but to a great extent retaining their separate form, climb up in a cluster, each to spread out into a separate branch. Each root is thus continuous with its own branch; and therefore, root and branch being inseparably one, it is possible to speak of the branch as descending to the earth, and of the root as rising aloft. This interpretation of the phrase not only explains the choice of the *aśvattha* as a symbol, but is an aid to the understanding of the figure. 'Above' then, means 'above the ground in the visible world'; 'below' means 'down to the hidden places below ground'. Root, and branch, as one, are *prakṛti*; below ground, *avyakta*; above ground, *vyakta*. There is no need to distinguish between the *mūla* of 1 and the *mūlāni* of 2." *Vyakta* and *avyakta* mean manifest and unmanifest, *mūla* and *mūlāni* are singular and plural of "root'.

3. Reading *prapadyet* (the Kashmir reading, according to Besant-Das) instead of *prapadye*. Cf. Hill's note on the point, p. 187.

4. XV.4: *pravṛttiḥ*.

5. XV.6: for a similar phrase, cf. *Kaṭha Upaniṣad*, II. 2. 15 (the same verse appears in *Śvetāśvatara Upaniṣad*, VI. 14, and *Muṇḍaka Upaniṣad*, II. 2. 11).

6. XV.9: *viṣayān upasevate* seems to carry two meanings at once, frequenting the realms of sense and cultivating what is to be found there.

7. XV.7-10: for similar thoughts, cf. *Kaṭha Upaniṣad*, I. 3. 4-9., and *Śvetāśvatara Upaniṣad*, I. 8-9; also *Praśna Upaniṣad*, III. 3-10.

8. XV.14: masticated, swallowed (or drunk), sucked, licked.

9. XV.15: *apohanaṁ*, loss, or, the dispelling of doubt.

10. XV.15: *vedānta-*, literally, end of the Veda; at that time in history, this would mean the Upaniṣads and perhaps (cf. Barnett) also the Āraṇyakas.

11. XV.16: *kūṭastho*.

12. XV.17: for a similar thought, cf. *Śvetāśvatara Upaniṣad*, I. 8-10.

13. XV.18: for a similar thought, cf. *Muṇḍaka Upaniṣad*, II. 1. 1-2.

14. XV.19: *-bhāvena*.

15. XV.20: *śāstram*.

16. XV.20: *buddhvā*.

CHAPTER XVI

1. XVI.1: cf. XVII.16. Also compare with *Muṇḍaka Upaniṣad*, III. 1. 8 (*viśuddha-sattvas*).
2. XVI.1: *jñāna-*.
3. XVI.1: *-yoga-*.
4. XVI.3: *sampadaṁ daivīm abhijātasya*: belong to one fit by birth for a divine issue (or for divine accomplishment), or, belong to one born to a divine destiny (or lot, or estate). Similarly in Verse 5, and correspondingly in Verse 4.
5. XVI.4: *ajñānam.*
6. XVI.4: *abhijātasya...sampadam āsurīm*: see note 4 above (to XVI. 3). For the meaning, see the account in the rest of this Chapter, of how some men achieve a demonic birth, fitting them for a demonic issue (or accomplishment), or constituting for them a demonic destiny (or lot, or estate).
7. XVI.5: *vimokṣāya.*
8. XVI.6: for a similar thought, cf. *Bṛhad-āraṇyaka-upaniṣad*, I. 3. 1.
9. XVI.8: apparently, it is denied that the world is constituted in a creational fashion, involving a source and a governing divine power, an ordainment toward an end beyond mere existence, a moral ordering of human life, and a truth that is more than worldly and that concerns this end, that moral order, and the beginning of things. Instead, the world is affirmed as simply there, to be enjoyed; and the enjoyers (living beings) are generated (not created) through the results of sexual passion.
10. XVI.11: *cintām.* Cf. the "endless" *buddhi* of II. 41.
11. XVI.11: cf. *Kaṭha Upaniṣad*, I. 2. 6 (see note 17 to Chapter VII).
12. XVI.23 and 24: *śāstra-*.

CHAPTER XVII

1. XVII.1: *niṣṭhā.*
2. XVII.1: note the connection of this question with the thought in Verses 23-24 in the previous Chapter.
3. XVII.3: compare with *Chāndogya Upaniṣad*, III. 14. 1 ("..now in truth, a person is made of purpose, according to the purpose a person had in this world so does he become on departing hence..."), and *Praśna Upaniṣad*, III. 10 ("What one's thinking is, with that one enters life; life united with vital heat together with self leads to a world that accords with one's purpose.").
4. XVII.4: cf. IX. 25.
5. XVII.5: *-śāstra-*.
6. XVII.8: that is, substantial and nourishing, so that it "stays with" one.
7. XVII.13: *mantra-*, hymns, or more broadly, sacred text.
8. XVII.16: *-prasādaḥ*, translated by Aurobindo as "clear and calm gladness". Cf. note 53 to Chapter II, as well as Aurobindo's comments in Notes II. 65.

9. XVII.16: purity of *bhāva-*.
10. XVII.18: that is, is not steady, undertaken with constancy and a sense of proportion (fluctuates between extremes).
11. XVII.27: *tadarthīyaṁ*, for the sake of that (such steadfastness), or, for such purposes (sacrifice, austerity, charity).

CHAPTER XVIII

1. XVIII.1: Keśin was a Daitya who attacked Kṛṣṇa in the form of a horse.
2. XVIII.1: *saṁnyāsasya* (*saṁnyāsa* in the genitive case).
3. XVIII.1: *tyāgasya* (*tyāga* in the genitive case).
4. XVIII.2: *nyāsaṁ*.
5. XVIII.3: perhaps because "all undertakings are clouded by defect" (XVIII. 48); but most likely, because of the identification of action with action that binds (it being inconceivable to some thoughtful men how social action, for example, could be undertaken, no matter how idealistic its forms, on grounds that were not implicitly egoistic).
6. XVIII.4: 'three-fold' here presumably means according to the *guṇas*; hence the reference is to Verses 7-9 to come, to which Verses 5-6 serve as introductory statement of the basic thought.
7. XVIII.5: *manīṣiṇām*.
8. XVIII.10: *medhāvī*.
9. XVIII.13: that is, at the end of the first or perfect age, when the Sāṁkhya teaching was still preserved uncorrupted. Cf. III. 3, and IV. 1-2.
10. XVIII.14: that is, the body. For *adhiṣṭhāna* in that meaning, cf. *Chāndogya Upaniṣad*, VIII. 12. 1.
11. XVIII.14: that is, the sense organs and powers of action.
12. XVIII.14: that is, the vital breaths (organic functions and the like).
13. XVIII.14: *daivaṁ*, that is, the world upheld by spirit and entering as environment and circumstance into the making of action. Cf. Hill, footnote 4, pp. 204-5 for a discussion of this and of the five-fold division as a whole.
14. XVIII.16: that is, sees only himself as active center to be responsible for the deed, as if this were not simply one of the five factors involved in the determination of action. The *guṇas* , or *prakṛti* articulated by the *guṇas*, accomplish actions in the conjunction of center and an environment of centers (both poles being qualified in many ways); within this conjunction, the center is simply one factor. Since this center is only one side of the self of the being in question, namely, the active side, there is also a second sense in which the mistaking of "I am the doer" is at times understood. And that is where this is a matter of identifying one's own self wholly with the active side of oneself.
15. XVIII.18: *jñānaṁ*.
16. XVIII.21: cf. VII. 12 and 13; X. 4 and 5, also 17; XIII. 30. "Knows separately" probably means "knows them in separation from the Lord, not knowing them in their expressing and manifesting the Lord". This could also

include knowing them as if they were isolated from each other and not interconnected in essence.

17. XVIII.22: that is, the five-fold cause (Verses 13-15 above); this verse echoes Verse 16 above.

18. XVIII.24: or, "with great exertion" (emphasizing thus the concentration and channelling of energy on a large scale, rather than the unnaturalness and distortion that ego-guided undertaking involves—and involves even though one becomes so used to it that it seems "natural" or is no longer even noticed).

19. XVIII.26: *-utsāha-*. Or, "confidence", perhaps "zeal".

20. XVIII.28: *ayuktaḥ*. Or, "undisciplined", "discordant, disharmonious".

21. XVIII.28: *prākṛtaḥ*. Or, "vulgar".

22. XVIII.30: cf. XVI. 7, for *pravṛtti* and *nivṛtti* , ways of action and inaction.

23. XVIII.33: compare with *Kaṭha Upaniṣad*, II. 3. 11 ("The steady control of the senses: that, they consider to be *yoga*; then one becomes vigilant-and-attentive (*apramattas*). *Yoga* indeed is an arising and vanishing." [That is, it is the ceasing of certain functionings and the arising of a stable state of vigilant awareness.]).

24. XVIII.37: Verses 36 and 37 could be taken together and divided differently, so as to read: "But hear now from me, Bull-of-the-Bharatas, the three-fold happiness. That in which, due to repeated practise, one takes delight and enters into the end of sorrow, and which, born of clarity in one's awareness of self, is at first like poison but in the end is the finest nectar: that happiness is sattvic."

25. XVIII.42: *jñānaṁ*.

26. XVIII.42: *vijñānaṁ*.

27. XVIII.45: *abhirataḥ*, attentive to, or, taking delight in.

28. XVIII.45: the achievement of success in the perfection of one's capacity for action as agent of Kṛṣṇa; such success in *kriyā-yoga* is succeeded then by a further stage, that of the meditative success in *rāja-yoga* which precedes final release (cf. Verses 49-56).

29. XVIII.47: *sva-bhāva*. Cf. III. 35.

30. XVIII.51: cf. Verse 33 above, for example.

31. XVIII.52: *dhyāna-*.

32. XVII.55: cf. XI. 54.

33. XVIII.59: *vyavasāyas*.

34. XVIII.59: *prakṛtis*.

35. XVIII.61: recall here the Lord as time (XI. 32). For the wheel-image, cf. *Śvetāśvatara Upaniṣad*, I. 6 and VI. 1. Though this imagery seems to invite a mechanistic view of things, keep in mind that through time the Lord (as a living power) enters beings into a vital and active existence which He pervades and (directly or indirectly) animates. Thus while the image of a wheel conveys that the unfolding of time is steady, circular, and beyond one's will to control, it also tempts one to a false understanding of this, since one's relation to time and to its source is inward and vital and active, not of the external and mechanical and inactive sort one has to such a wheel.

36. XVIII.62: cf. XV. 19.

37. XVIII.66: that is, *dharma* as something to be engaged in for its opening the way to heaven, hence as having the power to move one because of egoistic grounds.

38. XVIII.67: for similar prohibitions, cf. *Bṛhad-āraṇyaka-upaniṣad*, VI. 3. 12; *Chāndogya Upaniṣad*, III. 11. 5; *Muṇḍaka Upaniṣad*, III. 2. 10; *Maitrī Upaniṣad*, VI.29: *Śvetāśvatara Upaniṣad*, VI. 22-23.

39. XVIII.68: for a similar thought, cf. *Kaṭha Upaniṣad*, I. 3. 17.

40. XVIII.72: that is, attentive and concentrated.

41. XVIII.73: *acyuta*, the same epithet that Arjuna used when he first spoke to Kṛṣṇa in the poem (I. 21).

42. XVIII.73: cf. II. 63. Also compare with *Chāndogya Upaniṣad*, VII. 26. 2 ("...When nourishment is pure, essential-nature is pure; when essential-nature is pure, memory is firm-and-lasting; when memory is gained, there is release from all knots...").

43. XVIII.75: it was Vyāsa who gave Saṁjaya the super-natural power to see and hear at a distance.

44. XVIII.78: *nītir*. This has both a moral and a political significance; cf. X. 38.

Notes to the Commentary

1. In regard to the import of the drama for the interpretation of the meaning of the teaching, it is interesting to note Edgerton's response. To begin with, he is forceful in his recognition of the work as a poem: "a religious, devotional poem". And his sensitivity to its dramatic movement as such is implicit in his notice of the poem's structure. Trying to explain (in his Interpretation) why it is only in Chapter IX that he has come to discuss the relation of God to human salvation, he suggests: ". . . . the poem itself affords a precedent for approximately such an arrangement. The Gītā does not begin with this subject; and references to it in the early chapters are few and scattering. In the middle chapters of the work it gradually becomes more prominent, until it finally occupies the center of the stage, with the climax in the eleventh chapter, in which the mystic vision of God's supernal form is revealed to Arjuna. After this, somewhat anti-climatically, the Gītā gradually drops into other themes, again to return to the theme of salvation through God towards the end of its final, summary chapter (the eighteenth)" (p. 172). It is true that this characterization is in terms of content, explicitly; but it seems also to reflect Edgerton's awareness of, and response to, the poem's "poetic, emotional point of view".

However, this awareness and response are not allowed into his interpretation at all, presumably because as a poem the *Gītā* makes an appeal which is "to the emotions rather than to the intellect", or, which is "mystical" (and that means, for Edgerton, "emotional", without appeal to "the reasoning faculty of mankind"). It is the prevalence of this "rationalist" attitude (p. 106) which can see no more to a poem than the appeal to emotion and which can identify that with the mystical, that probably explains why Edgerton's interpretation does not, and will not, take its guidance from the poem as drama ("It is likely that the Bhagavad Gītā was not a part of the original epic narrative. Possibly it was composed, or inserted in its present position, by a later interpolator. To be sure, he must have had in mind the dramatic situation in which he has placed the *Gītā*, for he repeatedly makes reference to it. But these references are purely formal and external; they do not concern the essentials of the work. We must think of the Gītā primarily as a unit, complete in itself, without reference to its surroundings. Its author, or whoever placed it in its present position, was interested chiefly in the religious doctrines to be set forth, not in external dramatic forms" [pp. 105-6]). Perhaps it is his rationalism, and its false dichotomies, which also is in good measure responsible for his view of the *Gītā* as a "mixture of discordant theories" (p. 172). Yet despite the attitude with which Edgerton approaches his subject, the preliminary Chapters in his interpretation, and to a much lesser extent, that interpretation itself, contain much that is suggestive, at least if one can take them out of the philosophically inadequate framework into which Edgerton has placed them.

Almost at the other end of the spectrum philosophically, is Aurobindo, and his is also a quite different approach in regard to the dramatic character of the poem. Noting that the *Gītā* is peculiar among the great religious books of the world in that it does not stand apart as a work by itself but appears as an episode in an epic history, he understands this setting to mean that "the teaching of the Gītā must therefore be regarded not merely in the light of a general spiritual philosophy or ethical doctrine, but as bearing upon a practical crisis in the application of ethics and spirituality to human life" (p. 1, footnote). Despite the fact that this is still too narrow a grasp of the matter, Aurobindo is led to pay fairly close attention to the drama and its unfolding in his interpretation of the poem. Refusing the allegorical method of explaining the drama, and insisting on its literal meaning, he sees the drama as expressing something typical: "...setting of the doctrine, though not symbolical, is certainly typical, as indeed the setting of such a discourse as the Gita must necessarily be if it is to have any relation at all with that which it frames" (p. 4, footnote). For notes expressing his reading of the poem in this dimension, see references to be found in the Notes Concerning Text, cited under the Chapter-and-verse numbers as follows: I. 21; I. 29; I. 36; I. 42; II.1; II. 7; II. 10; II. 11; II. 31; II. 32; II.37; II. 54; X.1; XI. 2.

2. Cf. note 6 to Chapter II.

3. For the Sāṁkhya, cf. Barnett, pp. 15-29, but with this caution: after providing an account of the Sāṁkhya as it became formalized and systematized after the time of the *Gītā*, Barnett says (footnote, p. 72): "Much that is here (that is, in the *Gītā*) paraded under the name 'Sāṁkhya' seems to be not Sāṁkhyan at all, but of miscellaneous origin". Such an appearance is intelligible if the Sāṁkhya in the *Gītā* concerns that tradition in the making, not as it came to be in relatively finished form. In this regard, for example, Edgerton suggests: the existence of God is "denied by Sāṁkhya", "or rather, by certain representatives of the later Sāṁkhya, which have been, a little hastily, taken as typical of the whole school. As a matter of fact, a theistic Sāṁkhya has probably always existed, and was certainly known late as well as early" (p. 145, with footnote 29). Hill seems rather judicious in this matter: "It is probable that at the time when the Bhagavadgītā was being composed Sāṁkhya notions were afloat but had not yet been reduced to so dogmatic a scheme as the Kārikās present. One or two passages in the old Bṛhadāraṇyaka and Chāndogya Upaniṣads have been claimed as sources whence certain conceptions of the later Sāṁkhya were derived; but it is not till the Kaṭha and the Praśna, and especially the Śvetāśvatara and the Maitrī Upaniṣads, that any certain Sāṁkhya teaching is to be found, though even in these allied with a Supreme. The term Sāṁkhya first occurs in the Śvetāśvatara Upaniṣad compounded with *yoga*, with which it appears to be contrasted as meditation with practical devotion....In the Gītā Sāṁkhya is contrasted with Yoga, the former being the theoretical reflection of those who rely on knowledge alone for release, while the latter is practical endeavour and the systematic exercise of self-control; the two are, however, complementary systems and their goal is one. Sāṁkhya is becoming more defined as a system, and it is probable that Kapila is recognized as its founder. But there is no indication that a Supreme *puruṣa* has been abandoned; and, indeed, if the system had at that time been recognized as atheistic, Kṛṣṇa's exaltation of Kapila as chief of the perfected would not have been consistent with his scorn of those who deny a Lord" (pp. 36-7).

Yet Hill takes the Sāṁkhya to be "derived from the Upaniṣads" (p. 38), rather than as developing independently and influencing the seers and authors of the Upaniṣads. Aurobindo seems closer to the point. In his discussion of Sāṁkhya and Yoga (pp. 25-32), he says: "What, then, are the Sankhya and Yoga of which the Gita speaks? They are certainly not the systems which have come down to us under these names as enunciated respectively in the Sankhya Karika of Ishwara Krishna and the Yoga aphorisms of Patanjali. Still, all that is essential in the Sankhya and Yoga systems, all in them that is large, catholic and universally true, is admitted by the Gita, even though it does not limit itself by them like the opposing schools. Its Sankhya is the catholic and Vedantic Sankhya such as we find it in its first principles and elements in the great Vedantic synthesis of the Upanishads and in the later developments of the Puranas. Its idea of Yoga is that large idea of a principally subjective practice and inner change, necessary for the finding of the Self or the union with God, of which the Raja-Yoga is only one special application and not the most important and vital" (p. 25).

Aurobindo's discussion in these pages could be understood as presupposing a non-Vedāntic (and non-Vedic) Sāṁkhya and Yoga, which were gradually taken up into the Upaniṣads and entered into that (Vedāntic) mode of thought. In that assimilation, for example, the Upaniṣads seek to undercut the absolute dualism of Sāṁkhya. And the *Gītā* could then be understood as developing this effort of assimilation further, with emphasis upon *yoga* that deepened the notions of Yoga as well as those of Sāṁkhya (in its non-Vedic and in its Vedāntic forms). Yet I am not at all sure that this notion of the development is in Aurobindo's mind.

4. For the Yoga, cf. Barnett, pp. 29-36, but with a similar caution as in respect of his treatment of Sāṁkhya. Again, Hill shows a judiciousness, taking the Yoga as "beginning to take shape" at the time of the *Gītā* and saying: "...we must not read into the Gītā that strictly systematic philosophy of control which found expression so many centuries later in the Yogasūtras and which gave rise to so vast a literature in after days. It was, perhaps, the special merit of the author of the Gītā that he applied these current methods of control to man's whole personality, bringing into their right and balanced relationship the functions of reason and will and emotion. It must also be borne in mind that for the Gītā, unlike the Yogasūtras, yoga could retain its fuller, more original content—control that leads to union with Vāsudeva-Brahman" (pp. 53-54). Barnett recognizes that the Yoga of the *Gītā* is not that of Patanjali (p. 64), but he seeks to understand this as due to the fact that "in borrowing the Yoga of Patanjali the author of the Bhagavad-gītā has filled its outlines with a new content" (p. 71). This is so not simply in regard to the ideas of God and of isolation, but also to the phases of *kriyā-yoga* and *rāja-yoga* (pp. 65-66).

5. Hence the "bare" senses of V. 11; free of ego-guidance, they subserve *buddhi* and one's deeper self.

6. In his study of the *Gītā* Aurobindo works within a traditional Hindu way of dividing the poem, into sets of six Chapters; but he understands the nature of the focus in each set in his own fashion. According to it, the first six Chapters relate and synthesize works and knowledge in giving the primary basis for its teachings; the second set lays down a large metaphysical statement

of the nature of the Divine Being and on that foundation closely relates and synthetises knowledge and devotion. Then "the Gītā in its last six chapters, in order to found on a clear and complete knowledge the way of the soul's rising out of the lower into the divine nature, restates in another form the enlightenment the Teacher has already imparted to Arjuna. Essentially it is the same knowledge, but details and relations are now made prominent and assigned their entire significance, thoughts and truths brought out in their full value that were alluded to only in passing or generally stated in the light of another purpose" (p. 189).

Notes Concerning Text

CHAPTER I

I.1: in the Sanskrit, *dharma* is the first word of the poem, excluding "Dhṛtarāṣṭra said".

I.7: *saṁjñārthaṁ*, for the sake of mutual understanding. Other translations are "for thy information" (Radhakrishnan, hereafter R; Besant-Das, hereafter B-D; Gandhi-Desai, hereafter G-D); "for thy special notice" (Aurobindo, hereafter A); "for thy recognition" (Deutsch, hereafter D); "that thou mayest know" (Hill, hereafter H); and "so that you may be kept informed" (Zaehner, hereafter Z).

I.10: *aparyāptaṁ..paryāptaṁ*. Translators differ in their interpretation of the meaning of these terms. Thus H ("all too weak ..all too strong"), B-D, D, and Edgerton (hereafter, E) ("insufficient..sufficient"); Z ("imperfect.. perfect"); but Barnett (hereafter B) ("cannot be coped with..can be coped with") and R and A ("unlimited..limited") reverse the sense. The former alternative seems more natural, as Hill notes: it is supported by the special command to guard Bhīṣma, and by the effort of the latter (Verse 12) to encourage Duryodhana with his conch.

I.11: *ayaneṣu*, comings and goings of battle. E translates "movements" and Z "goings", but others are quite different. Thus "ranks" (H) or "rank and file" (B-D), "fronts" (R, D) or "fronts of the battle" (A), and even "entrance" (G-D).

I.12: *kuru-vṛddhaḥ pitāmahaḥ....pratāpavān*, literally, Kuru-aged-grandfather ..majestic. Since both sides are descended from Kuru, and since Bhīṣma is grandfather to members of both sides, the "Kuru" might signify this status (cf. Verse 25, similarly). Yet normally Kaurava (descendant of Kuru) is distinguished from Pāṇḍava, and the Kuru name signifies the one side preeminently. Given the context, then, I translate "Duryodhana's aged but majestic grandfather". In the remainder of the verse, some translators separate the lion's roar from the blowing of the conch; for example, "roared aloud like a lion and blew his conch" (R, but likewise A, G-D, E, D, Z; as against H, B, B-D).

I.14: *yukte*, harnessed. This reflects the basic meaning of *yuj*. Cf. note to II. 48.

I.20: in connection with note 30 to Chapter I, G-D and B translate "about to begin" whereas H, A, and E translate "having begun". D has "as (it) began", and Z "the clash of arms was on". R seeks to straddle the fence, as does B-D, in effect giving two translations, one on each side.

I.21: Aurobindo notes: "The Gita starts from action and Arjuna is the man of action and not of knowledge. It is typical of the pragmatic man that it is through his sensations that he awakens to the meaning of his action. He has asked his friend and charioteer to place him between the two armies, not with any profounder idea, but with the proud intention of viewing and looking in the face these myriads of the champions of unrighteousness whom he has to meet and conquer and slay 'in this holiday of right' so that the right may prevail. It is as he gazes that the revelation of the meaning of a civil and domestic war comes home to him, a war in which no only men of the same race, the same nation, the same clan, but those of the same family and household stand upon opposite sides. All whom the social man holds most dear and sacred, he must meet as enemies and slay, all these social ties have to be cut asunder by the sword. It is not that he did not know these things before, but he has never realised it all; obsessed by his claims and wrongs and by the principles of his life, the struggle for the right, the duty of the Kshatriya to protect justice and the law and fight and beat down injustice and lawless violence, he has neither thought out deeply nor felt it in his heart and at the core of his life. And now it is shown to his vision by the divine charioteer, placed sensationally before his eyes, and comes home to him like a blow delivered at the very centre of his sensational, vital and emotional being."

I.22: *nirīkṣe,* take a good look at. Other translations are "observe" (R), "behold" (H, B-D, G-D, B, D), "scan" (Z), and "view" (A).

I.23: *avekṣe,* carefully to observe. Other translations are "mark" (B), but simply "look at" (R) or "gaze on" (H, B-D) or "look upon" (A) or "survey" (G-D) or "see" (E, Z, D) otherwise.

I.25: *-pramukhataḥ,* facing. Other translations are "before the face of" (H), "before" (B), "in front of" (A, G-D, E, R, Z, D) and "over against" (B-D).

I.27: *samīkṣya,* having looked closely at. Other translations are simply "beholding" (G-D, B) or "saw" (R H, B-D, A, E) or "seeing" (Z, D).

I.28: *viṣīdan,* weighed down by his sorrow. Other translations are "sorrowfully" (D), "in sadness" (R, B-D), "in sadness and dejection" (A), "desponding" (Z), "despondent" (E), "in despair" (H, B) and "in anguish" (G-D).

I.29: Aurobindo notes: "The first result is a violent sensational and physical crisis which produces a disgust of the action and its material objects and of life itself. He rejects the vital aim pursued by egoistic humanity in its action—happiness and enjoyment; he rejects the vital aim of the Kshatriya, victory and rule and power and the government of men. What after all is this fight for justice when reduced to its practical terms, but just this, a fight for the interests of himself, his brothers and his party, for possession and enjoyment and rule? But at such a cost these things are not worth having. For they are of no value in themselves, but only as a means to the right maintenance of social and national life and it is these very aims that in the person of his kin and his race he is about to destroy. And then comes the cry of the emotions."

I.36: Aurobindo notes: "The whole thing is a dreadful sin,—for now the moral sense awakens to justify the revolt of the sensations and the emotions. It is a sin, there is no right nor justice in mutual slaughter; especially are those who are to be slain the natural objects of reverence and of love, those without whom one would not care to live, and to violate these sacred feelings can be no virtue. Granted that the offence, the aggression, the first sin, the crimes of greed and selfish passion which have brought things to such a pass came from the other side; yet armed resistance to wrong under such circumstances would be itself a sin and crime worse than theirs because they are blinded by passion and unconscious of guilt, while on this side it would be with a clear sense of guilt that the sin would be committed. And for what? For the maintenance of family morality, of the social law and the law of the nation? These are the very standards that will be destroyed by this civil war."

I.42: Aurobindo notes: "Although Arjuna is himself concerned only with his own situation, his inner struggle and the law of action he must follow, yet the particular question he raises, in the manner in which he raises it does really bring up the whole question of human life and action, what the world is and why it is and how possibly, it being what it is, life here in the world can be reconciled with life in the spirit. And all this deep and difficult matter the Teacher insists on resolving as the very foundation of his command to an action which must proceed from a new poise of being and by the light of a liberating knowledge. But what, then, is it that makes the difficulty for the man who has to take the world as it is and act in it and yet would live, within, the spiritual life? What is this aspect of existence which appals his awakened mind and brings about what the title of the first chapter of the Gita calls significantly the Yoga of the dejection of Arjuna, the dejection and discouragement felt by the human being when he is forced to face the spectacle of the universe as it really is with the veil of the ethical illusion, the illusion of self-righteousness torn from his eyes, before a higher reconciliation with himself is effected? It is that aspect which is figured outwardly in the carnage and massacre of Kuruksetra and spiritually by the vision of the Lord of all things as Time arising to devour and destroy the creatures whom it has made. The outward aspect is that of world-existence and human existence proceeding by struggle and slaughter; the inward aspect is that of the universal Being fulfilling himself in a vast creation and a vast destruction. Life a battle and a field of death, this is Kuruksetra; God the Terrible, this is the vision that Arjuna sees on that field of massacre."

I.46: *kṣemataraṁ*, better. Other translations of "safer" (E) or "more comfortable" (B) or "happier" (G-D, H) emphasize other sides to the word.

CHAPTER II

II.1: *āviṣṭam*, burdened with. Other translations are "overcome" (R, D, B-D, G-D), "stricken" (B), or "filled with" (H), "possessed by" (E) and "invaded by" (A).

viṣīdantam, sinking into depression. Other translations are "his heart overcome by depression and discouragement" (A), "much depressed in mind" (R), "despondent" (B-D, D, E), "desponding" (Z), "despairing" (H, B), and "sorrowing" (G-D).

Aurobindo notes: "This pity of Arjuna is quite different from the godlike compassion mentioned later on in the Gita, which observes with an eye of love and wisdom and calm strength the battle and the struggle, the strength and weakness of man, his virtues and sins, his joy and suffering, his knowledge and his ignorance, and enters into it all to help and to heal. Arjuna's pity is a form of self-indulgence; it is the physical shrinking of the nerves from the act of slaughter, the egoistic emotional shrinking of the heart from the destruction of the Dhritarashtrians because they are 'one's own people' and without them life will be empty."

And again, with respect to Verse 3, Aurobindo notes: "Arjuna's pity is a weakness of the mind and senses,—a weakness which may well be beneficial to men of a lower grade of development, who have to be weak; because otherwise they will be hard and cruel. But this way is not for the developed Aryan man who has to grow not by weakness, but by an ascension from strength to strength. Not this was fitting in the son of Pritha, not thus should the champion and chief hope of a righteous cause abandon it in the hour of crisis and peril or suffer the sudden amazement of his heart and senses, the clouding of his reason and the downfall of his will to betray him into the casting away of his divine weapons and the refusal of his God-given work."

II.5: *mahānubhāvān*, venerable. Other translations are "most reverend" (H) or "reverend.... of great dignity" (E), "of great dignity" (Z), "most noble" (B-D), "noble" (D), "honored" (R) and "high-souled" (A).

II.7: Aurobindo notes: "Arjuna is the man of action and not of knowledge, the fighter, never the seer or the thinker. In the Gita he typifies the human soul of action brought face to face through that action in its highest and most violent crisis with the problem of human life and its apparent incompatibility with the spiritual state or even with a purely ethical ideal of perfection. The nature of the crisis which he undergoes is an all-embracing inner bankruptcy which he expresses when he says that his whole conscious being, not the thought alone but heart and vital desires and all, are utterly bewildered and can find nowhere the *dharma*, nowhere any valid law of action. That for the soul of action in the mental being is the worst possible crisis, failure and overthrow. For this alone he takes refuge as a disciple with Krishna; give me, he practically asks, that which I have lost, a true law, a clear rule of action, a path by which I can again confidently walk. He does not ask for the secret of life or of the world, the meaning and purpose of it all, but for a *dharma*. Yet it is precisely this secret for which he does not ask, or at least so much of the knowledge as is necessary to lead him into a higher life, to which the divine Teacher intends to lead his disciple; for he means him to give up all *dharmas* except the one broad and vast rule of living consciously in the Divine and acting from that consciousness."

In a further note, Aurobindo says: "*Dharma* means literally that which lays hold of and which holds things together, the law, the norm, the rule of nature, action and life."

II.10: *viṣīdantam*, sinking into depression. Other translations are "depressed and discouraged" (A), "depressed" (R), "despondent" (E, B-D, D), "in his [deep] desponding" (Z), "despairing" (B) or "stricken with despair" (H), and "stricken with anguish" (G-D).

In comment on the verse Aurobindo notes: "Arjuna in his reply to Krishna admits the rebuke even while he strives against and refuses the command. He is aware of his weakness and yet accepts subjection to it. He attempts still to justify his refusal on ethical and rational grounds, but merely cloaks by words of apparent rationality the revolt of his ignorant and unchastened emotions. It is these claims of Arjuna's egoistic being that Krishna sets out first to destroy in order to make place for the higher law which shall transcend all egoistic motives of action."

II.11: Edgerton notes: "The meaning is that Arjuna shows ignorant presumption in daring to discuss learned topics while showing himself so uninformed as to mourn the dead. So essentially R(āmānuja). See JAOS 52.70 f.; and cf. *prājñavādikaḥ*, 'talking as (pretending to be) wise', Mbh ii. 2288 (Critical edition ii. 61.38)."

Aurobindo notes: "The answer of the Teacher proceeds upon two different lines, first, a brief reply founded upon the highest ideas of the general Aryan culture in which Arjuna has been educated, secondly, another and larger founded on a more intimate knowledge, opening into deeper truths of our being, which is the real starting point of the teaching of the Gita. This first answer relies on the philosophic and moral conceptions of the Vedantic philosophy and the social idea of duty and honour which formed the ethical basis of Aryan Society."

II.14: *mātrā-*, sense-objects. *Mātrās* seem to be the sensible properties of things. More deeply, following out the implication of the reference Edgerton makes in his note on this verse (to *Bṛhad-āraṇyaka-upaniṣad*, IV. 3. 10), his translation "matter" might be acceptable if divested of Western connotations and placed into the context of the *Gītā*, in particular, into the framework of its conception of creation through *māyā*. *Māyā* and *mātra* have the same root, *mā*, meaning both to lay out and display and to measure. The *mātrās* could then be the sensible world of things as layed out through *māyā* and as constituting (being things already there for perception) a limit to the reaching-out activity of the self (through the senses and *manas*).

II.15: Aurobindo notes: "By immortality is meant not the survival of death, —that is already given to every creature born with a mind,—but the transcendence of life and death. It means that ascension by which man ceases to live as a mind-informed body and lives at last as a spirit and in the Spirit."

II.20: the first half of this verse is subject to different readings grammatically, and thus to different translations. Edgerton translates the second *pāda* (half-line) "nor, having come to be, will he ever more come not to be". And he notes: "The text reads: *nā'yam bhūtvā bhavitā vā na bhūyaḥ*. The second *na* is to be taken closely with *bhavitā* (together, 'will come not to be') which compound expression is negated by the first *na*, as in vs. 12 *na...nāsam*." But as he goes on to say, there is this objection to such a reading, "that the soul should not be spoken of as having 'come to be', since it has existed from everlasting." Nonetheless, some such reading lies behind the translations of R, B-D, A, G-D, and B. Alternatively, H: "he came not into being, nor shall come hereafter." Presumably he has understood the grammar of the second half-line to involve a disjunction parallel to that in the first, with *bhūtvā* and *bhavitā* disjoined as the verbal forms were in the first half-line. Such a translation seems not only more consistent with what Kṛṣṇa says elsewhere, but more parallel to the *Kaṭha Upaniṣad* verse being fairly closely paralleled in these verses.

II.29: Edgerton translates (p. 127): "By a rare chance may a man see him (the Soul); by a rare chance likewise may another declare him; and by a rare chance may another hear (of) him. But even when he has heard (of) him, no one whatsoever knows him." Zaehner translates similarly, using the phrase "by a rare privilege". But Hill, noting that "it is not clear whether *āścaryavat* refers to *enam* or to the subjects of the verbs", translates: "Marvellous is one who sees him; marvellous, likewise, another who declares him; marvellous another who hears of him; yet even though one hear of him, one knows him not." Confirming the uncertainty of the adjectival reference, Radhakrishnan translates: "One looks upon Him as a marvel, another likewise speaks of Him as a marvel; another hears of Him as a marvel; and even after hearing, no one whatsoever has known Him." B, B-D, D, and A translate like R.

II.31: Aurobindo notes: How does this self-knowledge pointed to in Verses 11-30 "justify the action demanded of Arjuna and the slaughter of Kuruksetra? The answer is that this is the action required of Arjuna in the path he has to travel; it has come inevitably in the performance of the function demanded of him by his *swadharma*, his social duty, the law of his life and the law of his being. This world, this manifestation of the Self in the material universe is not only a cycle of inner development, but a field in which the external circumstances of life have to be accepted as an environment and an occasion for that development. It is a world of mutual help and struggle; not a serene and peaceful gliding through easy joys is the progress it allows us, but every step has to be gained by heroic effort and through a clash of opposing forces."

II.32: Aurobindo notes: "The Teacher turns aside for a moment to give another answer to the cry of Arjuna over the sorrow of the death of kindred which will empty his life of the causes and objects of living. What is the true object of the Kshatriya's life and his true happiness? Not self-pleasing and domestic happiness and a life of comfort and peaceful joy with friends and relatives, but to battle for the right is his true object of life and to find a cause for which he can lay down his life or by victory win the crown and glory of the hero's existence is his greatest happiness."

II.37: Aurobindo notes, in regard to Verses 11-37: "Indian ethics has always seen the practical necessity of graded ideals for the developing moral and spiritual life of man. This, says Krishna in effect, is my answer to you if you insist on joy and sorrow and the result of your actions as your motive of action. I have shown you in what direction the higher knowledge of self and the world points you; I have now shown you in what direction your social duty and the ethical standard of your order point you, *swadharmam api chavekshya.* Whichever you consider, the result is the same. But if you are not satisfied with your social duty and the virtue of your order, if you think that leads you to sorrow and sin, then I bid you rise to a higher and not sink to a lower ideal. Hence the next verse."

In regard to that verse, Aurobindo writes: "Put away all egoism from you, disregard joy and sorrow, disregard gain and loss and all worldly results; look only at the cause you must serve and the work that you must achieve by divine command; 'so thou shalt not incur sin'. Thus Arjuna's plea of sorrow, his plea of the recoil from slaughter, his plea of the sense of sin, his plea of the unhappy results of his action, are answered according to the highest knowledge and ethical ideals to which his race and age had attained."

II.41: Aurobindo notes: "Buddhi, the word used, means, properly speaking, the mental power of understanding, but it is evidently used by the Gita in a large philosophic sense for the whole action of the discriminating and deciding mind which determines both the direction and use of our thoughts and the direction and use of our acts; thought, intelligence, judgment, perceptive choice and aim are all included in its functioning; for the characteristic of the unified intelligence is not only concentration of the mind that knows, but especially concentration of the mind that decides and persists in the decision, *vyavasaya*, while the sign of the dissipated intelligence is not so much even discursiveness of the ideas and perceptions as discursiveness of the aims and desires, therefore of the will. Will, then, and knowledge are the two functions of the Buddhi. The unified intelligent will is fixed in the enlightened soul, it is concentrated in inner self-knowledge; the many-branching and multifarious, busied with many things, careless of the one thing needful is, on the contrary, subject to the restless and discursive action of the mind, dispersed in outward life and works and their fruits."

II.43: commenting on Verses 42-43, and suggesting that the *Gītā* gives to action and sacrifice much broader meanings than in the Vedic tradition of the time, Aurobindo notes: "It is the ignorant who worship the gods, not knowing whom they are worshipping ignorantly in these divine forms; for they are worshipping, though in ignorance, the One, the Lord, the only Deva, and it is He who accepts their offering. To that Lord must the sacrifice be offered, the true sacrifice of all the life's energies and activities, with devotion, without desire, for His sake and for the welfare of the peoples. It is because the Vedavada obscures this truth and with its tangle of ritual ties man down to the action of the three gunas that is has to be so severely censured and put roughly aside; but its central idea is not destroyed; transfigured and uplifted, it is turned into a most important part of the true spiritual experience and of the method of liberation."

II.44: cf. the translation of *vyavasāyātmikā* by Davies, quoted in a footnote to this verse by Hill: "having effort as its essence". Also R: "which discriminates between right and wrong". In contrast E ("resolute in nature"), H ("resolute"), B ("sure") and B-D (("determinate") make the same meaning for the term as in Verse 41. D slightly varies the two ("the resolute understanding" in 41, "the intelligence of those (who are intended to have) resolute understanding (but)...." in 44). Z makes the same translation by ignoring the grammar ("the essence of the soul is will").

II.45: *guṇas*. Though the conception of these seems to stem from Sāṁkhya as a non-Vedic mode of thought, this mode had its influence upon the Vedic tradition. Hill suggests (p. 41) that the term begins to be used in the technical Sāṁkhya sense first (in the Vedic tradition) in the *Śvetāśvatara Upaniṣad* (e.g., I. 3), which also contains picturesque metaphors (the 'triple tyre', I. 4; the 'one she-goat, red, white, and black', IV. 5) which have been plausibly interpreted as alluding to the three *guṇas* of *prakṛti*. "The *Maitrī Upaniṣad*, composed like the Gītā at a time when the Sāṁkhya was developing into a more definite system, gives the *guṇas* their names. The Gītā develops the *guṇa* idea very completely." In regard to that developed notion and the function it attributes to the *guṇas* Hill comments: "it is their interaction and relative proportion in things that cause the manifold differences of character and function in the world" (p. 40). Barnett comments (p. 18, on the Sāṁkhya notion): "The Guṇas are the phases into which Matter or Nature by its own essence is determined for the fulfilment of its immanent activities, without losing thereby its ultimate unity."

sattva: Edgerton notes: "both Ś(aṁkara) and R(āmānuja), followed by Barnett, take it to mean the 'Strand' (*guṇa*) of that name. This may be right, though seemingly inconsistent with the context. But *sattva* may also mean 'truth, reality' (so Deussen, Hill), 'purity' or 'courage' (so Telang, Garbe)." Edgerton translates "goodness", R "purity", B-D "purity" also, Hill "eternal truth", and Barnett "everlasting goodness".

II.46: Hill's note on this verse reads: "The meaning of this śloka is obscure, and commentators differ widely in their interpretations. Does the author mean that the enlightened Brāhmaṇa can find *no* utility in the Vedas (i.e., in the work-section of the Vedas), or that there are certain uses that he alone can detect? Those commentators who are afraid of allowing the teaching to depart too far from the old paths take the latter view; while others, such as Śaṁkara, limit the uses of the Veda to those aspirants who are just setting out on the *karma-mārga*, saying that for the truly enlightened Brāhmaṇa the utility of the Vedic ritual is comprehended in Right Knowledge, just as the utility of the tank is comprehended in that of the all-spreading flood of water. This seems to be the more reasonable view of the sense. Th(omson) writes: 'As a full tank of fresh water may be used for drinking, bathing, washing one's clothes, and numerous other purposes, so the texts of the Vedas may be turned to any object of self-interest by a Brāhman who is well acquainted with them and knows how to wield them.' B(arnett) has the following note: 'The sense of this obscure and much-disputed passage seems to me to be that a large pool has many uses, the thirsty traveller using it to assuage his thirst, the farmer to water his field, the religious man to perform his baths of purification; and in the same way the Vedas are used by various sorts of men to attain their several objects, the worldly man employing them for rituals to secure his own worldly benefit, and the enlightened sage using them in the same rites, but solely for the worldly benefit of others. The sage thereby practises Yoga, and secures for himself spiritual grace.' " Translations vary: "As much use as there is in a tank flooded with waters from all sides, so much there is in all the Vedas for a Brāhmaṇa of wisdom" (H); "as much profit as there is in a water-tank when on all sides there is a flood of water, no more is there in all the Vedas for a brahman who (truly) understands" (E); "as is the use of a pond in a place flooded with water everywhere, so is that of all the Vedas for the Brāhmin who understands" (R); "as much profit as is in a pool of waters gathered from all sides lies in all the Vedas, for the discerning Brahman" (B); "all the Vedas are as useful to an enlightened Brāhmaṇa as is a tank in a place covered all over with water" (B-D); "to the extent that a well is of use when there is a flood of water on all sides, to the same extent are all the Vedas of use to an enlightened *Brahmana*" (G-D); "as much use as there is in a well with water in flood on every side, so much is there in all the Vedas for the Brahmin who has the knowledge" (A).

II.47: Other translations of the first half-verse: "On action alone let thy interest be fixed, never on its fruits...." (E, p. 160); "In work thy rightful interest should lie, nor ever on its fruits...." (H); "In Works be thine office, in their fruits must it never be...." (B); "Thy business is with action only, never with its fruits.." (B-D); "To action alone hast thou a right and never at all to its fruits..." (R); "in action alone hast thou a right and never in its fruits" (D); "Action alone is thy province, never the fruits thereof.." (G-D); "[But] work alone is *your* proper business, never the fruits [it may produce]" (Z).

II.48: Edgerton (pp. 165-6) says of *yoga*: "It is necessary to consider what the author means by the 'Sāṁkhya discipline' and the 'discipline of action'. These are technical terms, which require very careful definition. The word which I translate 'discipline' is *yoga*. The phrase 'discipline of action' renders a Sanskrit compound, *karma-yoga*. Elsewhere the word *yoga* alone is used in the sense of *karma-yoga*; that is, 'discipline', when otherwise undefined, means in the *Gītā* frequently (and indeed usually) the 'discipline of action'. The word *yoga* is unfortunately a very fluid one, used in a great variety of senses; this makes it often hard to give an exact definition of its meaning in any given occurrence. It may mean simply 'method, means'. It also means 'exertion, diligence, zeal'. And especially it is used to describe a regular, disciplined course of *action* leading to a definite end; in the Gītā and works of its type, to the end of emancipation. In some contemporary works it connotes a system of ascetic practices culminating in a sort of self-hypnosis, conceived as leading to emancipation, or to some supernatural attainment. When used alone, without qualifying epithet, it always denotes, in works of the time of the Gītā, a *practical* method, as distinguished from an *intellectual* method. But in the Gītā its meaning is narrowed down. Here it means the method of salvation which is characterized by participation in normal, worldly action (hence the fuller expression *karma-yoga*, which is synonymous with *yoga* alone in this sense) without interest in the fruits of action. Action characterized by indifference is the central principle. 'Yoga is defined as Indifference', says one verse (ii. 48). But it is always an indifference *in action*. The word *yoga* definitely implies *activity*, as it is used in this connection in the Gītā, where it is constantly colored by (often unformulated) association with the other meaning of the word, 'energetic performance, exertion'. It is then opposed to the system or 'rule' or 'discipline' (the same word *yoga* is also used, confusingly) of the Sāṁkhya, which is elsewhere called the *jñāna-yoga* or 'discipline of knowledge'...."

II.50: *yujyasva*, become ready for. Other translations are "strive to be in" (A), "strive for" (R, D), "gird yourself up for" (G-D), "set thyself to" (B), "discipline yourself into" (E), "practise" (H), "cleave to" (B-D), "brace yourself for [this]" (Z).

II.52: According to Hill, the reference here and in the next verse to *śruti* (what is heard) must (in this context) be to the *karmakāṇḍa* (work-section) of the Veda, whose teaching the *yogin* is expected to transcend.

Aurobindo notes: "The Vedas and the Upanishads are declared to be unnecessary for the man who knows (Sl. 46). Nay, they are even a stumbling-block; for the letter of the Word—perhaps because of its conflict of texts and its various and mutually dissentient interpretations—bewilders the understanding, which can only find certainty and concentration by the light within."

II.53: Aurobindo, taking *śruti* to refer here to the Vedas and Upaniṣads, comments: "this criticism of the Śruti is so offensive to conventional religious sentiment that attempts are naturally made by the convenient and indispensable human faculty of text-twisting to put a different sense on some of these verses, but the meaning is plain and hangs together from beginning to end. It is confirmed and emphasised by a subsequent passage in which the knowledge of the knower is described as passing beyond the range of Veda and Upanishad, *shabdabrahmativartate* (Ch. VI, Sl. 44). At the same time, as we have already seen, the Gita does not treat such important parts of the Aryan Culture in a spirit of mere negation and repudiation."

II.54: Aurobindo notes: "Arjuna, voicing the average human mind, asks for some outward, physical, practically discernible sign of Samadhi. No such signs can be given, nor does the Teacher attempt to supply them; for the only possible test of its possession is inward and that there are plenty of hostile psychological forces to apply. Equality is the great stamp of the liberated soul and of that equality even the most discernible signs are still subjective."

In a note to this note, he adds: "The sign of the man in Samadhi is not that he loses consciousness of objects and surroundings and of his mental and physical self and cannot be recalled to it even by burning or torture of the body,— the ordinary idea of the matter; trance is a particular intensity, not the essential sign."

II.55: Aurobindo notes: "The test of Samadhi is the expulsion of all desires, their inability to get at the mind, and it is the inner state from which this freedom arises, the delight of the soul gathered within itself with the mind equal and still and high-poised above the attractions and repulsions, the alternations of sunshine and storm and stress of the external life. It is drawn inward even when acting outwardly; it is concentrated in self even when gazing out upon things; it is directed wholly to the Divine even when to the outward vision of others busy and preoccupied with the affairs of the world."

II.58: In speaking of traditional Sāṁkhya (that of Kapila), Barnett says: "The activity (*vṛtti*) of an outer sense-organ, according to Hindu psychology, consists in the organ projecting itself outwards and imposing itself upon its objects, thereby receiving from them an impression corresponding to their real character. Thus if I become conscious of seeing a jar, the reason is, according to the Sāṁkhya, that my sense-organ of sight applies itself to the real jar, and takes an imprint thereof, which it conveys to the *Manas* or internal sense-organ; and this in turn carries on the impression to *Buddhi* and *Ahaṁkāra*. The *Buddhi* within me decides that this is a true particular cognition, formulating the proposition 'this is a jar'; and the *Ahaṁkāra* within me leads me to the consciousness that this proposition is mine, suggesting to me that I know the thing to be a jar."

Aurobindo notes: "The first movement must be obviously to get rid of desire which is the whole root of the evil and suffering ; and in order to get rid of desire, we must put an end to the cause of desire, the rushing out of the senses to seize and enjoy their objects. We must draw them back when they are inclined thus to rush out, draw them away from their objects into their source, quiescent in the mind, the mind quiescent in the intelligence, the intelligence quiescent in the soul and its self-knowledge, observing anything that the objective life can give. It is not an external asceticism, the physical renunciation of the objects of sense that I am teaching, suggests Krishna immediately to avoid a misunderstanding which is likely at once to arise; I speak of an inner withdrawal, a renunciation of desire."

II.60: *yatato*, endeavoring to make his way toward fulfillment. Other translations are "though he be striving" (B-D) and "even though... (he) strive" (H, B), also "ever strive (for perfection)" (R), "who labours for perfection" (A); also "in spite of... (his) endeavour" (G-D), and "one who strives" (E).

II.64: *prasādam*, calm. Other translations are "large and sweet clearness of soul and temperament" (A), "tranquillity" (E) or "serenity" (H) or "peace" (B-D) or "calm serenity" (Z), "clearness" (B), "peace of mind" (G-D), "serenity of mind" (D), "purity of spirit" (R).

II.65: commenting on Verses 64-65, and observing that "desireless contact with objects" is possible through "vision of the Supreme" and through "living in the Yoga, in union or oneness of the whole subjective being with that", Aurobindo continues: "Then free from reactions, the senses will be delivered from the affections of liking and disliking, escape the duality of positive and negative desire, and calm, peace, clearness, happy tranquillity, *atmaprasada*, will settle upon the man. That clear tranquillity is the source of the soul's felicity; all grief begins to lose its power of touching the tranquil soul; the intelligence is rapidly established in the peace of the self; suffering is destroyed. It is this calm, desireless, griefless, fixity of the buddhi in self-poise and self-knowledge to which the Gita gives name of Samadhi".

II.66: *bhāvanā*, contemplative steeping of himself. Other translations are "concentration" (B-D, D) and "power of concentration" (R), "inspiration" (B), "devotion" (B-D), "contentment of thought" (A), "reflection" (H), "efficient force" (E), "development" (Z). Hill quotes other translations, for example "right condition" and "perseverance in the pursuit of self-knowledge"; while Edgerton notes: "*Bhāvanā*: here, 'effective religious impulse': the word *bhāvanā* means 'bringing to be, tendency to produce something (here, religious effort).' It is a technical word of the Mīmāṁsā system." Zaehner notes (p. 155): "...Both in Sanskrit and Pāli the normal meaning of *bhāvaya-* is 'nourish' or 'develop'. In the Gītā itself (3.11) the word is used of the sacrifice to the gods. By sacrifice man *nourishes* the gods and the gods in turn nourish man."

II.72: *nirvāṇa*, extinction. Edgerton notes (p. 125) that this word "means 'extinction', originally of a fire or flame; then of the flames of desire, as the cause of continued rebirth..The Bhagavad Gītā uses the word *nirvāṇa* several times, generally in the compound *brahmanirvāṇa*, 'extinction in Brahman', or 'the extinction which is Brahman'." Aurobindo translates "extinction in the Brahman", and notes: "Nirvāṇa is not the negative self-annihilation of the Buddhists, but the great immergence of the separate personal self into the vast reality of the one infinite impersonal Existence." A. B. Keith, in his *Buddhist Philosophy in India and Ceylon* (pp. 65-66) says: "...There is no doubt that the Indian idea of the extinction of fire was not that which occurs to us of utter annihilation, but rather that the flame returns to the primitive, pure, invisible state of fire in which it existed prior to its manifestation in the form of visible fire."

CHAPTER III

III.3: *niṣṭhā*, way of devotedly applying oneself (or, form of self-dedication). Other translations are "self-application of the soul (by which it enters into the

Brahmic condition)" (A) , but also: "path" (B-D, D), "way of life" (R), "system" (H), "law" (Z), "basis (of religion)" (E), "foundation" (B), "attitudes" (G-D).

III.4: Aurobindo notes: "Naishkarmya, a calm voidness from works, is no doubt that to which the soul, the Purusha has to attain; for it is Prakriti which does the work and the soul has to rise above involution in the activities of the being and attain to a free serenity and poise watching over the operations of Prakriti, but not affected by them. That, and not cessation of the work of Prakriti, is what is really meant by the soul's *naishkarmya*. But if the works of Prakriti continue, how can the soul help being involved in them? How can I fight and yet in my soul not think or feel that I the individual am fighting, not desire victory nor be inwardly touched by defeat? This is the teaching of the Sāṅkhyas that the intelligence of the man who engages in the activities of Nature, is entangled in egoism, ignorance and desire and therefore drawn to action; on the contrary, if the intelligence draws back, then the action must cease with the cessation of the desire and the ignorance. Therefore the giving up of life and works is a necessary part, an inevitable circumstance and an indispensable last means to the movement to liberation. This objection of a current logic, the Teacher immediately anticipates. No, he says, such renunciation, far from being indispensable, is not even possible."

III.12: Barnett's note reads: "Compare the Laws of Manu, iii. 117-8, 'After worshipping Gods, Sages, men, Ancestors and household deities, the householder shall then eat of the remains; he eats sheer guilt who cooks only for himself; this eating of the leavings of sacrifice is the food ordained for good men.' The daily ritual of the householder includes the Five Great Sacrifices, viz. to gods (*deva-yajna*), to ghosts (*bhūta-yajna*), to ancestors (*pitṛi-yajna*), of the Veda (*brahma-yajna*, viz. recitation of scriptural texts), and to men (*nṛi-yajna*, viz. feeding guests and beggars)."

III.15: *brahman*, holy power. Hill indicates various explanations that have been proposed for this word in this verse: "Ś. says: 'Sacrifice is enjoined in the Veda, and the Veda comes from the Imperishable *paramātman*: the Veda treats mainly of sacrifices and the mode of their performance'. R. takes Brahman to mean the body, and *akṣara* to be the *jīvātman*, from which the body is said to proceed, because it serves as its instrument for work. Thus the body is the requisite for sacrifice. M. says that the Supreme Spirit is revealed by the Veda (*akṣara*); the Supreme Spirit is revealed to man through sacrifice and is thus said to be established in it. D. translates: 'Know that action springs from Brahmā: Brahmā proceeds from the Indivisible one. Wherefore Brahmā the all-pervading is ever present in sacrifice.' TG. follows Ś. B. has a note: 'Brahma in the first instance is probably the Veda...and secondly it is the Cosmic Spirit, or *jīvabhūta*.' RANG identifies Brahman with *prakṛiti*, an interpretation which appears to be the most satisfactory for the first two mentions. The third 'Brahman all-pervading' must be, more generally, the sum of all things; or perhaps, as B., *jīvabhūta*. For Brahman identified with *prakṛiti*, cf. xiv. 3. 4."

akṣara-, the imperishable. But given the "identity" of *aum*, the holy syllable (*akṣara*), and the imperishable (*akṣara*) expressed in *Kaṭha Upaniṣad*, I. 2. 15-6 (cf. footnote 11 to Chapter VIII), the *akṣara* here could be thought additionally as *aum*, that from which the Vedas arise (cf. *Chāndogya Upaniṣad*, I. 1, for example). Thus as Aurobindo notes (in footnote 3, p. 113): "The basic syllable OM is the foundation of all the potent creative sounds of the revealed word; OM is the one universal formulation of the energy of sound and speech, that which contains and sums up, synthetises and releases, all the spiritual power and all the potentiality of *vak* and *shabda* and of which the other sounds, out of whose stuff words of speech are woven, are supposed to be the developed evolutions...."

III. 20: *lokasaṁgraham*, holding together of the world. Other translations are "holding together of the peoples" (A), "maintenance of the world" (R, D), "order of the world" (B), "guidance of the world" (H) or "of mankind" (G-D), "welfare of the world" (B-D), "welfare [and coherence] of the world" (Z).

III.28: *-vibhāgayoḥ*, differentiation-and-relation. Other translations are "distinctions" (B-D) or "divisions" (A), "distribution" (H); or, taking the meaning of differentiation in a different direction, "the two distinctions (of the soul) from" (R) and "separation (of the soul) from" (E, D). Z has "how (constituents and works) are parcelled out in categories." In a footnote to this verse, Hill clarifies by "the works appropriate to the various characters caused by varying proportions of the three Strands".

III.30: *adhyātma-*, what stands over your self. Other translations are "founded in the self" (A) and "(your thoughts [withdrawn]) in what appertains to self" (Z), or, taking the term more technically: "fixed in the Self" (R), "resting on the Supreme Self" (B-D), "(fixed) on the supreme Self" (D), "fix...on the Essential Self" (H), "fixed on the indwelling Atman" (G-D), "on the over-soul" (E) or "on the One over Self" (B).

III.32: in Section 31 of his introduction, Hill speaks of Kṛṣṇa's account of knowledge ("...theory and practice, knowledge and work, are not opposed, but, as the learned realize, two sides of one well-balanced mode of life. Knowledge must find its complement in work; its function is to bring all work to true fulfillment."), and says this of *jñāna*: "Apart from this insistence on the union of work with knowledge there is no great difference between the Gītā doctrine of *jñāna* and that of the Upaniṣads. In both alike *jñāna* bears a higher and a lower sense; the higher *jñāna* differs from the lower, not so much in its content as in its nature; the higher is uncaused, direct and personal; the lower is obtained by ordinary means, dependent on authority. Yet, though the higher knowledge dawns uncaused, the acquisition of the lower fits a person to receive the higher revelation. Four times in the Gītā the higher knowledge is associated with the lower, as *vijñāna* with *jñāna*. *jñāna*, says Śaṁkara, is 'the knowledge of the Self and other things, acquired from scriptures and from a teacher', while *vijñāna* is 'personal experience of the things so taught'. *jñāna*, then is primarily concerned with the self, and aims at realizing the oneness of the Self with the Absolute. In a secondary, auxiliary sense, it has for its object the contents of sacred books, the interpretation of those books by the teacher, and in general, the solution of all religious and metaphysical problems."

III.35: *viguṇaḥ*, even when not done perfectly. Other translations are "though imperfectly carried out" (R), "(tho) imperfect" (E, D), "though ill-done" (H), "without excellence" (B), "bereft of merit" (G-D), "though in itself faulty" (A), "though destitute of merit" (B-D), "though void of merit" (Z).

III.41: *jñānavijñāna-*, *jñāna* and discrimination. Other translations are "(spiritual) wisdom and discrimination (logical knowledge)" (R), "wisdom and knowledge" (B-D), "knowledge and discrimination" (G-D), "knowledge and experience" (H), "knowledge and discernment" (B), "theoretical and practical knowledge" (E), "spiritual and practical knowledge" (D), "what we learn from holy books and what we learn from life" (Z).

CHAPTER IV

IV.2: *naṣṭaḥ*, corrupted. Other translations are "decayed" (B-D), "dwindled away" (G-D), "lost" (R, A, E, B, D, Z) and "perished" (H).

IV.6: *adhiṣṭhāya*, having taken my stand over. Other translations are "establishing Myself in" (R, D), "stand upon" (A), "in My sway over" (B), "governing" (H), "assuming control over" (G-D), "resorting to" (E), "consort with" (Z), "brooding over" (B-D). Zaehner notes: "*adhiṣṭhāya*, 'I consort with...': Ś. glosses *vaśī-kṛtya*, 'brings under his power', and this would appear to be about right...In Ch(āndogya) U(paniṣad) 5.19.2 to 5.23.2 the word seems to mean 'rule over' while in P(raśna) U(paniṣad) 3.4. it certainly means to 'govern' a group of villages. In Ś(vetāśvatara) U(paniṣad), as we might expect, the word is used in more 'theological' passages. Here again 'govern', 'preside over', or 'direct' seems to fit.... [At] Ś(vetāśvatara) U(paniṣad), 4.11....we read: *yoniṁ yoniṁ adhitiṣṭhaty eko*, which may either mean, 'He alone governs every cause', or 'He alone approaches every womb'. This second translation seems the more likely since the same idea is expressed in the Gītā 14.3 where Krishna says: 'Great Brahman (meaning here "material Nature") is to Me a womb, in it I plant the seed'. As usual in such cases, I prefer to think that the author of the Gītā had both senses in mind."

IV.11: *bhajāmy*, apportion. Other translations are "render to" (G-D), "return their love" (Z), "accept to My love" (A), "welcome" (B-D), "grant favor" (E) or "show favor" (H) or "am gracious to" (D), "accept" (R), "deal with" (B). One might translate: "I share with men according as they approach me." The verbal root here, *bhaj-* (meaning "to allot or apportion, to share with, to participate in"), is the basis for such terms as *bhaktaḥ* ("devoted, loyal" : IV. 3) and *bhakti* ("devotion": VIII. 10 and 22, e.g.). With such terms, we find expressed a sense of participation in the divine which, in its fullest and transparent form, involves clear-sighted mutuality of loyal devotion and love (from the human side) and of care and love (from the divine side). Since *prapadyante* (meaning "approach") comes from a verbal root (*pra-pad-*) meaning not simply "go forward" but "go forward to take refuge with" and "fall down (at a person's feet)", what is being spoken of here is an interplay of human with divine in which differing degrees and forms of devotional approach by human beings to the divine are received and responded to by the ultimate divine power in appropriate and correspondent degrees and forms, all expressing the divine care and love.

IV.18: *kṛtsna-karma-kṛt*, doing action whole. Other translations are "doing work perfectly" (H), "doer of perfect work" (B), "done all he need to do" (G-D), "a many-sided universal worker (for the good of the world, for God in the world)" (A), "has accomplished all his work" (R), "while performing all action" (B-D), "performing every work" (Z), and "does all actions" (ED).

IV.24: *brahmaiva tena gantavyaṁ brahmakarmasamādhinā*, what is to be partaken of by him who is ingathered in the midst of his active effort (which itself is the holy power) (is) the holy power itself. Other translations are "God is that which is to be attained by him who realizes God in his works" (R), "to Brahman must he come who contemplates a work that is Brahman" (H), "Brahman is that which is to be attained by samadhi in Brahman-action" (A), "he whose mind is fixed on acts dedicated to *Brahman* must needs pass on to Brahman" (G-D), "just to Brahman must he go, being concentrated upon the (sacrificial) action that is Brahman" (E), "unto the Eternal verily shall he go who in his action meditateth wholly upon the Eternal" (B-D), "to Brahma shall he go who dwells in concent with the Works that are Brahma" (B), "Brahman is to be attained by him who concentrates his actions upon Brahman" (D), "who sinks himself in this [sacrificial] act which is Brahman, to Brahman must he thereby go" (Z).

IV.25: Hill's note reads: "the first part of this śloka refers to ordinary sacrifice offered to *devas*. The second part presents difficulty, and opinions differ widely with regard to its meaning. Ś explains: 'in the fire of Brahman others offer the self by the self', making *yajña*=*ātman*; i.e., 'know their conditioned self as identical with the unconditioned Brahman.'..R explains *yajñena* as 'with apparatus used in Vedic sacrifice', and considers that such sacrifice, performed in consonance with the ideal presented in 24, is here intended. Th., following SCH., considers this sacrifice to be purely mental. B. writes: 'It may be a mere repetition of the thought of v. 24; or it may mean that the devotees, while actually performing the rite, identify their sacrifice with Viṣṇu as *adhiyajña* and thus symbolically interpret the rite as the identification of the conditioned Self with the Absolute Brahma.' RANG. supposes that the sacrifice here is in itself the same as that performed in the first part of the śloka, but that the sacrificer thinks of the *devas* as equivalent to, or culminating in, Brahman. He translates *yajñenaiva* 'in the manner of the sacrifice itself. *Yajñenaiva* seems to me to mean 'merely performing the ordianry outward ceremonial acts' while the mind is fixed, not on any *deva* (as in the first part) but on the Absolute Brahman. The sacrifice is actually performed, but its value lies in the mental attitude of the sacrificer."

Edgerton comments on the last part of the verse, which he takes to refer to "philosophical mystics": "the following is a cryptically figurative way of saying that they abandon ritual action and devote their thoughts to the Brahman alone."

Aurobindo notes: "Those who follow after the sacrifice of the gods, conceive of the Divine in various forms and powers and seek him by various means, ordinances, *dharmas*, laws or, as we might say, settled rites of action, self-discipline, consecrated works; but for those who have the knowledge, the simple fact of sacrifice, of offering whatever work to the Divine itself, of casting all their activities into the unified divine consciousness and energy, is their one means, their one *dharma*."

IV.27: Edgerton suggests that this refers to "followers of the 'Sāṁkhya' way of knowledge with complete renunciation of action". Similarly Barnett: "Some, who practise the austerities of an intellectual Yoga, regard all their physical activities as a sacrifice of devotion offered by means of this Yoga." Aurobindo says: "There is the discipline by which, when the self is known, all the actions of the sense-perceptions and all the actions of the vital being are received into that one still and tranquil soul."

IV.32: *vitatā brahmaṇo mukhe*, spread out in the mouth of the holy power. Hill translates "outspread at the gate of Brahman" and notes: "this phrase has been variously interpreted: 'are known from the Vedas' (Ś, followed by Galanos, TG., and B.); 'expounded as means to attaining the true nature of *ātman*' (B. note); 'offered to Brahman' (M.); so also Th.: 'performed in the presence of the Supreme Spirit' and D: 'offered in the presence of Brahman'. RANG. translates: 'spread out in the mouth of the Brahman', and adds that 'Brahman is the one ultimate goal of all religions, as also of all forms and processes of religious worship'. The interpretation of Brahman as the Veda may be definitely rejected; as also R.'s explanation. The third interpretation is very possible; but I would suggest that the phrase carries on the idea in the previous śloka of 'going to Brahman', and that all these various forms of sacrifice, provided that they are performed by 'knowers of sacrifice', are represented as 'spread out at the gate to Brahman', that each one may adopt for performance the sacrifice he prefers, and none the less enter through the door to Brahman."

Edgerton suggests that "spread out" might be instead "performed, carried out", and that *brahmaṇo mukhe* might mean "in the fire (of sacrifice)", this being the mouth by which the gods eat the offerings. Similarly, Aurobindo translates: "Therefore all these and many other forms of sacrifice have been extended in the mouth of the Brahman (the mouth of that Fire which receives all offerings)..."

IV.33: *-akhilaṁ*, complete. Other translations are "without exception" (D, Z), "without any exception" (R, H), "without remainder" (E), "in their entirety" (B-D).

IV.35: *ātmany*, in your self. Other translations are "in [your] self" (Z), "in Self" (R, B-D, A), "in the Self" (D), "in Thyself" (H, G- D, E), "in thy Self" (B).

CHAPTER V

V.16: in the first half of this verse, the *ātmanaḥ* could be taken with *jñāna* or with *ajñāna*. G-D, B-D, and A take it with *jñāna*, whereas H, B, Z, and E take it with *ajñāna*. Even then, and disregarding still the precise meaning of *ātman*, it remains a question of whether, for example, the *jñāna* is into *ātman* or simply belongs to *ātman*.

Commenting on *jñāna* here, Aurobindo says: "this knowledge of which the Gita speaks, is not an intellectual activity of the mind; it is a luminous growth into the highest state of being by the outshining of the light of the divine sun of Truth, 'that Truth, the Sun lying concealed in the darkness' of our ignorance of which the Rigveda speaks...."

V.17: the first half of this verse is translated by others as follows: "thinking of that, directing their whole conscious being to that, making that their whole aim, with that as the sole object of their devotion" (R, with A essentially the same, but with replacement of "thinking" by "turning their discerning mind"); "thinking on that, merged in that, established in that, solely devoted to that" (B-D); "thinking on that (highest Self), their self fixed on that, devoted to that" (D); "their reason that, and that their self, that their devotion, that their aim" (H); "whose intellect is suffused with that, whose self has become one with that, who abide in that, and whose end and aim is that" (G-D); "their consciousness and soul fixed on that (Highest), with that as their final goal, supremely devoted to that" (E); "with understanding set on That, with Self at one with That, with heart in That, with That for their supreme path" (B); "souls [bent on] that, selves [bent on] that, with that their aim and that their aspiration" (Z).

V.23: *soḍhuṁ*, overcome. Other translations are "bear" (H, A, B), "resist" (R), "endure" (B-D, D), "hold out against" (G-D), "stand fast against" (Z), "control" (E).

CHAPTER VI

VI.6: Or, put with less attention to the many forms of *ātman* used here: "the self of one whose self is self-subdued is its own friend; but the self of one not having such a self, will be hostile like an enemy." In any case, this verse allows of a variety of interpretations and translations. For example: "Self is a friend of that Self by which self has been conquered; but in its enmity toward him who has not Self, like a true enemy the self shall be" (H); "The self is a friend to that self by which self the very self is subdued; but to him that does not possess the self, in enmity will abide his very self, like an enemy" (E); "For him who has conquered his (lower) self by the (higher) Self his Self is a friend but for him who has not possessed his (higher) Self, his very Self will act in enmity, like an enemy" (R); "For him who has conquered his self by the self, his Self is a friend; but for him who has not conquered his self, the Self becomes hostile, like an enemy" (D); "The Self is friend to that self that has by self conquered self; but Self will be a very foe warring against him who possesses not his self" (B); "SELF is the friend of the self of him in whom the self by SELF is vanquished; but to the unsubdued self, SELF verily becometh hostile as an enemy" (B-D); "Self is the friend to the self of him whose self is by the self subdued; but for the man bereft of self will act as an enemy indeed" (Z); "His Self alone is friend, who has conquered himself by his Self; but to him who has not conquered himself and is thus inimical to himself, even his Self behaves as foe" (G-D); "To the man is his self a friend in whom the (lower) self has been conquered by the (higher) self, but to him who is not in possession of his (higher) self, the (lower) self is as if an enemy and it acts as an enemy" (A).

VI.7: Hill takes *param* and *ātmā* separately and translates: "Of him who has conquered self and come to peace the Self remains absorbed in contemplation of the Highest...." In his footnote he quotes commentators who take *param* adverbially, as modifying *samāhitaḥ* ("supremely well collected", "sublimely realized"). And so, likewise, G-D, "completely composed".

VI.8: Edgerton notes that *kūṭastha* ("stands on high") "perhaps" means "literally 'abiding on a mountaintop', as if 'above the battle', not subject to external influences."

VI.15: other translations of the last half of this verse are "attains to peace, the supreme nirvāṇa, which abides in Me" (R: D is essentially the same, but translates *nirvāṇa* as "bliss"); "goeth to Peace, to the supreme Bliss that abideth in Me" (B-D); "attains to the supreme peace of Nirvāṇa which has its foundation in Me" (A); "wins the peace which culminates in *Nirvāṇa*, the peace that is in Me" (G-D); "comes to the peace whose end is calm, the peace that is in me" (H); "to peace that culminates in nirvāṇa, and rests in Me, attains" (E); "comes to the peace that ends in extinction and that abides with Me" (B); "approach that peace which has Nirvāṇa as its end and which subsists in Me" (Z)

VI.24: Hill's footnote reads: "R. explains the desires 'born of *saṁkalpa*' as such mental desires as love for sons &c, to be contrasted with physical desires 'born of *sparśa*.' "

VI.29: the first half of this verse is translated by others as "the Self abiding in all beings and all beings in the Self (R, but similarly, B-D, H, B, D, Z), "*Ātman* in all beings and all beings in *Ātman*" (G-D), "the self in all beings and all beings in the self" (A); but E, translating "himself as in all beings, and all beings in himself", notes: "Himself. So Garbe and Deussen with both Ś and R, *svātman* or *svam ātmānam*. Surely not 'Self' abstractly (Barnett, Hill) or '*l'ātman*' (Senart)."

VI.31: *sarvathā vartamāno'pi*, whatever directions the turns of his existing take him in. Other translations are "howsoever he may be active" (R), "no matter how he live and move" (G-D), "however and in all ways he lives and acts" (A), "in whatever state he be" (Z), "in whatsoever state he may abide" (H), "tho abiding in any possible condition" (E), "wheresoever he may abide" (B), "whatever his mode of living" (B-D), "no matter how otherwise he exists" (D).

VI.32: Hill's note reads: "in vv. 29-32 Kṛiṣṇa sums up the Ascetic's progressive meditation on the Self. First, he beholds the universal, all-pervading Self as one unalterable essence dwelling in all sentient beings. In that Self all live and move and have their being. Next, he identifies that universal, all-pervading Self with Kṛiṣṇa, the Blessed Lord, the object of devotion, the gracious friend of every votary. Thus he begins to realize that he who enjoys the vision of the oneness of all Selves, and the knowledge that that one Self is Kṛiṣṇa, to whom devotion is due, must himself be one with Kṛiṣṇa, in whatsoever state he may chance to be—high or low, rich or poor, or worldly-wise or foolish, active or contemplative. Thus, understanding that all Selves are one, his sympathies extend to all the world, to every sentient being; their pleasure is his own, their pain his own..."

VI.36: *duṣprāpa*, impossible to attain. Other translations are "hard to attain"

(R, B-D, B, D), "hard to win" (H), "hard to reach" (E), "hard to come by" (Z), "difficult to attain" (A, G-D).

VI.47: speaking of the last two verses, Hill says: ". . . . the superiority of the true *yogin* consists in the combination in himself of all those elements which up to the time of the Bhagavadgītā had been too severely separated; and especially in the addition of devotion, *bhakti*, as the most essential element of all. D. sees in 47 a sectarian emphasis, which would surely be most inappropriate in this place. Kṛiṣṇa is laying stress, not on his own unique position, but on the supreme importance of devotion; and with this final śloka unites the colder philosophical teaching of the first section of the poem with the doctrine of devotion to be expanded in the second."

CHAPTER VII

VII.1: in the course of commenting on the "fully" ("integrally", he translates it) of this verse, Aurobindo says: "The implication of the phrase is that the Divine Being is all, *vasudevah sarvam*, and therefore if he is known integrally in all his powers and principles, then all is known, not only the pure Self, but the world and action and Nature. There is then nothing else here left to be known, because all is that Divine Existence. It is only because our view here is not thus integral, because it rests on the dividing mind and reason and the separative idea of the ego, that our mental perception of things, is an ignorance. We have to get away from this mental and egoistic view to the true unifying knowledge, and that has two aspects, the essential, *jñāna*, and the comprehensive, *vijñāna*, the direct spiritual awareness of the supreme Being and the right intimate knowledge of the principles of his existence, Prakriti, Purusha and the rest, by which all that is can be known in its divine origin and in the supreme truth of its nature. That integral knowledge, says the Gita, is a rare and difficult thing."

VII.2: Hill, referring to his note to III. 41, suggests here that "ancient commentators agree that *vijñāna* is higher and deeper than *jñāna*, M(adhvācārya) suggests that *vijñāna*, or the more detailed comprehension of God, finds exposition in 8-12."

In a note to this verse, Desai says: "I am inclined to think that the explanation of these terms is to be sought in the *samkhyan* use of them. There *jnana* is experience of the Self, and *vijnana* is discriminative knowledge of the Self as distant from all that is not-Self."

VII.3: *yatatāṁ ca sahasrāṇāṁ*, of the thousands of those who strive. Another reading is *yatatām api siddhānāṁ*, of the strivers who achieve perfection. If this is correct, presumably this refers to the perfection in *kriyā-yoga*, not ultimate and complete perfection. Hill suggests that the "phrase *yatatāṁ siddhānām* is equivalent to *yatatāṁ siddhaye*".

VII.5: *jīvabhūtam*, endowed with life. Other translations are "the soul" (R), "Life (soul)" (E), "Very Life" (H), "Jiva (the Vital Essence)" (G-D), "which becomes the Jiva" (A), "which is the life-soul" (D), "[Nature] developed into life" (Z), "the life-element" (B-D), "Elemental-Soul" (B).

VII.6: Edgerton translates "Beings spring from it" and notes: "Both Ś and R, followed by Telang, Garbe, Deussen, Barnett and Hill take this to refer to both the 'natures' of vss. 4 and 5. This is verbally possible, and certainly better than Senart's interpretation, which refers it to the 'lower' nature alone. If to either, the pronoun must refer rather to the last mentioned ('higher') nature; so I understand it....As the following verses show, the author is thinking primarily of God's supreme essence."

VII.8 : Hill's note on "sacred syllable" reads: "*praṇava*, i.e., OM, derived from *praṇu-*, to praise. The syllable OM appears in the Upaniṣads as a mystic word, meditation on each of whose elements—A, U, and M—is of the highest spiritual value. In Chānd. Up. i, 1.3 OM (identified with the *udgītha*) is called the 'quintessence of all essences (*rasānām rasatamaḥ*).' The syllable is pronounced by a Brāhmaṇa at the beginning and end of every reading of the Veda. See Mān. ii.74."

VII.16: *arthārthī*, seeker of purpose. Other translations are "seeker for wealth" (R., B-D, H, D), "material seeker" (G-D), "desirer of substance" (B), "the man who strives for gain" (Z); but also "seeker for good in the world" (A), and "he who seeks personal ends" (E). In a note Edgerton refers to the interpretation of Rāmānuja, who takes *artha* as *aiśvarya* (that is, lordship, power).

VII.24: *avyaktaṁ vyaktim āpannaṁ manyante mām*, think me, the unmanifest, to be exhausted by a manifestation. Other translations are "think of Me, the unmanifest, as having manifestation" (R, B-D); "think of Me, the unmanifest, as having (only) come into manifestation" (D); "think that I am the unmanifest that has come to manifestation" (H); "think of Me, the unmanifest, as being limited by manifestation" (A); "think Me, who am unmanifest, to have become manifest" (G-D); "conceive Me, Unmanifest, as having come into manifestation" (E); "think of Me as one unmanifest [before] who has reached [the stage of] manifestation" (Z); "deem Me to have come from the unshown, to the shown state" (B). Understanding of the phrase is aided by considering it in connection with IX. 11. Nonetheless, commentators differ widely in their interpretation of the verse. Edgerton notes: " 'Fools' take the external manifestation of Kṛṣṇa to be all there is to Kṛṣṇa. Whether they think him a man or a 'god', they are equally in error; the author does not distinguish between these two possible errors." Zaehner says: The first sentence seems to mean that Krishna, like any other mortal, 'appears' at birth and 'disappears' at death...Fools think He is a human being like every one else, here today and gone tomorrow." Hill notes: "commentators vary widely in their interpretations. The majority consider that reference is made to Kṛṣṇa as incarnate. Thus Ś. explains: 'Not knowing my higher nature as the Supreme Self, the ignorant think that I have *just now* come into manifestation, having been unmanifested hitherto, though I am the ever-luminous Lord.' R. says that the ignorant regard the incarnate God as an ordinary mortal, whose birth as a Kṣatriya prince is due to *karman*. M. has more than one suggestion to make, of which the most sensible is as follows: 'Fools think me to be the manifest *jīva*, who can be fully understood, whereas I am the unmanifest, not able to be fully comprehended.' TG. writes: 'The ignorant do not know the real divinity of Viṣṇu, thinking him to be no higher than as he is seen in the human form.' This last explanation may be right; but the use of *avyakta* and *vyakti*, and a comparison with 5 and 13 above, lead me to believe that the reference here is solely to *prakṛti*, Kṛṣṇa's 'lower Nature'. This view is taken by B., who translates: 'Men of no understanding deem me to have come from the unshown to the shown state;' and writes on this the following note: 'Some misguided men regard the Supreme who is substrate of the universe as essentially material, existing either in a potentially determinable (*avyakta*) or actually determinate (*vyakta*) condition; but in truth He is fundamentally absolute and immaterial.' "

CHAPTER VIII

VIII.4: the meaning of the terms in Verses 3 and 4 is subject to widely differing interpretation. R translates: "Brahman (or the Absolute) is the indestructible, the Supreme (higher than all else), essential nature is called the Self, Karma is the name given to the creative force that brings beings into existence. The basis of all created things is the mutable nature; the basis of the divine elements is the cosmic spirit. And the basis of all sacrifices, here in the body is Myself, O Best of embodied beings (Arjuna)." Taking *svabhāva* to signify "Brahman assumes the form of *jīva*, Chap. XV. 7", and *adhyātma* to mean "the lord of the body, the enjoyer. It is the phase of the Divine which constitutes the individual self", R writes: "Here again the author wishes us to possess an integral knowledge of the Divine in all aspects. There is the Immutable Divine, Brahman; there is the Personal God, Īśvara, the object of all devotion; there is the Cosmic Self, Hiraṇyagarbha, the presiding deity of the cosmos, and the jīva the individual soul which partakes of the higher nature of the Divine and prakṛti the mutable nature. See VII. 4 ff."

Edgerton translates: "Brahman is the supreme imperishable; the over-soul is called innate nature; that which causes the origin of states of beings, the creative force, is known as action. The over-being is the perishable condition (of a being), and the spirit is the over-divinity; the over-worship am I myself, here in the body, O best of embodied ones." But he notes: "All the terms used here are somewhat loose and vague; the language is grandiloquent."

Hill translates: "Brahman is the Imperishable, the Supreme; Its Being is called Essential Self; the creative force that causes beings to spring into existence is called Work; Essential Being is perishable existence; Essential Deity is the person; Essential Sacrifice am I, here in the body, O best of men embodied." And he refers the reader to his Introduction, Sections 14, 15, 16, 19, and 21, for his explanation of the terms.

Barnett translates: "Brahma is the Imperishable, the Supreme; the Nature of each is called the One over Self; the creative force that makes born beings arise into existence bears the name of Works. The One over Born Beings is perishable existence; the One over Gods is the Male; the One over Sacrifice am I in this body, O Best of men." And he refers the reader to his Introduction, Sections 68-69, for the meaning of the terms he uses.

Deutsch translates: "Brahman is the indestructible, the supreme; the Self is called essential nature; and *karma* is the name of the creative power that causes beings to exist. A perishable condition is the basis of all material things; the spirit (*purusha*) is the basis of divine elements, and I am the basis of all sacrifice here in the body, O best of embodied ones."

Aurobindo translates by maintaining the Sanskrit terms for the most part and comments: "Here we find the universal principles enumerated. By that Brahman, a phrase which in the Upanishads is more than once used for the self-existent as opposed to the phenomenal being, the Gita intends, it appears, the immutable self-existence which is the highest self-expression of the Divine and on whose unalterable eternity all the rest, all that moves and evolves, is founded, *aksharam paramam*. By adhyatma it means *swabhava*, the spiritual way and law of being of the soul in the supreme Nature. Karma, it says, is the name given to the creative impulse and energy, *visarga*, which looses out things from this first essential self-becoming, this swabhava, and effects, creates, works out under its influence the cosmic becoming of existences in Prakriti. By *adhibhuta* is to be understood all the result of mutable becoming, *Ksharobhava*. By *adhidaiva* is intended the Purusha, the soul in Nature, the subjective being who observes and enjoys as the object of his consciousness all that is this mutable becoming of his essential existence worked out here by Karma in Nature. By *adhiyajna*, the Lord of works and sacrifice, I mean, says Krishna, myself, the Divine, the Godhead, the Purushottama here secret in the body of all these embodied existences. All that is, therefore, falls within this formula."

Finally, Zaehner translates: "The Imperishable is the highest Brahman; it is called 'inherent nature' in so far as it appertains to [an individual] self,—as the creative force known as 'works' which gives rise to the [separate] natures of contingent beings. In so far as it appertains to [all] contingent beings, it is [their] perishable nature, and in so far as it appertains to the gods, [it is] 'person (spirit)'. In so far as it appertains to sacrifice [it is] I here in this body, O best of men who bodies bear." He notes in relation to *adhyātmam*: "modern translators have gone strangely wrong here. E's 'over-soul' which he would distinguish from the Supreme Self and matter, H's 'Essential Self', Rk.'s 'Self', and Barnett's 'One over Self' all ignore not only Ś. but the combined witness of Upanishadic usage. Ś correctly translates, 'with reference to self, i.e. the body' ...*Adhyātman*, *adhibhūtam*, and *adhidaivatam* are all common Upanishadic adverbs meaning 'with reference to the individual',...'with reference to creatures or contingent beings in general', and 'with reference to the gods or external phenomena'...Here they may be treated as adverbs or as adjectives agreeing with *brahman*. To translate them as if they were independent substantives is quite contrary to Upanishadic usage and therefore inadmissible."

CHAPTER IX

IX.8: *avaṣṭabhya*, resting on. Other translations are "leaning—pressing down upon" (A), "holding under My sway" (B), "subduing" (Z), "taking hold of"

(R, D), "having embraced" (B-D), "resorting to" (H, G-D), "taking as base" (E).

IX.15: *mām upāsate ekatvena pṛthaktvena bahudhā viśvatomukham*, attend in manifold ways upon me who face in all directions, attending with *jñāna* into my oneness and into my distinctness. Other translations are "worship Me as the one, as the distinct and as the manifold, facing in all directions (R, with D being the same except having "many" for "manifold"); "worship Me as the One and the Manifold everywhere present" (B-D); "worship me as One and yet as Manifold, in many a guise with face turned every way" (Z); "regarding me as one, as separate—me, who in various forms face every way" (H); "worship Me in My oneness and in every separate being and in all My million universal faces (fronting them in the world and its creatures)" (A); "worship Me, who am to be seen everywhere, as one, as different or as many" (G-D); "wait upon Me, in my unique and manifold forms, (Me as) variously (manifested), facing in all directions" (E); "wait on Me.... according to My unity, or My severalty, or My manifold aspects that face all ways" (B). Barnett notes: "These worshippers contemplate the Supreme either (1) as the universal One, the Whole of existence, or (2) as specially manifested in any phenomenon that they may choose to meditate upon e.g., the sun or moon, or (3) as combining an infinite number of aspects, such as are detailed in xi. 5ff." And Hill notes: "Ś and other commentators interpret: 'either as one, or as many *devas*, &c.' But there is no alternative conjunction, and certainly to fix the mind on God's manifoldness is not a mark of the 'sacrifice of knowledge'. We have already seen (4-10) how Kṛṣṇa claims to be one with all beings, and at the same time free from contact with them. It is with this knowledge that these men worship him, both 'with the idea of his oneness' with all existences, and at the same time 'with the idea of his separateness' from them." Deutsch notes alternatives to the key words: "*ekatvena*: as the one or 'by the oneness'; *pṛthaktvena*: as the distinct or 'by the manifoldness' or 'in many different manifestations'; *bahudhā*: as the many or 'in many particular things'."

IX.17: Barnett notes that "Grandsire" (*pitāmaha*) is a title of Brahmā the Demiurge.

CHAPTER X

X.1: *bhūya*, still further. Other translations are "yet further" (E), "again" (R, B-D, A, B, D), "once more" (H, G-D), "once again" (Z).

Concerning the reference in this verse to Arjuna's "taking delight in" "me" (so he understands it), Aurobindo notes: "this delight of the heart in God is the whole constituent and essence of true bhakti, *bhajanti prītipūrvakam*; this is put as a condition for the further development by which the final command to action comes at last to be given to the human instrument, Arjuna. This supreme word of the Lord contains the declaration of a unified knowledge and bhakti as the supreme Yoga."

X. 7: Hill notes: "the word *vibhūti* contains an idea of 'power' or 'lordship' and also an idea of 'pervasion' or 'immanence'. Later in the Reading, Kṛṣṇa recounts to Arjuna some of his *vibhūtis*; he speaks of himself(a) as the chief of each class of beings, e.g., as the sun among lights, and (b) as that without participation in which each member of the class could not exist as it is; for example, any lights owe their possession of light to the sun. Any translation of *vibhūti*, then, which ignores this double aspect..must be considered inadequate." Similarly Edgerton: "both meanings, 'lordship, power'....and 'varied manifestation', are contained in the word."

Zaehner translates: "whoso should know this my far-flung power and how I use it, [whoso should know these] as they really are, is [truly] integrated; and this his integration can never be undone. Herein there is no doubt." In a note, he says: "Here once again the Gītā is playing on the various meanings of the word *yoga* and its verbal root *yuj-*: if a man knows God's far-flung power and his *yoga*—his mode of operation, his way of putting it into practise—if his knowledge is not merely theoretical but a practical participation in it..., then he himself will be 'exercised by an unshakeable spiritual exercise (an integration that can never be undone)', that is, firmly integrated within himself. In other words God's *yoga* in the universe is like the *yoga* conducted by the *buddhi*, the 'soul', in man: it is the orderly integration of all things about their immortal centre. To take the analogy a stage further, it might be said that God's 'far-flung power' corresponds to the senses in man: He controls and integrates into an orderly and unitary whole just as the soul co-ordinates and integrates the senses into and around the immortal self. This play on the word *yoga* is not only exceedingly subtle, but also throws a flood of light onto the central philosophy of the Gītā—the ultimate inseparability of eternal being from existence in time, and the interdependence of man's integration of himself and the cosmic integration around him and in God."

X.9: *-prāṇā*, life-breaths, that is, vital energies, and more broadly, life. That such translations as "their lives (are wholly) given up to Me" (R), "their life rooted in Me" (B-D), "their life absorbed in Me" (H), "their life wholly given up to Me" (A), "with life concentrated on me" (E), "their lives centered on me" (D).

X.11: *ātmabhāvastho*, standing over my own nature. Other translations are "remaining within My own true state" (R, E) and "remaining in My own self-nature" (D), or, "dwelling within their Self" (B-D) and "abiding in their souls" (H) and "lodged in their self" (A) and "dwell in their hearts" (G-D) and "present in their spirit's mood" (B). Zaehner translates to convey a (probably intended—so he claims) double meaning, both "abiding [ever] in my own [true] nature" and "abiding in the state of being peculiar to the self".

X.18: *vistareṇa..bhūyaḥ*, further in full detail. Other translations are "again in detail" (R, B-D), "yet again, in full detail" (G-D), "again in full" (H), "again..in fulness" (B), "in full detail....further" (E), "in detail... ever more of it" (A), "again in complete detail" (D), "again in detail full" (Z).

X.22 : *cetanā*, consciousness, is also translated "intelligence" (B, B-D) or "intellect" (E).

X.25: *japa-*, repetition of the name of the divine. Other translations are "silent repetitions" (B-D) or "silent repetition of sacred names etc." (A), "repetition of God's name" (G-D), "muttered worship" (E) or "muttered prayer" (H, B, Z), "silent meditation" (R), "the silent sacrifice" (D).

X.29: *saṁyamatām*, subduers. Other translations are "chastisers" (G-D, B) and "governors" (B-D), or "those who maintain law and order" (R, or "rule and law", A), "guardians" (D), "those who subdue" (Z).

X.30: *kalayatām*, reckoners. Other translations are "calculators" (R, D, B-D), "them that make count" (B), "those who reckon" (Z), "the head of all reckoning to those who reckon and measure" (A), "impellent forces" (E). Barnett notes: "The next words contain a verbal play upon *kāla*, 'time', and *kalayati*, 'to count'. The meaning is rather abstruse. The fundamental conception in counting is that of succession in time. Now in Hindu logic Time is a single omnipresent and eternal *substance* in which all determinate existence is lodged, and the instrumental cause by which the mind is led to formulate the terms 'past', 'present', and 'future', which are the basis of all reckoning. Thus time, not the mind, is the fundamental principle that is at work when we are reckoning, the moving spirit of calculation."

X.32: *pravadatām*, speakers. Other translations are "those who debate" (R, A, G-D), "orators" (B-D) or "them that speak" (E, B) or "those who speak" (D, Z); also "arguments" (H). Edgerton notes: "..*pravadatām* can only be personal, and is therefore not partitive genitive but possessive. R. and (alternatively) Ś, followed by many moderns, would make it refer to various kinds of argument (as a partitive genitive), which seems to me a grammatical impossibility."

X.33: *dhātā-*, supporter. Other translations are "creator" (R, H, G-D, D), "Ordainer" (B, Z), "Ordainer (Creator)" (E); also "Master and Ruler" (A).

X.36: *sattvaṁ*, courage. Other translations are "goodness" (R, H, D, G-D, B) and "truth" (B-D). Edgerton notes: "*sattva* has many meanings, among them 'courage'. But *sattvavant* is regularly used only in the sense of 'courageous'. This interpretation accords with the rest of the verse, which clearly deals with warlike and royal matters, which to the Hindus are identical (the warrior caste, *kṣatriya*, is the same as the royal caste, *rājanya*). Even gambling belongs specifically to this social group."

X.38: *damayatām*, tamers. Other translations are "those who chastise" (R) or "punish" (G-D) or "subdue" (B, Z); "those who rule and tame and vanquish" (A), "stern controllers" (E), "rulers" (B-D, D); and "things that punish" (H).

jigīṣatām, those seeking victory. Other translations are "those who seek the upper hand" (Z), "those who succeed and conquer" (A), and "them that seek political success" (E).

nītir, wise conduct. Other translations are "wise policy" (R: A, D, and B omit the "wise"), "statesmanship" (B-D) or "statecraft" (H, Z, E), "strategy" (G-D).

X.42: *viṣṭabhya-...sthito*, keep continually pervading. Other translations are "pervading...support" (R), "having pervaded ... remain" (B-D), "having established abide" (H), "support...am here" (A), "upholding...stand" (G-D), "stand supporting" (D), "support...remain" (E), "having established... is" (B), "hold apart [supporting it]...abide [unchanging]" (Z).

CHAPTER XI

XI.1 : *-saṁjñitam*, making known. Other translations are "revealing the knowledge of" (G-D)) or "called" (H, E, D, Z).

XI.2: commenting on the vision of this Chapter Aurobindo notes: "It is invited by Arjuna in his desire to see the living image, the visible greatness of the unseen Divine, the very embodiment of the Spirit and Power that governs the universe. For this greatest all-comprehending vision he is made to ask because it is so, from the Spirit revealed in the universe, that he must receive the command to his part in the world-action."

XI.18: *akṣaraṁ paramaṁ veditavyaṁ*, to be known as the supreme imperishable. With a different division and connection, other translations read "supreme imperishable, the one to be known" (B, A: or "worthy to be known", G-D), "Imperishable, Supreme Object of knowledge" (E) or "Imperishable, learning's highest theme" (H) or "Imperishable, the Supreme to be realized" (R), or "the imperishable, the highest to be known" (D). Claiming that *paramam* (supreme, highest) qualifies both 'imperishable' and 'wisdom's goal', Zaehner translates: "(You are) the Imperishable, [You] wisdom's highest goal".

XI.25: Hill notes: "here, and in 32, *kāla* bears the double sense of 'time' and 'death' : cf. the phrase 'your *time* has come'. The 'fire of doom' is that which consumes the world at the time of dissolution."

XI.37: *tvam akṣaraṁ sad asat tatparaṁ yat*, you are the imperishable, being and not-being, that which is supreme; or, you are the imperishable which is beyond being and not being; or, you are the imperishable which is being and not-being and what is beyond (see IX. 19 for the identification with being and not-being). Other translations are "Thou art the Imperishable, the being and the non-being and what is beyond that" (R); "Thou art the Immutable and Thou art what is and is not, and Thou art that which is the Supreme" (A); "Thou art the Imperishable, Being, Not-being, That Supreme" (H); "Thou art the Imperishable, Being, not-Being, and That which transcends even these" (G-D); "Thou art the Imperishable, being and no-being the Supreme Verity" (B); "Thou the imperishable, existent, non-existent, and beyond both" (E); "Thou art the imperishable; Thou art being and non-being, and that which is beyond both" (D); "You are the Imperishable, what IS and what is not and what surpasses both" (Z).

XI.39 : *prapitāmahaś*, the Great Grandfather; Barnett translates "Grandsire's sire" and refers to IX. 17 (his note to that verse).

CHAPTER XII

XII.1: *paryupāsate*, attend upon. This recurs in Verse 3, while in Verses 2 and 6 (where it is a matter simply of worship of the incarnate divinity) one finds *upāsate* instead. Translators seem to make no distinction, yet perhaps one should: for example, taking *paryupāsate* in the sense of attend, approach, draw near, but *upāsate* in the sense of worship. However that may be, other translations of *paryupāsate* here are "worship" (R, B-D, H, G-D, B), "seek after" (A), "revere" (E), "serve" (Z), "honor (and)...worship" (D).

XII.12: Hill attempts to give meaning to Verses 9-11, then 12, as follows: "in vv. 9-11 Kṛṣṇa has graded devotional practices. He recommends to Arjuna above all other methods the *steady concentration* of his thoughts on him. If Arjuna is unable to practise such concentration, then let him fix his mind on Kṛṣṇa not without interruption but *again and again*. If that, too, be beyond his strength, at least let him do all his *work as a sacrifice*, as an offering, to Kṛṣṇa; even so much will lead him to release. If such positive devotion be too hard, he should *give up desire for fruit of work* and act with negative control, as taught by Kṛṣṇa. He now stresses the importance of devotion. Even the abandonment of the fruit of work, if practised with devotion as Kṛṣṇa taught it, is a method superior to those colder intellectual methods that exclude devotion altogether. This is an attempt to give v. 12 some meaning; but it must be confessed that the attempt is desperate. The difficulty is a real one; ancient commentators vainly grapple with it; many modern commentators...preserve a discreet silence...The solution indicated above is to be found in the fact that the message of this Reading is the praise of devotion in contrast with the colder forms of intellectual contemplation. The concentration recommended in 9 is concentration *on me*; the constant practice is to *win me*; work, in 10, is *for me*; and even abandonment of the fruit of work, in 11, is connected with *the control that I have taught*. The methods of this śloka, then, are understood to be divorced from the devotion that Kṛṣṇa here exalts. Even the last of the first list is better than any method that excludes devotion. 'Abandonment of the fruit of work' in a spirit of devotion is better than mere 'meditation' that would reject all loving service; and 'meditation', better than 'knowledge' of the intellect, that would dispense with work and yet not know the warmth of love; while 'constant practice' that lacks the steadiness of knowledge, and shares its cold indifference to devotion, is lowest of all methods. The exaltation of devotion is measured by the violence of the paradox."

Desai, in a note to Verse 12, puts an interpretation offered by Vinoba and adopted by himself in the following way: "'Renunciation of the fruit of all action' is, it must be remembered, suggested as the easiest method in Shl. 11. Shl. 12 explains how it is the easiest. Constant practice of the method is the first stage; the next higher stage, and the natural result of the first is a knowledge of the secret of renunciation; the stage still higher and again the natural result of the lower is concentration, i.e., concentrated devotion to the method; which last results in perfected renunciation of the fruit of all action. This perfected renunciation means lasting peace." Adding a comment, he says: "much of the difficulty is caused by the author's practice of using one and the same word in varying senses, and by the commentator's attempt to relate the 12th *shloka* to *shls*. 8-10."

Aurobindo, commenting on *abhyāsa* in this verse, says: "*Abhyasa*, practice of a method, repetition of an effort and experience is a great and powerful thing; but better than this is knowledge, the successful and luminous turning of the thought to the Truth behind things. This thought knowledge too is excelled by a silent complete concentration on the Truth so that the consciousness shall eventually live in it and be always one with it. But more powerful still is the giving up of the fruit of one's works, because that immediately destroys all causes of disturbance and brings and preserves automatically an inner calm and peace, and calm and peace are the foundation on which all else becomes perfect and secure in possession by the tranquil spirit."

If this verse is retained, then an explanation along the lines suggested by Hill and Aurobindo would seem most plausible, making renunciation of ego (in the encounter with the Lord) the grounding element in all action undertaken on the path of devotion which Kṛṣṇa is teaching; meditation, knowledge, practice, which are not so undertaken may indeed lead one to something like the end Kṛṣṇa teaches, but only as they are sustained in that devotional renunciation of the ego that places one on Kṛṣṇa's path will they enable one to reach the end or fulfilment with the fulness of one's being, with the kind of integration and richness in being that Kṛṣṇa teaches.

XII.20: *dharmyāmṛtam*, nectar teaching about practice. Other translations are "nectar of duty" (E), "nectar of righteousness" (D), "deathless [words] of righteousness" (Z), "life-giving wisdom" (B-D), "immortal wisdom" (R), "immortalizing Dharma" (A), "holy law of deathlessness" (H), "lawful power of immortality" (B), "essence of *dharma*" (G-D). In a footnote Hill says: "lit. 'the holy or righteous, immortality'; i.e., the method of devotion which is in accord with duty and leads to release." Aurobindo notes: "Dharma in the language of the Gita means the innate law of the being and its works and an action proceeding from and determined by the inner nature, *swabhavaniyatam karma*. In the lower ignorant consciousness of mind, life and body there are many dharmas, many rules, many standards and laws, because there are many varying determinations and types of the mental, vital and physical nature. The immortal Dharma is one; it is that of the highest spiritual divine consciousness and its powers, *para prakritih*. It is beyond the three gunas, and to reach it all these lower dharmas have to be abandoned, *sarva-dharman parityajya*. Alone in their place the one liberating unifying consciousness and power of the Eternal has to become the infinite source of our action, its mould, determinant and exemplar. To rise out of our lower personal egoism, to enter into the impersonal and equal calm of the immutable eternal all-pervading Akshara Purusha, to aspire from that calm by a perfect self-surrender of all one's nature and existence to that which is other and higher than the Akshara, is the first necessity of this Yoga. In the strength of that aspiration one can rise to the immortal Dharma. There, made one in being, consciousness and divine bliss with the greatest *Uttama Purusha*, made one with his supreme dynamic nature-force, *swaprakriti*, the liberated spirit can know infinitely, love illimitably, act unfalteringly in the authentic power of a highest immortality and a perfect freedom. The rest of the Gita is written to throw a fuller light on this immortal Dharma."

Paryupāsate, partake of. Other translations are "follow" (R, D, G-D), "follow out" (A), "serve" (H, B), "revere" (E), "reverence" (Z).

CHAPTER XIII

XIII.4: Hill, Edgerton, Radhakrishnan, and Barnett take the "hymns" specifically to be the Vedic hymns, but Hill and Edgerton dispute identification of the "verses of the Sūtras on the holy power" with the *Brahma-sūtra* attributed to Bādarāyaṇa, both considering that, that work was probably written later than the *Gītā*. Edgerton takes the reference to be to the Upaniṣads, whereas Hill suggests the term "perhaps includes Upaniṣadic passages and verses in the current Vedāntic schools". Zaehner translates "aphoristic verses concerning Brahman" and argues that the *Brahma-sūtra* of Bādarāyaṇa "may not have existed in their present form" at the time of the *Gītā*, "but it seems more than likely that collections of aphorisms concerning the nature of the Brahman, that is, the nature of the Absolute, were already in circulation."

XIII.6: *saṁghātaś*, the bodily aggregate. Other translations are "the aggregate (the organism)" (R), "organism" (B-D, D), "bodily whole" (B), and "association" (H, G-D, E) or "collocation" (A), also "'*sensus communis*'" (Z). Hill notes: "the appearance of this word *saṁghāta*—among the modifications of mind is not easy to explain." Normally it is taken as something like "bodily whole", yet (Hill continues) the "introduction of such an idea between 'desire, hate, &c.' and 'intelligence, constancy' remains unexplained... *Saṁghāta* usually means "collection'. As an abstract noun, which the context here seems to demand, it can only mean 'the idea of combination, or association'; but even so the meaning is obscure."

Perhaps *saṁghāta* here should be connected with *saṁgraha* in XVIII. 18, which refers to the unity of active center, action, and instrumental powers in the constitution of activity; though this is a somewhat different sort of factor than the others in the list here, its placing is quite to the point in making a transition from the factors which move toward action (desire and hatred, pleasure and pain) and the factors involved in its essential determination in regard to such moving powers (consciousness and firmness).

XIII.17: Edgerton takes *jyotiṣām* to be partitive genitive, and translates "among lights it is that light which is beyond darkness."

XIII.20: Edgerton suggests that "the only natural interpretation" of the Sanskrit compound here is to take "*karya-karaṇakartṛ* as a three-member dvandva, made into an abstract by adding the suffix *-tva*. The three nouns derived from the root *kṛ*, 'act', are meant to include all phases of action (cf. xviii. 18 for a very close parallel, where *karman* replaces *kārya*): *kārya*, 'thing to be done'; *karaṇa*, 'means of doing it'; *kartṛ*, 'doer, agent'; the addition of *-tva* makes the whole compound mean approximately 'effectuation, instrumentality, and agency'. *Prakṛti* alone is at the bottom of all that concerns all of these, that is, all phases of action." Barnett, Hill, and Besant-Das, as well as Aurobindo and Gandhi-Desai, more or less follow Śaṁkara and Rāmānuja in the division of the compound, leading to a translation like "in the production of effects and causes" (H) or "of the generation of causes and agents" (D). Radhakrishnan divides differently again, and translates: "Nature is said to be the cause of effect, instrument and agent (ness)." Similarly, Zaehner has "the cause of cause, effect, and agency" (following the reading of *-kāraṇa-*, 'cause', for *-karaṇa-*, 'instrument').

XIII.25 : the last half of this verse is translated by others as "and they too cross beyond death by their devotion to what they have heard" (R: similarly D with the exception of "the scripture which they have heard", and B-D with the exception of "adhering to", and H, with the exception of "wholly intent on", and G-D with the exception of "devoted adherence to"); also, "even they also, nevertheless, cross over Death, devoted to the holy revelation which they hear" (E), and "they likewise, though having hearsay for their highest way, pass beyond death" (B). Zaehner has: "and even these, taking this stand on what they hear, overcome death indeed."

XIII.28: Edgerton notes: "Since the same Lord (=soul, cf. v.15) is in all beings, the self of others is one's own self, and if he injures others, he injures himself." Most others interpret differently: Hill, e.g., by reference to VI. 5 and 6 ("he does not cause his own destruction by dragging down the Great Self in him through the 'enmity' of the lower self").

CHAPTER XIV

XIV.1: *bhūyaḥ*, still further. Other translations are "further" (E), "again" (R, B-D, A, H, B, D, Z), "yet again" (G-D). *ito*, from that. Other translations are "from this world" (R, D, E), "hence" (B-D, A, H, G-D, B, Z).

XIV.7 : *tṛṣṇāsaṅgasamudbhavam*, the source of attachment in the form of craving. Other translations are "source of attachment and thirst for life" (B-D, G-D); or "springing from craving and attachment" (R), "child of the attachment of soul to desire of objects" (A), "sprung from thirst and attachment" (H, E), "whose source is thirst and attachment" (D), "sprung from yearnings and cravings" (B), "from craving and attachment it wells up" (Z).

XIV.16: Desai notes: "the usual text is '*Karmanah sukrutasyahus sattvikam nirmalam phalam*'....It is obviously a kind of spoonerism. It should read: '*Karmanah sattvikasyahus sukrutam nirmalam phalam*'.." Accepting this, perhaps one should translate: "the fruit of sattvic action (*karman*) is well-formed and spotless".

XIV.20: *dehasamudbhavān*, springing from the body. Hill translates "which owe their being to the body" and notes: "i.e., which exist in relation to the Self because it is embodied. Most commentators and translators have found the compound...difficult, because it seems to imply that *guṇas* are caused by the body, whereas the body is rather caused by the *guṇas*. Ś. explains: 'which are the seed out of which the body is evolved...' So TG.: 'from which bodies are produced'; and B.: 'whence body has its rise'. This is a forced translation of the compound. R. takes *deha* as equivalent to *prakṛti*, but the close proximity of *dehī* renders this improbable. Th. lays stress on the *sam-*, and translates: 'Which co-originates with the body'. D. approves this rendering in a note, but himself follows Ś.: 'from which all bodies have sprung'."

XIV.23: *udāsīnavad*, seated as if unconcerned. Aurobindo notes: "He has seated himself in the conscious light of another principle than the nature of the gunas and that greater consciousness remains steadfast in him, above these powers and unshaken by their motions like the sun above clouds to one who has risen into a higher atmosphere.He from that height sees that it is the gunas that are in process of action and that their storm and calm are not himself but only a movement of Prakṛti; his self is immovable above and his spirit does not participate in that shifting mutability of things unstable. This is the impersonality of the Brahmic status; for that higher principle, that greater wide high-seated consciousness, *kutashta*, is the immutable Brahman."

XIV.27: *pratiṣṭhā-*, dwelling-place. Hill notes: "Ś says: 'Brahman is *paramātman*, immortal and indestructible; that abides in me, who am *pratyagātma*... that being so, one sees by right knowledge the identity of the two...it is through the power that Brahman has to manifest itself as Lord (*īśvaraśakti*) that Brahman shows grace to devotees. I am that power in manifestation, and therefore Brahman itself.'..The phrase probably means that Kṛṣṇa is Brahman for the purpose of the votary. Thus T.: 'I am the representative of the Supreme Spirit'; D.: 'I am the seat of Brahman', with a reference to BF's 'la demeure de Dieu', and a note: 'Brahman dwelt in Kṛṣṇa, was incarnated in him'. TG.: 'I am the embodiment of the Brahman.' "

dharmasya, truth. Other translations are "law" (R, B), "righteousness' (B-D), "right" (H, E).

CHAPTER XV

XV.1: Barnett's note reads : "...The sacred Fig-tree (see x. 26) typifies the eternal *saṁsāra*, the physical existence in which souls are bound to successive bodies. Its upper roots, which rise above the level of the earth, typify *avyakta*, primal matter; its branches typify *Buddhi*, *Ahaṁkāra*, the subtle elements, and other forms of physical being evolved from primal matter; they spread upward and downward, that is, they fill the whole of conditioned life. From them issue as leaves the Vedas, the divine rules for the works of the world (ii. 42 etc.), and as fruits issue works. The general influence of the latter in forming a sequence of fetters to the Soul (passion, hate, etc.) and thus maintaining physical being is typified by the lower roots clinging deep in the earth."

XV.4: Barnett translates *pravṛtti* (manifestation) as "energy" and notes that it is the "eternal force by which the Supreme maintains the conditioned universe alternately in actual and in potential being."

XV.5: *adhyātmanityā*, constant in regard to their self. Other translations are "ever devoted to the Supreme Spirit" (R), "established in the inner self" (D), "dwelling constantly in the Self" (B-D), "ever abiding in what appertains to self" (Z), "always to be fixed in a pure spiritual consciousness" (A), "constant to the Essential Self" (H), "constant in the over-soul" (E), "constant to the One over Self" (B).

XV.7: *jīvabhūtaḥ*, endowed with life. Other translations are "transformed... into a living Spirit" (B-D), "having become a soul" (R) or "becomes the Jiva" (A) or "becomes the individual-soul" (E) or "becomes a living soul" (D) or "becomes a living [self]" (Z), "has been the...Jiva" (G-D); also "Essential Life" (H) and "Elemental Soul" (B).

XV.8: The "fragrant odors" here remind of the "*vāsanās*" or "scents" which are the impressions stamped on the "characteristic body" by previous acts and which predispose the possessor to new acts of the same kind; cf. Barnett, Introduction, pp. 25 and 27.

XV.9: *adhiṣṭhāya*, having inhabited. Other translations are "using" (R, A, E), "making use of" (D), "having settled himself in" (G-D), "enshrined in" (B-D); also "presiding over" (H, B), and "turns to due account" (Z).

CHAPTER XVI

XVI.1: *jñānayogavyavasthitiḥ*, perseverance in knowledge and action. Other translations are "wise apportionment of knowledge and concentration" (R), "steadfastness in the Yoga of wisdom" (B-D, D; or, "of knowledge" A), "steadfastness in devotion to knowledge" (H), "steadfast in the exercise of wisdom" (Z).

XVI.3: *bhavanti saṁpadaṁ daivīm abhijātasya*, belong to one fit by birth for a divine issue. Other translations are "are the endowments of him who is born with the divine nature" (R, D), "are in him that is born to Gods' estate" (B), "are the wealth of the man born into the Deva nature" (A), "are his who is born with the divine properties" (B-D), "are (the qualities) of him that to the divine lot is born" (E), "are to be found in one born with the divine heritage" (G-D), "are his who is born to Divine estate" (H), "such is the man who is born to [inherit] a godly destiny" (Z).

XVI.6: Aurobindo notes: "The distinction between the Deva and the Asura is not comprehensive of all humanity, not rigidly applicable to all its individuals, neither is it sharp and definite in all stages of the moral or spiritual history of the race or in all phases of the individual evolution. The tamasic man who makes so large a part of the whole, falls into neither category as it is here described, though he may have both elements in him in a low degree and for the most part serves tepidly the lower qualities. The normal man is ordinarily a mixture; but one or the other tendency is more pronounced, tends to make him predominantly rajaso-tamasic or sattvo-rajasic and can be said to be preparing him for either culmination, for the divine clarity or the titanic turbulence. For here what is in question is a certain culmination in the evolution of the qualitative nature, as will be evident from the descriptions given in the text..." And in commenting on Verse 20, he says: "When it is said that there are two creations of being in this material world, Deva and Asura, it is not meant that human souls are so created by God from the beginning each with its own inevitable career in Nature, nor is it meant that there is a rigid spiritual predestination and those rejected from the beginning by the Divine are blinded by him so that they may be thrust down to eternal perdition and the impurity of Hell. All souls are eternal portions of the Divine, the Asura as well as the Deva, all can come to salvation: even the greatest sinner can turn to the Divine. But the evolution of the soul in Nature is an adventure of which Swabhava and the Karma governed by the Swabhava are ever the chief powers; and if an excess in the manifestation of the Swabhava, the self-becoming of the soul, a disorder in its play turns the law of being to the perverse side, if the rajasic qualities are given the upper hand, cultured to the diminution of sattva, then the trend of Karma and its results necessarily culminate not in the sattvic height which is capable of the movement of liberation, but in the highest exaggeration of the perversities of the lower nature. The man, if he does not stop short and abandon his way of error, has eventually the Asura full-born in him, and once he has taken that enormous turn away from the Light and Truth, he can no more reverse the fatal speed of his course because of the very immensity of the misused divine power in him until he has plumbed the depths to which it falls, found bottom and seen where the way has led him, the power exhausted and misspent, himself down in the lowest state of the soul nature, which is Hell. . . ."

XVI.7: Hill notes: "Ś interprets: 'neither those acts which ought to be performed to achieve the end of man, nor those acts from which they should abstain to avert evil.' . . . . B. writes: '"action" seemingly means here, as often, the pursuance of religious and moral objects by a course of works, and "inaction" the pursuance of the same ends by ascetic withdrawal from the works of the world, i.e., Sannyāsa.' "

XVI.8: *aparasparasaṁbhūtaṁ kim anyat kāmahaitukam,* nor is it produced in orderly fashion, what else is the case but that it is produced by desire. Other translations are "it has not come to be by mutual causal law; desire alone has caused it, nothing else" (Z); "brought about by mutual union, and caused by lust and nothing else" (B-D); "brought about by a mutual union, with Desire for its sole cause, a world of Chance" (A); "born of the union of the sexes, prompted by naught but lust" (G-D); "born of mutual union, caused by lust—naught else !" (H); "that it is not originated by regular causation, but that it is caused by desire" (D). In a note, Das explains that, alternatively to the way he has translated it, the phrase *a-paraspara-saṁbhūtam* "might also mean 'without mutual cooperation', without mutual co-ordination, without any guiding and synthesising Principle, a matter of mere blind competition and chance desires." Hill says: "Ś notes: 'this is the view of the Lokāyatikas (materialists), that sexual passion is the sole cause of all living creatures.' Th., following SCH., whose view is defended by Lassen, translates: 'They deny that the Universe. . . . has arisen in certain succession, or anything else, save that it is there for the sake of enjoyment.' So also D., who notes: 'they deny such a succession in the order of development or creation as the Sāṁkhya or Yoga system taught.' "

XVI.23: Hill notes: "*śāstra* is a wide term, which may include the Veda and the Dharmaśāstras. These are to be the canon in matters of morality, with which this Reading has been dealing."

CHAPTER XVII

XVII.1: *niṣṭhā,* state. Other translations are "condition" (B-D) or "position" (R, G-D) or "standing" (H), "basis" (E) or "foundation" (B), "that concentrated will of devotion...which gives them this faith and moves them to this kind of action" (A).

XVII.3: Commenting on XVI. 20, Aurobindo has said that "the evolution of the soul in Nature is an adventure"; continuing that line of thought in the discussion that precedes Chapter XVII, he says: "But what then shall be the secure base of an action which departs both from the guidance of desire and from the normal law? For the rule of desire has an authority of its own, no longer safe or satisfactory to us as it is to the animal or as it might have been to a primitive humanity, but still, so far as it goes, founded on a very living part of our nature and fortified by its strong indications ; and the law, the Shastra, has behind it all the authority of long-established rule, old successful sanctions and a secure past experience. But this new movement is of the nature of a powerful adventure into the unknown or partly known, a daring development and a new conquest, and what then is the clue to be followed, the guiding light on which it can depend or its strong basis in our being? The answer is that the clue and support is to be found in man's *shraddha*, his faith, his will to believe, to live what he sees or thinks to be the truth of himself and of existence. In other words, this movement is man's appeal to himself or to something potent and compelling in himself or in universal existence for the discovery of his truth, his law of living, his way to fulness and perfection. And everything depends on the nature of his faith, the thing in himself or in the universal soul—of which he is a portion or manifestation—to which he directs it and on how near he gets by it to his real self and the Self or true being of the universe...." Then, in comment on Verse 28 of this Chapter, he says: "Because *shraddha* is the central principle of our existence, any of these things done without *shraddha* is a falsity and has no true meaning or true substance on earth or beyond, no reality, no power to endure or create in life here or after the mortal life in greater regions of our conscious spirit. The soul's faith, not a mere intellectual belief, but its concordant will to know, to see, to believe and to do and be according to its vision and knowledge, is that which determines by its power the measure of our possibilities of becoming, and it is this faith and will turned in all our inner and outer self, nature and action towards all that is highest, most divine, most real and eternal that will enable us to reach the supreme perfection."

XVII.23: Hill notes: "The intimate, indissoluble connexion between all true sacrifice, austerity, and almsgiving, and the authority of Scripture, is indicated by the use of the mystic syllables—OM TAT SAT. These form the threefold designation of Brahman, OM expressing its absolute supremacy, TAT its universality, and SAT its reality, reflected as goodness in the world of men. The castes (with Brāhmaṇas at their head), the Vedas, and the Sacrifices proceed from this one source, and are thus inseparable. Therefore all Vedic rites of sacrifice, austerity, and almsgiving begin with the utterance of OM. Those, too, whose aim is liberation, and in whose works is no desire for fruit, knowing that all is Brahman, perform their rites with thought of Brahman as TAT. And all who would continue in sacrifice, austerity, and almsgiving, or any work that has these for its end, and make them real and good and auspicious, must join with them the thought of Brahman as SAT. For whatsoever sacrifice is offered, or austerity practised, or alms given, without the thought and utterance of the sacred threefold name, and therefore contrary to rule and without faith, is ASAT, having neither reality nor goodness; such work is of no value in this world, and bears no fruit of happiness hereafter. Commentators vary considerably in their interpretations of this rather obscure passage. The view taken above is in accordance with the general view of Kṛṣṇa's answer to Arjuna's question. No rite is valid unless it follows scriptural rule and is referred with faith to OM TAT SAT, which is the author of both Scripture and sacrifice." And yet, in his footnote to Verse 24, Hill says: "The questions arise: (a) Why is the triple designation divided in 24-7? (b) Is any distinction intended between the *brahmavādin*, the *mokṣākāṅkṣin*, and the worshipper who uses SAT? Probably both worshipper and Name are divisible in theory alone; in actual fact, the one man worships with the threefold Name throughout. In so far as he is a Vedic student, he thinks of OM; as eager for release, he thinks of TAT; as anxious that his rites should be well and auspiciously performed, he thinks of SAT. Thus the utterance of OM TAT SAT leaves nothing imperfect in his worship."

CHAPTER XVIII

XVIII.3: Desai, in a note to Verse 2 of this Chapter, says about this matter of giving up actions: "The reference here is to the doctrine which must have been prevalent at the time and which we find defined in *Manusmṛti* thus: 'No action is here seen to be done by one who is without desire ; the spring of whatever action one does is desire.' Hence the extreme position of the school of *sannyāsa* that all action should be abandoned."

XVIII.6 : Hill's introduction, Section 30, outlines the kinds of work involved here and later in this Chapter, indeed, throughout the poem: (1) *nitya* (regular religious ceremonies and observances) and (2) *naimittika* (occasional ones), appearing in the *Gītā* under the triad of sacrifice, austerity, and charity; (3) *sahaja* or 'innate' works, appropriate to caste and for each man his *svadharma*; (4) works performed for the maintenance of the body; (5) all other works. All works but the last fall into the class of *niyata* (obligatory or inevitable).

XVIII.13: *kṛtānte* is normally translated something like "decisive" (B), "doctrine" (R, E), "dogmas" (H); but as Radhakrishnan and Das both note, the compound can be understood as meaning "at the end of the *Kṛta yuga*", that is, "as taught in the original Sāṁkhya" (R).

XVIII.14: Hill notes: "this fivefold division is obscure; and the various explanations of commentators are not helpful. It is generally agreed that *adhiṣṭhāna* means 'body'. Ś glosses *kartā* with *upādhilakṣaṇo bhoktā*. R.: *jīvātman*, M. : *Viṣṇu*. The *karaṇas* are agreed to be the sense-organs.... Ś and R consider the *ceṣṭās* to be the breaths.... ; M., the movements involved in the performance of sacrifice. *Daiva* causes great difficulty....Th..calls *daiva* 'Divine will' (or circumstance, destiny). D.: 'the divine part'. B.: 'Providence'. The following suggestion is intended to preserve the consistency of Gītā doctrine, and to account for the reference to Sāṁkhya in 13. (a) The *adhiṣṭhāna* or basis, is *avyakta prakṛiti*, the *mūla* from which all springs. (b) *Kartā* includes *buddhi* and *ahaṁkāra*; for the former issues orders to the organs of action, and the latter causes the idea of personal agency. (c) The *karaṇas* are the mind and the five organs of perception. (d) The *ceṣṭās* are the five organs of action. (e) *daiva* is the realm of the elements, gross and subtle, presided over by the *devas*, Agni being lord of fire, Vāyu lord of air, &c. The fivefold division thus corresponds to the usual twentyfourfold division of *prakṛiti* in the Sāṁkhya. This interpretation of *daiva* may be regarded as forced: but the introduction in this place of Fate as an agent would be very strange indeed. It must also be remembered that, with the rise of Vedāntic monism and of theistic devotion, the *devas* had sunk to the position of 'superintendents of elemental departments', and little more..."

XVIII.18 : Hill notes : "as Ś points out, *karma* here means *the end*—'that which is sought for, that which is reached through action by the agent'." And Edgerton notes: "Cf. xiii.20, where the three elements are *kārya, karaṇa,* and *kartṛ*. Here *kārya* is (rather poorly) replaced by *karman*."

XVIII.21: alternative translations of the major share of this verse are as follows: "the knowledge which sees multiplicity of beings in the different creatures, by reason of their separateness" (R); "that knowledge which regardeth the manifold existences of different kinds in all beings as separate" (B-D); "that knowledge which sees the multiplicity of things only in their separateness and variety of operation in all these existences" (A); "that knowledge which perceives severally in all beings many existences of diverse kinds" (H); "what knowledge in various fashion different conditions of various sorts sees in all beings" (E); "that knowledge which perceives separately in all beings several entities of diverse kinds" (G-D); "the knowledge whereby one severally perceives diverse and various existences in all born beings" (B) ; "that knowledge which sees various beings of different kinds in all beings, because of their separateness" (D); "that [kind] of knowledge which in all contingent beings discerns in separation all manner of modes of being, different and distinct" (Z).

XVIII.22: *kārye*, causal factor. Other translations are "effect" (R, D, Z, H, B), "thing" (B-D, G-D), "thing to be done" (E), "movement or routine" (A).

XVIII.37: *ātmabuddhiprasādajam*, born of clarity in one's awareness of self. Other translations are "springs from a clear understanding of the Self" (R), "born of satisfaction of the higher mind and spirit" (A), "born of the blissful knowledge of SELF" (B-D), "born of the serenity of his own reason" (H), "born of the serene realization of the true nature of Ātman" (G-D), "sprung from serenity of soul and of intellect" (E), "springs from that serenity which comes from apperception of the self" (Z), "born from the serenity of self and intellect" (D), "born of the clearness of one's own understanding" (B).

XVIII.58: Das notes: "Kashmir reading *ahaṁkāram na mokṣyasi*, 'wilt not give up egoism', seems better." This, instead of: from egoism, you will not listen (*śroṣyasi*).

General Index of Themes and Ideas

Index of Epithets for Arjuna and Krsna

...

ARJUNA

KṚṢṆA

Slayer-of-Madhu I/35; II/1, 4; VI/33; VIII/2
Exciter-of-Men I/36, 39, 44; III/1; X/18; XI/51
Descendant-of-Vṛṣṇi I/41; III/36
Slayer-of-Foes II/4
Strong-Armed VI/38; XI/23
Vāsudeva VII/19; X/37; XI/50; XVIII/74
Supreme Spirit VIII/1; X/15; XI/3
Magic One X/17
Lotus-eyed XI/2
Supreme Lord XI/3
Presiding One XI/4, XIV/21
Lord-of-Magic (-and-Discipline) XI/4, 9; XVIII, 75, 78
Hari XI/9; XVIII/77
Lord-of-All XI-16
Form-of-All XI/16, 46
One-of-Great-Self XI/20, 37, 50
Viṣṇu XI/25, 30
Lord-of-Gods XI/25, 37, 45
Abode-of-the-World XI/25, 37, 45
Best of Gods XI/31
Boundless-Form XI/39
All XI/40
Immeasurable One XI/42
One-of-Incomparable-Power XI/43
Thousand-Armed-One XI/46
Slayer-of-Keśin XVIII/1

Subject Index to Commentary